THE GOOD GUYS, THE BAD GUYS
and the
FIRST AMENDMENT

FRED W. FRIENDLY

THE GOOD GUYS, THE BAD GUYS
and the
FIRST AMENDMENT

Free Speech
vs.
Fairness in Broadcasting

VINTAGE BOOKS
A Division of Random House
New York

VINTAGE BOOKS EDITION, February 1977
Copyright © 1975, 1976 by Fred W. Friendly

All rights reserved under International and Pan-American
Copyright Conventions. Published in the United States by
Random House, Inc., New York, and simultaneously in
Canada by Random House of Canada Limited, Toronto.
Originally published by Random House, Inc., in May 1976.

Library of Congress Cataloging in Publication Data
Friendly, Fred W.
The good guys, the bad guys and the first amendment.

Bibliography: p.
Includes index.
1. Broadcasting—Law and legislation—United States.
2. Broadcasting policy—United States.
I. Title.
[KF2805.F7 1977]   343'.73'0994   76-13144
ISBN 0-394-72320-1

Manufactured in the United States of America

For
RUTH W. FRIENDLY,
who traveled all the way
from Red Lion to Tulsa,
from Media to Culpepper

THE FIRST AMENDMENT
TO THE CONSTITUTION OF THE UNITED STATES

Congress shall make no law respecting an establishment of religion, or prohibiting the free exercise thereof; or abridging the freedom of speech, or of the press; or the right of the people peaceably to assemble, and to petition the Government for a redress of grievances.

RATIFIED DECEMBER 16, 1791

THE FAIRNESS DOCTRINE

To devote a reasonable amount of broadcast time to the discussion of controversial issues; and
To do so fairly, in order to afford reasonable opportunity for opposing viewpoints.

FCC, 1949; CODIFIED IN LAW, 1959

THE PROBLEM

. . . [in] some areas of the law it is easy to tell the good guys from the bad guys . . . In the current debate over the broadcast media and the First Amendment . . . each debator claims to be the real protector of the First Amendment, and the analytical problems are much more difficult than in ordinary constitutional adjudication . . . the answers are not easy.

JUDGE J. SKELLY WRIGHT
U. S. COURT OF APPEALS (D.C.)
IN A SPEECH BEFORE THE NATIONAL
LAW CENTER, GEORGE WASHINGTON
UNIVERSITY, JUNE 3, 1973

CONTENTS

FOREWORD

~~~~~~~~~~~~~~~~~~~~~~~~~~

"Television writes on the wind," as one President of the United
States put it.[1] "There is no accumulated record which the historian can examine later with a 20-20 vision of hindsight, asking . . . How fair was he tonight? How impartial was he today?
How honest was he all along?" That question of fairness has preoccupied American Presidents ever since Calvin Coolidge talked
into the first carbon microphone. It must also concern the millions of citizens who depend upon radio and television as their
swiftest and often primary source of news. It was this concern of
the Congress and the Federal Communications Commission which
created the Fairness Doctrine.

Once, in a classroom of journalism and law students at Columbia University, I experienced one of those awkward moments
when a seemingly elementary question forced my rhetoric to out-
run my analysis. The question was, "What are the origins of the
Fairness Doctrine, and what is the relationship of the *Red Lion*
case to *Brandywine* and Carl McIntire?" The answers satisfied
neither me nor the class. Subsidiary questions from the same student: "How did the landmark *Red Lion* case get its name, and if
the equal-time rule is different from the Fairness Doctrine, why
do both regulations contain some of the same language?" Further,
"Why did *Red Lion* reach the Supreme Court and how long did it
take?"

I finally sought relief by saying that I did not know, and I
promised to be better informed by next week. The answers took
two years, and involved a trip to Red Lion, Pennsylvania, and a

twenty-thousand-mile excursion through the fifty-year thicket of regulatory history. It also involved a search through the murky record of the 1964 presidential election, in which the roots of *Red Lion* are intertwined. More than seventy-five participants in this drama were willing witnesses, although a few will not view the facts exactly as I do, and not all will share the conclusions I reach.

One of the earliest lessons I learned as a documentary producer was to keep the focus narrow, to use the "little picture" to illuminate the whole. In this inquiry the larger picture is broadcast regulation and the quality and freedom of radio and television news in America. The small picture is a view of the Fairness Doctrine, one hopes without the subjective bias of one who has spent all his professional life practicing or teaching journalism. This book is basically a documentary about *Red Lion,* its ghosts and a series of other fairness cases which grew out of that historic decision. It is not intended as an examination of the equal-time provisions of Section 315 of the Communications Act of 1934 (which apply only to elections). The equal-time provision is a crucial subject for another book, perhaps to be written in the wake of the 1976 election, when the stopgap decision making, confusion and posturing involving debates, news conferences and "bona-fide news events" concerning candidates have subsided sufficiently to determine whether Section 315 should be repealed or drastically revised. This volume does not concern itself directly with public broadcasting, prime-time access, violence on television, multiple or newspaper ownership, children's programing or any of the other critical, yet unresolved conflicts of our national communications policy.

The story of *Red Lion* is traced in detail, not only because of its impact on broadcasting, but because it dramatizes the method by which a well-intentioned law can be manipulated to mute "noxious views," as perceived by one group of politicians. *Red Lion* also provides an opportunity to study the complex route by which an obscure case, involving air time costing less than the retail price of one copy of this book, worked its way up through the regulatory process to the Supreme Court of the United States.

One of the temptations I have tried to avoid is projecting the founding fathers' eighteenth-century vision of free speech to the limited-access miracle of telecommunications in the last third of the twentieth century. Their Constitution, and especially the Bill of Rights, is a constantly evolving instrument, and the prior-restraint, freedom-of-the-press protections we live under are much more the product of Holmes, Brandeis and Black than of Jefferson, Madison or even Patrick Henry. To claim that they would turn in their graves at the idea of the Fairness Doctrine, or at the thought that the First Amendment does not apply absolutely to radio and television, is, to quote historian Leonard Levy, to "anticipate the past by succumbing to an impulse to re-create it so that its image may be seen in a manner consistent with our rhetorical tradition of freedom, thereby yielding a message that will instruct the present."[2]

Newspersons are comforted by the Jeffersonian ideal that "our liberty depends upon the freedom of the press and that cannot be limited." But there is equal discomfiture in Jefferson's 1804 letter to Abigail Adams: "While we deny that Congress have a right to controul the freedom of the press, we have ever asserted the right of the states and their exclusive right to do so."[3] Indeed, Jefferson's draft of the First Amendment was considerably less absolute than Madison's and that which the Congress finally adopted.*

In anticipating the past and projecting the 1791 Bill of Rights, each segment of our society has selected its own sacred cows. Journalists seek their protections in the absolutism of the First Amendment words: "Congress shall make no law . . . abridging the freedom of speech or of the press . . ." Others interpret the First Amendment to mean that Congress did not surrender its censorial power only to have it monopolized by powerful corporations answerable primarily to their stockholders. "Freedom of speech for whom?" asks one scholar. Caught between those two extreme

---

* Jefferson's concept of freedom of speech and of the press would have included certain limiting exceptions. In 1789, Congressman James Madison sent Thomas Jefferson, then U.S. Minister to France, an early draft of what was to become the Bill of Rights. The Madison version said: "The people shall not be deprived or abridged of their right to speak, to write, or to publish their sentiments; and the freedom of the press, as one of the great bulwarks of liberty, shall be inviolable."[4] Jefferson approved of "the declaration of rights" in principle, but cautioned Madison to include certain limitations: "The people shall not be deprived or abridged of their right to speak, to write or *otherwise* to publish anything *but false facts affecting injuriously the life, liberty, property or reputation of others or affecting the peace of the confederacy with other nations.*"[5] (Emphasis added.)

positions is the viewing and listening public. To bridge that gulf between protection of the broadcasters and the public's right of access on controversial issues of public importance, the Fairness Doctrine was formulated.

Whether this regulatory apparatus, constructed by lawyers and politicians on an ad hoc basis to meet the sudden stresses of a communications revolution, has become a strait jacket is the crux of the current constitutional debate. In this confrontation, all ideological labels lose their meaning. Strange alliances form: Justice William O. Douglas, Reverend Carl McIntire, Sam Ervin and the presidents of CBS and NBC on one side, against Chief Justice Warren Burger, Nicholas Johnson, Senator Robert Griffin and the president of ABC News on the other. Judge Wright is correct; you can't tell the good guys from the bad guys.

F.W.F.

October 1, 1975
Columbia University, New York City

THE GOOD GUYS,
THE BAD GUYS
and the
FIRST AMENDMENT

1

RED LION:
The Attack Lasted Two Minutes

~~~~~~~~~~~~~~~~~~~~~~~~~~~~~~~~~~

"John, get a radio station and preach the gospel from that pulpit."

"But it takes two things to run a radio station that I don't have—brains and money."

"Nonsense! You've got the brains and the Good Lord has the money."

CONVERSATION BETWEEN REVEREND A. L. LATHAM
AND REVEREND JOHN M. NORRIS, 1950

"This is WGCB, the World for God, Christ and the Bible in Red Lion, Pennsylvania . . ."

On that late November morning, the sun rose over the transmitter towers on Windsor Hill at 6:44. Because of a complaint of interference by a radio station in Worcester, Massachusetts, the Red Lion station is prohibited by the Federal Communications Commission from beginning its broadcast day until sunrise and must cease operations at sunset. According to the transmitter log, eleven hard-line right-wing programs were crowded into that ten-hour day for its "primarily Christian clientele," as defined by its owner. It was a rich diet of conservative, anti-Communist opinion derived from the evangelical vision of "the infallible word of God" and country. There were a few local commercials, and some gospel hymns, but mostly there was message. The messages were that Southeast Asia must be saved from the "Red menace" and that the United States must be protected from the Supreme Court, mongrelization of the races, and "the Satanization of the

Gospel from liberal forces in the church." The spectrum of crusading commentators ranged from the fundamentalism of Dr. Carl McIntire to the absolutist views of Reverend Billy James Hargis, an Oklahoma evangelist preacher.

WGCB in Red Lion is not so much a radio station disseminating news or the top twenty tunes or Madison Avenue advertising as it is a cassette deck radiating a blend of evangelical "Christian Crusade" and radical-right politics. There are hundreds of stations like it throughout the United States, many of them clustered in the Bible belts of Pennsylvania, Texas and Oklahoma. What distinguished Red Lion Broadcasting was the circuit-riding commitment of octogenarian Reverend John M. Norris against the regulatory lightning which in 1964 struck his transmitter.

At 1:12 P.M. on November 25, 1964, the announcer on duty, Bob Barry, threaded a tape recorded in the "Christian Crusade's" Tulsa, Oklahoma, studio. At 1:14 he began reading a commercial for Mailman's Department Store. Sixty seconds later he gave station identification, pushed the button on tape recorder one and raised the level of the audio pot in time for the opening fanfare of "The Battle Hymn of the Republic"; Billy James Hargis was on the air in Red Lion, York, Spry, Dallastown . . . but the button Barry pushed started more than a tape recorder.

In a stinging personal attack Reverend Hargis lashed out at Fred J. Cook, an investigative reporter who in his own crusades had taken aim at a wide range of targets, from Richard M. Nixon to J. Edgar Hoover, from the CIA to the FBI. Cook's most recent book had been a highly critical biography of the Republican candidate for President, Barry Goldwater, whom Hargis had vigorously supported.

Hargis views himself as "a watchman at the wall." He is convinced that "Communism is the devil himself," and he blames liberals, agnostics and "all men who reject the Second Coming of Christ" for a "destroyed church and enslaved America." His heroes are Senator Joseph McCarthy ("I was with Joe the day he died") and General Edwin Walker. Hargis and the extremist general traveled fifty thousand miles in 1963, and "on a midnight ride like Paul Revere's . . . Walker warned America about the arming of Russia, the UN and the threat to the military, while I explained the dangers of left-wing socialism in government and church." Hargis and Walker "alerted America" to Robert Kennedy, Martin Luther King, Jr., the "distorted liberal press" and Walter Reuther, "the single most dangerous individual in the United States."

Hargis has no reservations about his condemnation of the United Nations: "We slapped Christ in the face at the setting up of the United Nations in San Francisco in April 1945, just as surely as the Jews slapped Him on the night of His betrayal two thousand years ago."

In 1964 Hargis believed that the election of Barry Goldwater was essential "to the survival of a free America," and he was outraged by Cook for writing *Goldwater: Extremist on the Right*. In the broadcast on November 25, Hargis attacked Fred Cook as "a professional mudslinger," and accused him of dishonesty, of falsifying stories and of defending Alger Hiss. He also denounced a magazine that had published a number of Cook's articles, *The Nation,* as a "scurrilous magazine which has championed many Communist causes."

The Hargis attack lasted less than two minutes. The air time for the entire fifteen minutes cost $7.50—plus more than a quarter of a million dollars in legal fees and costs. Caught in the constitutional cross fire that resulted were the independence of 8,500 radio and television stations and the rights of 200 million Americans. Today, learned judges and powerful broadcast executives who hardly know there is a town called Red Lion use the name as a code word for government interference with freedom of the press.

A somnolent little town with a population of 5,684 in lush, rolling Pennsylvania Dutch country, Red Lion is seven miles from York, thirty miles from Harrisburg, and some seventy-five miles from Media in eastern Pennsylvania, another way stop on the circuitous path of communications law. It is one of those places more famous for what it stands for than for what it is. The sign on Highway 70 going east reads: "Red Lion, founded 1736, named from a nearby tavern." Once the town was known as the cigar capital of American "Dutch Masters," and for H. L. Mencken's short story about morality in the newsroom at the turn of the century, "A Girl from Red Lion, P.A."; now it is a name which rolls off law professors' tongues.

WGCB in Red Lion, with 1,000 watts of power at 1,440 kilocycles on the AM dial and at 96.1 megacycles on FM, is an exclusive franchise and has all the punch of the $25 it charges for an hour of prime time. This "religious commercial station," as the FCC designates it, hardly dominates the hearts and minds of its community. But though WGCB is its only broadcast outlet, Red Lion is not electronically isolated. There are 2,080 homes which subscribe to cable television, and they can watch twelve stations, some as distant as Baltimore, Washington and Harrisburg. Even without the cable, direct reception brings in seven television signals from York and Lancaster providing CBS, NBC, ABC and PBS programs. At least twenty AM and ten or fifteen FM radio transmitters from York, Coatesville and Chester provide a "multitude of tongues."

The Norris family, who still control the station, enjoy telling the story of how their father got into radio. Reverend John M. Norris, once a member of the United Presbyterian Church, was "not exactly defrocked," according to his son, John H. Norris: "He just sort of dropped out of the order to help form a new center"—the Bible Presbyterian Church. After a brief circuit-riding mission in South Dakota he returned to his native state of Pennsylvania in the forties and founded the Bethany Presbyterian Church in South Chester. There he met Reverend A. L. Latham, another refugee from the United Presbyterian Church in the United States. Latham suggested that Norris "get a radio station and preach the gospel from that pulpit."

"But it takes two things to run a radio station that I don't have—brains and money," Norris protested.

"Nonsense!" Latham retorted. "You've got the brains and the Good Lord has the money." So Reverend John Norris applied to the FCC, and in 1950 Red Lion Broadcasting Company was awarded a license to operate WGCB.

Not even Norris' worst enemies could suggest that the Red Lion station ever made him rich. The rate card of WGCB is considerably lower than that of competing stations in York, in Hanover and of many colleges, and the merchants of Red Lion and York County have never considered WGCB a must-buy. Less than one third of the station's time is sold to local merchants or regional sponsors, and there is virtually no national-product advertising.

The station's superstars have included Reverend Carl McIntire, whom Norris had discovered and later recruited to broadcast on

WGCB; at the height of his sensational career, McIntire was carried by six hundred radio stations. In addition, the station carried Reverend Billy James Hargis, Dan Smoot and Dean Manion, and "Life Line," the widely syndicated anti-Communist crusade of the late H. L. Hunt. Today, just as in 1964, most of these programs arrive by mail on cassettes or tape reels, and WGCB's announcer/technicians put them on the air with a religious chatter of grass-roots appeals for God, the United States and the sponsors.

The sponsors, like Hunt, Hargis and Smoot, paid the WGCB rate card (with certain discounts for frequency) of about $7.50 per fifteen minutes or $35 for five times a week, or $70 for a half-hour each weekday with a Sunday special thrown in. "Life Line" was the largest customer, accounting for some $900 a month, which included two playings of their tape each day on WGCB-AM. This sum also bought exposure on the FM transmitter and on the international shortwave station WINB, licensed since 1962, which sends the Norris gospel to Europe, South Africa and other distant lands. Recently "Life Line" terminated its sponsorship on WGCB. Now even a "Jewish Voice" program is aired—written by a Jew converted to Christianity named Kaplan who sends his tapes from Phoenix.

These sponsored religious-political broadcasts can afford to pay their own freight by appealing for funds over WGCB and over similar stations in Watseka, Illinois; Neon, Kentucky; and Vinita, Oklahoma. A more subtle ploy is to offer free scripts or booklets on "The Battles of Communism" or "Is the School House the Place to Teach Raw Sex?" or bargain-priced cassettes of programs in order to acquire mailing lists for future fund raising. Although this is reported to be big business for some of the more spellbinding performers, one has only to examine WGCB's $25 an hour, $1 per twenty-second-spot rate to realize that for station owners such as Reverend John M. Norris, radio was hardly "a license to print money!"[1] His home up near the transmitters was as simple as was his life until that fateful day in November 1964 when Billy James Hargis attacked Fred Cook. Norris was eighty-one years old at the time, and his son, John H. Norris, who helped him run the radio stations, says that neither he nor his father knew much about the Fairness Doctrine until it was brought to their attention after the Hargis attack.

This was not the first salvo exchanged between Cook and Hargis. In its May 25, 1964, issue *The Nation* had published Cook's 4,500-word investigative report "Radio Right: Hate Clubs of the Air." The piece examined nine such syndicated broadcasts, and was critical of the political motives and practices of the Hargis organization. Accusing Hargis of using a million dollars a year in tax-free funds to spread his own propaganda and hate, Cook summarized the broad list of targets the evangelist had condemned in a single broadcast: "communism, liberalism, the National Council of Churches, federal aid to education, Jack Paar, federal medical care for the aged, Ed Sullivan, the Kennedy-Khrushchev meeting, Eleanor Roosevelt, disarmament, Steve Allen and the Freedom Riders."[2] The article also reported that Hargis violently opposed "integration, which he called 'mongrelization.'"[3]*

"Hate Clubs of the Air" also included a paragraph which, if read in the light of subsequent events, almost blueprints the course of action which Hargis' attack and Cook's response were to set in motion:

> One recourse for liberal forces would appear to be to demand free time to counter some of the radical Right's wild-swinging charges. The Federal Communications Commission's "primer on fairness" provides that, where such controversial programs are aired, the opposing point of view must be presented if offended parties demand equal time. The object is to prevent just the kind of one-sided debate that is now going on, and to guarantee a balance that, in practice, is rarely achieved.[5]

In his denunciation of Cook, Hargis did not refer to the *Nation* article, nor did he take note of the trap that Cook, perhaps unwittingly, was setting for him. As Hargis remembers it now, "You know how I do these broadcasts, I don't even script them. I go into that little booth with a pile of clippings from *Time, U.S. News & World Report* or the Tulsa newspapers. On this particular day I had Cook's book about Goldwater and a five-year-old *Newsweek* clipping about Cook's phony attempt to smear New York officials."

---

* Norris received several copies of the *Nation* article and early in 1965 wrote to "thank" Cook for writing "'Hate Clubs of the Air,' which alerted us to several of the broadcasts which we later acquired, so that now we carry them all. Your article has resulted in cutting our deficit spending by almost one half, thus the harm that was intended has greatly benefited us."[4]

Hargis felt that Cook's book on Goldwater was part of the left-wing press conspiracy that contributed to the Johnson landslide. "Without thinking much about it," he says, "I took aim on Cook."

> This paperback book by Fred J. Cook is entitled *Goldwater: Extremist on the Right*. Now, who is Cook? Cook was fired from the New York *World-Telegram* after he made a false charge publicly on television against an un-named official of the New York City government. New York publishers and *Newsweek* magazine for December 7, 1959, showed that Fred Cook and his pal, Eugene Gleason, had made up the whole story and this confession was made to [New York] District Attorney, Frank Hogan. After losing his job, Cook went to work for the left-wing publication, *The Nation,* one of the most scurrilous publications of the left which has championed many communist causes over many years. Its editor, Carey McWilliams, has been affiliated with many Communist enterprises, scores of which have been cited as subversive by the Attorney General of the United States or by other government agencies. . . . Now, among other things Fred Cook wrote for *The Nation* was an article absolving Alger Hiss of any wrongdoing . . . There was a 208-page attack on the FBI and J. Edgar Hoover; another attack by Mr. Cook was on the Central Intelligence Agency . . . Now this is the man who wrote the book to smear and destroy Barry Goldwater called *Barry Goldwater: Extremist on the Right!*[6]

Hargis never told his listeners that he and his "Christian Crusade" had also been attacked in the Goldwater book and in Cook's article.

The Nation was aware of the Hargis broadside but did not raise the issue of reply time. "For one hundred and nine years we've been catching hell from all quarters," said editor Carey McWilliams, "but we've been dishing a lot of it out ourselves. *The Nation* is fair game. It may be different for an individual."

Cook had been an aggressive, muckraking reporter for the now-defunct New York *World-Telegram & Sun,* and had written numerous prize-winning exposés on organized crime. Studs Terkel once referred to him as "a modern Lincoln Steffens." However, it is true, as Hargis claimed, that Cook was discharged from the *World-Telegram & Sun* in 1959 under cloudy circumstances. With another *World-Telegram* reporter, Eugene Gleason, he had

written "The Shame of New York," a searching 70,000-word report on slum-clearance mismanagement. During the research on
the story Gleason told his partner that he had been offered a
$75–$100-a-week bribe by a city official. In a television interview
on *Open End* with David Susskind, Cook told of the bribe attempt to influence their reporting, but the next day Gleason admitted to the District Attorney that he had fabricated most of the
incident. The *World-Telegram,* insisting that its editors had
never been told of the attempted bribe and embarrassed by the
hoax, discharged Cook along with Gleason. Cook has always
claimed that he was a victim of Gleason's bravado, and believes
that the management of the *World-Telegram* "had been looking
for an excuse to fire me ever since the Hiss article in *The Nation.*" *Newsweek* magazine pulled no punches in reporting the
firings, and its article "Retreat of the Crusaders" provided grist
for Hargis' mill. After Cook's book on Goldwater appeared, the
preacher circulated reprints of the *Newsweek* article and enlarged on it for his "Christian Crusade" broadcast of November 25.

Twenty-four days later Fred Cook, then a free-lance author
living in Interlaken, New Jersey, wrote a letter to WGCB and the
more than two hundred other stations who had broadcast the
tape, asking: "Since your station is listed as one of those that has
carried the Rev. Billy James Hargis's Christian Crusade broadcasts, did you in fact put on the air this attack against me made
by the Rev. Billy James Hargis? I expect an answer, yes or no."

Cook also served notice in his letter that "I shall expect you to
grant me equal time, at your expense, as provided in FCC regulations, to answer in appropriate fashion this scandalous and
libelous attack."[7] (It should be noted that the FCC regulations do
not use the term "equal time"; their wording is "reasonable opportunity to respond."[8])

There is still some dispute about how Cook, residing as he did
at the time near Asbury Park, well beyond the range of WGCB,
knew about the Hargis broadcast in Red Lion. Hargis claims
that a "leftist smear outfit" called the National Council for Civic
Responsibility monitored the broadcast and "put Cook up to
demanding equal time." The reverend thereupon told his followers and the stations that carried him that the FCC was out to
get him and other conservative commentators, and that "there is

no doubt in my mind that the liberals intended the Fairness Doctrine to be their sole possession—a mandate from the government to coerce those who differ with their opinions."

Cook is certain that KXEN in St. Louis* was the only station out of the two hundred which carried the Hargis attack to notify him, as was its FCC requirement, and that this was his only motivation to act. He sees himself as "a private citizen trying to protect my own good name, and to teach those hysterical hate mongers like Hargis that they can't make irresponsible charges."

The origins of the case are part of a much more tangled web. The Hargis attack and the Cook response were not the opening scene; rather, they were the second act of a drama that the Oklahoma preacher and the New Jersey journalist never fully understood. Five years earlier, no case would have come out of the Hargis broadcast; there were no personal-attack requirements, and the Fairness Doctrine existed more as a hortatory summons to the licensee than as a sharp-edged sword which could command air time. The Red Lion attack changed all that. To grasp the full meaning of the case, one has to go back and trace the evolution of that benign regulatory principle which became a law almost by accident. It is against this hazy backdrop that *Red Lion* and all controversy on the air must be viewed.

* Although the management of KXEN complied with the FCC requirement to give notice of a personal attack, they refused to run the Cook reply except on a paid basis.

2

THE BIRTH OF THE FAIRNESS DOCTRINE:
From Aimee Semple McPherson to Red Lion

~~~~~~~~~~~~~~~~~~~~~~~~

"This is my station and I'll do what I want with it."

GEORGE A. RICHARDS, WJR, DETROIT;
WGAR, CLEVELAND; KMPC, LOS ANGELES

On March 8, 1954, the day before the *See It Now* broadcast on Senator Joseph McCarthy, Edward R. Murrow told CBS board chairman William S. Paley that the program about the powerful senator would be highly critical. The CBS chairman did not ask to examine the film or Murrow's conclusions, but he did offer some advice.

"Ed, if I were you, I'd play it smart," he said. "McCarthy is going to demand reply time, so beat him to the punch and offer him a half-hour on *See It Now* before he can ask for it; then the public won't believe you were forced into it." Then he added, "Besides, if the program is as hard-hitting as you say it is, it's only fair to offer the time."

Murrow needed no urging. He and the staff of *See It Now* had discussed such a plan—not just because it was fair, but because it was good journalism. *See It Now* was on the CBS television network for a half-hour every Tuesday night under the sponsorship of Alcoa, and the clearance of rebuttal time for Senator McCarthy was completely in the producers' hands. Murrow began the broadcast with the statement:

Tonight *See It Now* devotes its entire half-hour to a report on Senator Joseph R. McCarthy, told mainly in his own words and pictures. . . . If the senator believes we have done violence to his words or pictures, and desires to speak, to answer himself, an opportunity will be afforded him on this program.

Those two programs—the Murrow broadcast, which made no attempt to balance the senator's virtues with his abuses, and the senator's attack on Murrow a month later—were a demonstration of the broad goals of fairness as prescribed by the Federal Communications Commission. But in all the years of *See It Now,* I never heard Murrow speak of "the Fairness Doctrine," and I doubt if he thought much about this FCC guideline. In the nineteen-fifties, it was lawyer's language.

The Fairness Doctrine requires that television and radio stations devote adequate time to controversial issues of public importance, and that they do so fairly by affording reasonable opportunity for the opposing viewpoint.[1] The Murrow broadcast of March 9 was not fair in itself, nor was McCarthy's answer, but together the two thirty-minute programs amounted to a practical demonstration of the Fairness Doctrine. Many viewers considered the senator's personal attack on Murrow to be a more devastating illustration of the McCarthy smear technique than the examples provided in the original broadcast, but that is sometimes the nature of access.

Not all who witnessed the two broadcasts believed them to fulfill fairness standards, and perhaps this is an argument against the FCC Doctrine that reply time is the most effective method of ensuring fairness on a controversial issue. After the McCarthy answer to Murrow, a highly respected television critic of the *Saturday Review* wrote a stinging indictment of the two broadcasts. Gilbert Seldes said that the Murrow program was not a report but an attack that showed McCarthy at his worst and claimed that it was a dangerous precedent which may have "placed new weapons in the hands of [future] demagogues." The reply a month later was equally unfair, the critic wrote, because Murrow and his staff were masters of the technique of film, while McCarthy was a clumsy novice who could come up with nothing more than "a feebly handled newsreel talk . . . Because a broadcaster cannot provide equal skill and equal prestige to an adversary, the offer

of equal time isn't good enough."[2] It is true that McCarthy's reply was produced by Roy M. Cohn, chief counsel for the Senate
Investigations Subcommittee, and by advertising executives and
newsreel producers loyal to the senator, but CBS stood ready to
provide McCarthy with film or live production facilities if he so
requested.

Others besides Seldes found the formula of attack and response
unsatisfactory, which may demonstrate that even a voluntary application of the FCC's personal-attack rule and the Fairness Doctrine does not always provide "reasonable balance." Fairness is in
the eyes and ears of the beholder as much as in the motivation of
the broadcaster. One man's fairness may be another man's bias.

The government, which necessarily assigns frequencies to some
and denies it to others, has the responsibility to demand an effort
at overall fairness and to require a sufficient amount of news or
public-affairs programing to make fairness relevant. The dilemma
comes when the FCC orders radio and television stations—and in-
directly the networks—to achieve fairness without telling them
how to produce programs. Ostensibly this puts the government
in conflict with the constitutional prohibitions of the Bill of
Rights.

One of those who believes that the Fairness Doctrine does not
contradict but, rather, reinforces the First Amendment is Rhode
Island's John O. Pastore, chairman of the Senate Commerce Subcommittee on Communications. An advocate of bold documentaries, Pastore is not impressed with the argument that CBS and
Murrow displayed fairness overall by voluntarily offering Senator
McCarthy thirty minutes of response time. "Why should that decision be the prerogative of an individual broadcaster, no matter
how good he may be?" Pastore asks. "Reply time should be the
public's prerogative." By "the public" the senator means the FCC
and, if necessary, the courts.

Like many in the Congress who have shaped broadcast policy
for the last fifty years, Pastore is not willing to let the industry's
absolutist view of the First Amendment prevent the government
from keeping the air fair and free—in that order. While acknowledging the accomplishments of electronic journalism, such
disciples of the Fairness Doctrine cite the abuses of much of the
broadcast industry and deny that there is constitutional conflict
between fairness regulation and the First Amendment. They re-

cite the long history of shoddy practices perpetrated by a band of willful owners who claimed that it was their air and that they were protected by the Bill of Rights.

The drafters of the First Amendment assumed that all citizens speak with equal tongues at reasonably equal decibels. The pamphlets of Tom Paine, beyond their biting eloquence, afforded him no strong advantage over Alexander Hamilton. In turn, Hamilton wielded great power, but he could not drown out the iconoclastic Paine by amplifying his own words through an exclusive bullhorn. Similarly, Daniel Webster and John Calhoun faced the states' rights issue with the same equipment and opportunity. One could outwit or outdebate the other, as Abraham Lincoln and Stephen Douglas did, but neither of them had access to the one soapbox or the only printing plant in town.

The advent of radio forever eliminated this equality, and whatever radio did to the speakers' platform, television has done to radio. Politics, civil rights and war have not been the same since KDKA, Pittsburgh, went on the air in 1920. To deny the implications of this new revolution is akin to misreading the atomic bomb as a new variety of gunpowder.

New technologies often bring changes unanticipated by their inventors. The day the first horseless carriage puttered down Main Street, no one had considered traffic lights, driver's licenses, the future of the downtown department stores, or the sexual impact of the back seat or the motel. The night KDKA sent a saxophone solo and the results of the Harding-Cox election through its listeners' crystal sets, no one anticipated the need for rules preventing a station in Pittsburgh from drowning out one in Detroit, or an incumbent politician from denying his opponent access to the air, or quiz programs from being rigged. In each such case the invention eventually became the mother of the necessity.

Many of the pioneer radio stations went on the air to spur the sale of receivers, for without programing, the public had no reason to purchase the new product. Soon set manufacturers and department-store owners discovered that stations, begun as a merchandising loss-leader, might well become an economic bonanza. On September 15, 1921, there was one licensed radio station on the air; by 1922, thirty had been licensed, and no one could say how many illegal ones were on the air. "A raggle-taggle mob of free enterprisers was running away with the business," as one historian put it.[3]

The birth of the commercial was almost an accident. In August of 1922 a real estate developer in Jackson Heights, Long Island, was stuck with cooperative apartments he couldn't sell. Station WEAF in New York declined to sell advertising as such, but permitted the owner of Hawthorne Court to buy ten minutes of air time for $50 to deliver a speech in memory of Nathaniel Hawthorne and the joys of living in the rural beauty of Jackson Heights. It worked, and the Cliquot Club Eskimos and the Ipana Troubadors were not far behind. Radio had found its source of revenue.

The chaotic radio boom of the early twenties roused a conservative Secretary of Commerce, Herbert Hoover, to call for regulation. Describing the Radio Act of 1912, which assigned wireless operations to the Commerce Department, as "a very weak rudder to steer so powerful a development,"[4] Hoover struggled for an alternative to the law which forbade the use of wireless transmitters without a license from the Secretary of Commerce and Labor. First he tried to deal with the explosion by selecting two frequencies, 750 and 833, and licensing all broadcasters to operate on one of them. When this produced a wireless traffic jam, he assigned the AM frequencies (550 to 1,500 megacycles), ninety-six channels in all, to stations applying for licenses, but this failed to meet the extraordinary demands of a nation captivated by the Dempsey-Carpentier fight, Babe Ruth in the World Series, the Happiness Boys, the songs of Vaughn De Leath, and nightly lectures by H. V. Kaltenborn. (In July 1925, those Midwesterners who listened to Chicago's station WGN heard on earphones the final day of the Scopes "Monkey Trial," in Dayton, Tennessee, with Clarence Darrow confronting the aging William Jennings Bryan.)

The entire regulatory scheme collapsed when Secretary Hoover next attempted to find room for all applicants by limiting the power and hours of stations so that several broadcasters might utilize the same channel. Over two hundred new stations came on the air using any frequency and power they desired, regardless of the interference they caused. When Hoover tried to clamp down, the federal courts ruled that he was powerless to deal with the situation or to impose restrictions. The result "was confusion and chaos. With everybody on the air, nobody could be heard."[5]

Pleading for extensive controls, Hoover observed: "This is one of the few instances where the country is unanimous in its desire for more regulation."[6] Even the infant broadcasters' lobby supported the regulatory concept. As Erik Barnouw noted in his illuminating and entertaining history, *A Tower in Babel*, "A spokesman for Westinghouse, which already had four stations on the air, expressed the view that fifteen stations could serve the whole country adequately." "For him," Barnouw wrote, "the purpose of regulation would presumably be to stop in their tracks the hundreds of new stations about to invade the air."[7]

Hoover, who was hardly an advocate of excessive government regulation, called nationwide conferences asking for an orderly master plan and warning against "ether advertising." "It is inconceivable," he said, "that we should allow so great a possibility for service to be drowned in advertising chatter."[8]

In those hectic days when the electronic frontier was vulnerable to marauders—opportunistic stations in search of a place on the dial—one chronic squatter was the Los Angeles evangelist, Aimee Semple McPherson. When Secretary Hoover and his Department of Commerce inspectors finally closed her down, Sister Aimee telegraphed him: PLEASE ORDER YOUR MINIONS OF SATAN TO LEAVE MY STATION ALONE STOP YOU CANNOT EXPECT THE ALMIGHTY TO ABIDE BY YOUR WAVE-LENGTH NONSENSE STOP WHEN I OFFER PRAYERS TO HIM I MUST FIT INTO HIS WAVE RECEPTION.[9]

Watching the birth of a billion-dollar industry and network broadcasting (NBC in 1926 and CBS one year later), Hoover also understood the impact that radio news and public-affairs programing would have on freedom of speech in America. While fearing the excesses of unbridled industry control and demanding regulation, he warned of the threat in permitting any government control of content: "We cannot allow any single person or group to place themselves in a position where they can censor the material which shall be broadcast to the public, nor do I believe that the government should ever be placed in a position of censoring this material."[10]

In 1927, the year that Lindbergh's flight to Paris provided radio with its first major international story and Amos 'n Andy invented the nightly situation comedy, Congress responded to Hoover's plea and established the Federal Radio Commission.

On Hoover's recommendation, President Calvin Coolidge appointed the first five commissioners, and in the spring of 1928 the FRC opened for business with one desk, two chairs, a table and a packing box—and presumably a wireless receiver, although history does not record this.

In the debate to set up controls for radio, a few congressmen, particularly young Fiorello LaGuardia of New York, were concerned that the heavy hand of government, and specifically that of the Secretary of Commerce, might acquire a power "akin to censorship." An exchange between LaGuardia and Representative Wallace H. White of Maine, the father of the Radio Act, testifies to their intent and offers a hint of debates to come:

WHITE: . . . The pending bill gives the Secretary no power of interfering with freedom of speech in any degree.

LaGUARDIA: Is it the belief of the gentleman and the intent of the Congress in passing this bill not to give the Secretary any power whatever in that respect [program control] in considering a license or the revocation of a license?

WHITE: No power at all! [11]

Terms like "access," "equal time" and "Fairness Doctrine" were not yet in the electronic lexicon, but in one of its first and boldest rulings the FRC declared its policy on the side of unpopular ideas as well as the will of the majority. The limitations of the electromagnetic spectrum required that some 164 of the then-operating stations be eliminated, and these managements were summoned to the FRC to show cause why their licenses should not be revoked. One of those called was a New York station, WEVD, an acronym for Eugene V. Debs, the Socialist party candidate for President and a draft resister who had served time in a federal penitentiary. The WEVD petition is a small footnote in the struggle for diversification:

This station exists for the purpose of maintaining at least one channel of air free and open to the use of the workers. We admit without apology that this station has no deep concern with reporting polo matches . . . if WEVD is taken off the air and in fact if it is not to be treated on a parity with others who are richer and more influential with the government, the people of the nation can truly recognize that radio which might be such a splendid force for the honest clash of ideas—creating a free market for thought—is nothing but a tool to be used by the powerful against any form of disagreement or any species of protest.[12]

The Federal Radio Commission's unpopular decision to renew WEVD's license was a hopeful step in regulatory history.

The FRC became the Federal Communications Commission with the passage of the more comprehensive Communications Act of 1934, which centralized all interstate radio and wire operations, including the American Telephone & Telegraph Company and Western Union, under one regulatory agency.[13] But even today the loose provisions of the FRC are the root of the regulations that govern radio and television. For example, the FCC's ambiguous phrase "public interest, convenience, and necessity," which survives to this day as the criteria for granting and renewing a station's license, came out of the deliberations over the original FRC. Senator Clarence Dill once told Newton Minow, then the FCC chairman, that he had borrowed this phrase from the provisions of the Transportation Act of 1920. Thus, the standard for railroad franchises or discontinuance was applied to what was, for better or worse, to become the chief source of information for the American people.

The concept of fairness as a subject for regulation emerged from the early programing of some station managements who used their privileged microphones to drown their communities in the management's own politics or religious tenets. Finally, in 1929, the Federal Radio Commission took action, denying the application for a license modification from the single-minded Great Lakes Broadcasting Company, whose management regularly broadcast material propagating its own dogmas to the exclusion of all others. In its decision, the FRC stated:

> Broadcasting stations are licensed to serve the public, and not for the purpose of furthering the private or selfish interests of individuals or groups of individuals. The standard of public interest, convenience or necessity means nothing if it does not mean this. . . .
> In so far as a program consists of discussion of public questions, public interest requires ample play for the free and fair compe-

tition of opposing views, and the commission believes that the principle applies . . . to all discussions of issues of importance to the public.

In such a scheme there is no room for the operation of broadcasting stations exclusively by or in the private interests of individuals or groups so far as the nature of the programs is concerned. . . .[14]

In 1930 a Kansas doctor used his station, WFBK of Milford, to promote his hospital, which specialized in a radical operation utilizing goat glands to rejuvenate masculine virility. Not only did the local AMA protest Dr. Brinkley's ethics, but the Federal Radio Commission ordered Brinkley off the air for operating WFBK for his own private purposes.[15]

Some other early decisions reaffirmed this policy and removed the licenses of a Muscatine, Iowa, station which promoted a cancer "cure," and of a station in Los Angeles which attacked opposing religious groups.[16] In 1938 the application of the Young People's Association for the Propagation of the Gospel was rejected because the station's policy specifically denied use of its broadcast facilities by persons of differing religious viewpoints. Clearly, this differed from that of WEVD, whose policy was to provide access for Socialist Labor views, but not to the exclusion of others.

The thirties also witnessed the birth of serious radio journalism: H. V. Kaltenborn during the Munich crisis; William Shirer reporting the rise of Hitler; Raymond Gram Swing as France and the Low Countries fell; Edward R. Murrow at the Battle of Britain. These and others who followed, such as Howard K. Smith, Eric Sevareid, Charles Collingwood and Robert Trout, were responsible journalists imbued with professional codes of fairness and generally against preaching designed to make up the listener's mind for him. But there were other, more strident voices: commentator Boake Carter out of Philadelphia; Walter Winchell from the gossip pages of the New York tabloids; and Father Charles Coughlin, whose anti–"Franklin Doublecrossing Roosevelt," anti-Semitic, anti–World Court orations from the Shrine of the Little Flower in Royal Oak, Michigan, so embarrassed CBS that it eventually dropped him. Whereupon the radio priest bought lines from the telephone company and organized his own Sunday-afternoon network, which commanded such an audience that one broadcast against international "non-Gentile" bankers stimulated 200,000 telegrams. The FCC was powerless to control this demagogue, and only the disciplinary action of the Roman Catholic Church finally silenced him. Coughlin's discoverer and mentor was G. A. Richards of WJR, Detroit, who was to be to FCC regulations what the Triangle Shirtwaist factory fire was to the establishment of labor-reform laws.

Curiously, the FCC entered the sensitive zone of program content not because of radio news programs or the controversies triggered by the Winchells and the Coughlins, but because of the specter of editorializing by station owners, most of whom viewed politics with a conservative, big-business bias. Besides George A. Richards, another of the barons who strenuously resisted the FCC's attempts to establish fairness standards was John Shepard of the Yankee and Colonial Networks, owner of two Boston stations, WNAC and WAAB, and WEAN in Providence, Rhode Island.

Shepard's political broadcasts led to the surprising Mayflower decision of 1941. The newly formed Mayflower Broadcasting Company of Boston challenged Shepard's WAAB license, charging that this powerful station broadcast political endorsements and supported partisan positions in public controversies with no effort toward fairness or balance. After exhaustive hearings, the FCC reprimanded WAAB for its abject one-sidedness and political bias, but in a burst of faint-heartedness renewed the license after Shepard promised not to editorialize in the future. The decision affected all broadcasters; the Commission would henceforth prohibit licensees from expressing opinions—or so it was interpreted. In its decision, the FCC stated:

Radio can serve as an instrument of democracy only when devoted to the communication of information and the exchange of ideas fairly and objectively presented. A truly free radio cannot be used to advocate the causes of the licensee. It cannot be used to support the candidacies of his friends. It cannot be devoted to the support of principles he happens to regard most favorably. In brief, the broadcaster cannot be an advocate.

Freedom of speech on the radio must be broad enough to provide full and equal opportunity for the presentation to the public of all sides of public issues. Indeed, as one licensed to operate in a public domain the licensee has assumed the obligation of pre-

senting all sides of important public questions, fairly, objectively
and without bias. The public interest—not the private—is paramount.[17]

Doubts about the Mayflower decision continued until 1949.*
In 1946 the FCC, in an attempt to clarify the "public interest,"
institutionalized the confusion by publishing the notorious "Blue
Book," officially entitled "Public Service Responsibility of Broadcast Licensees." This document was designed to apprise licensees
of the FCC's policies and procedures in reviewing renewal policy,
practices and revenues. A Senate report called it "by far the most
comprehensive statement of its sort in the history of the Commission."[18] The "Blue Book" deals at length with the handling of
controversial public issues:

> Probably no other type of problem in the entire broadcasting
> industry is as important or requires of the broadcaster a greater
> sense of objectivity, responsibility and fair play. . . . Accordingly,
> the carrying of such programs in reasonable sufficiency and during
> good listening hours is a factor to be considered in any finding of
> public interest.[19]

Industry reaction to the "Blue Book" was explosive. Justin
Miller, a former federal judge and president of the National Association of Broadcasters, denounced the "Blue Book" as violating
the First Amendment and accused the FCC of being "stooges for
the Communists."[20]

In an attempt to correct the ambiguities of its actions, in 1949
the Commission published "Report on Editorializing by Broadcast Licensees," a document which many consider to have been
the first basic articulation of the Fairness Doctrine. It was written

* During that period, the Supreme Court decided *National Broadcasting
Company* v. *U.S.* (1943). NBC had objected to some FCC rules which required that it divest itself of one of its two networks. The regulations also
forced affiliated stations of all networks to retain control of their own programing. The Supreme Court ruled against NBC. As Justice Felix Frank-
furter wrote for the majority: "The act itself establishes that the commission's
powers are not limited to the engineering and technical aspects of regulation
of radio communication. Yet, we are asked to regard the commission as a kind
of traffic officer, policing the wavelengths to prevent stations from interfering with each other. But the act does not restrict the commission merely to
supervision of the traffic. *It puts upon the commission the burden of determining the composition of that traffic.*" (Emphasis added.)

against the ominous backdrop of the Richards case,[21] then pending before the FCC. The Commission staff was attempting to curb the political, flagrantly dishonest news policies of George A. Richards, owner and sole stockholder of the 50,000-watt stations WJR in Detroit, WGAR in Cleveland, and KMPC in Los Angeles. His three powerful stations had crusaded for the presidential candidacy of Thomas E. Dewey in 1944 and of Douglas MacArthur in 1948, and he had summarily discharged a reporter who in a documentary had dared to observe that the general seemed to suffer from palsy and other symptoms of old age. Richards violently opposed the congressional candidacy of Helen Gahagan Douglas, and said of her actor husband, Melvyn Douglas, "We've got to get these kike actors out of Hollywood."[22]

Richards' news staff signed affidavits giving testimony to the fact that they had been ordered to slant, distort and falsify news against Richards' enemies. Richards' pet hate had been President Roosevelt, to whom he referred as that " 'Jew-lover' who was out to communize the nation."[23] No stories favorable to the President were allowed; in fact, he had instructed his news staff to juxtapose stories about Roosevelt with those about Communists and criminals so that they might seem related. After the President's death, the attack was shifted to members of his family. When Mrs. Roosevelt, whom Richards called "the old bitch," was in an auto accident, he asked if the news story could be phrased in such a way as to make it appear she was drunk.[24]

As Richards wrote to Clete Roberts, the news director of his Los Angeles station, his aim was to "beat the New Dealers" and "accuse them of everything under the sun."[25] When the multiple-station operator was reminded of fairness regulations, he retorted, "This is my station and I'll do what I want with it."

Other multiple licensees who gave the public short shrift included Powell Crosley of WLW, Cincinnati, and the Hearst group with three AM and two FM stations, part of the vast William Randolph Hearst communications empire. In 1949 columnist Drew Pearson and his partner Robert Allen challenged WBAL, the Hearst station in Baltimore, asking that its license be awarded to them. The FCC ran extensive hearings, but eventually Hearst kept his valuable Baltimore franchise.

During much of the late forties, the Richards case occupied the FCC's deliberations, as it attempted to use and then strengthen fairness concepts intended to control Richards' operation without discouraging those networks or stations which were building responsible news organizations. Finally, in 1951, just as the FCC hearings on Richards climaxed with dozens of witnesses testifying about his orders to slant and falsify the news, and after an expenditure of $2 million in a frantic defense to save his three stations, the ruthless pioneer dropped dead. The FCC examiners were determined to make an example of him, even posthumously, but after endless lobbying and bargaining, Richards' licenses in Detroit, Cleveland and Los Angeles were renewed by the commissioners upon a written promise from his widow that the station's deceptive practices would cease. All three stations were sold soon afterward.

The Richards case was a traumatic embarrassment to both the industry and the FCC. As the Commission was trying to come to grips with a defiant challenge from a media baron, it was also attempting to bring stability and cohesion to its erratic formulations of licensee responsibility in dealing with news and public issues. The early, sometimes vague, often conflicting pronouncements of the *Great Lakes* and *Mayflower* decisions and the "Blue Book" were now synthesized in the 1949 "Report on Editorializing by Broadcast Licensees." Stripped to the core, its basic proposition—later called the Fairness Doctrine—directed licensees "to operate in the public interest," and

1. to devote a reasonable amount of time to the coverage of controversial issues of public importance; and
2. to do so fairly by affording a reasonable opportunity for contrasting viewpoints to be voiced on these issues.[26]

The report rejected all implications that the *Mayflower* decision denied broadcast stations the right to editorialize, and urged them to deal with controversial issues, with the caveat that fair opportunity for reply be made available:

. . . it is evident that broadcast licensees have an affirmative duty generally to encourage and implement the broadcast of all sides of controversial public issues over the facilities, over and beyond their obligation to make available on demand opportunities for the expression of opposing views. It is clear that any approximation of fairness in the presentation of any controversy will be difficult if not impossible of achievement unless the licensee plays a conscious and positive role in bringing about balanced presentation of the opposing viewpoints.[27]

Further, without mentioning Richards by name, the report stressed that this right to editorialize did not empower any station to distort or suppress the news.

It was the sudden about-face on editorials which received the public's and press's attention, but the shock waves felt a decade later did not have to do with editorials, but with fairness standards. In the 1949 report, however, the FCC was careful to state that in requiring standards of reasonableness and fair play, the Commission would not enforce "rigid" fairness controls:

> . . . it is clear that the standard of public interest is not so rigid that an honest mistake or error in judgment on the part of the licensee will be or should be condemned where his overall record demonstrates a reasonable effort to provide a balanced presentation of comment and opinion on such issues.[28]

This may have seemed reasonable to the FCC, but the broadcast industry attacked any regulatory oversight of content as a violation of the First Amendment and of Section 326 of the Communications Act of 1934.

Ten years later, Congress legitimized the shaky status of the Fairness Doctrine. Clarification grew out of a rough-and-tumble debate on the issue of election coverage, which at that time had no relationship to the Fairness Doctrine. Senator William Proxmire, who had only recently succeeded the late Joseph McCarthy as the junior senator from Wisconsin, bears responsibility for providing statutory language to the Fairness Doctrine—though ironically, in 1975 he was an aggressive opponent.

The 1959 debate over equal time (Section 315 of the Communications Act) involved a mathematical formula requiring that equal opportunities be afforded all legally qualified candidates for all public offices. Section 315 is a congressional enactment, whereas the Fairness Doctrine, which applies to all programing except attacks upon foreign leaders, was never specifically voted into law.

In 1959 the FCC had ruled that Lar Daly, an iconoclastic Chicago candidate for political offices ranging from the Presidency to the mayoralty of Chicago, was entitled to an equal opportunity on the air whenever Mayor Richard Daley appeared in a newscast. The FCC's decision overruled previous precedents of the Commission by rigidly applying Section 315 to all radio and television appearances. As a consequence, the discretion and flexibility that licensees had previously enjoyed was eliminated. In the summer of 1959, Senator Pastore led the legislative fight that created a series of exemptions from Section 315 as they applied to legally qualified candidates. What Pastore, Senator Hugh Scott and others in the Senate were trying to do was to remove the shackles from broadcast journalists so that they could cover the events involving political candidates without the obligation of the equal-time provision as interpreted in the Lar Daly decision.

Therefore, in the summer of 1959, in anticipation of the upcoming presidential election, it was understandable that Congress accorded the Fairness Doctrine a glancing acknowledgment. Senator Pastore had introduced a bill amending the equal-time rule in order to permit bona-fide news coverage and interviews of candidates during a campaign, and exempting documentaries if the appearance of the candidate was incidental to the subject being covered. But Senator Proxmire strongly objected to the modification because he feared the bias of broadcasters in his home state of Wisconsin:

. . . television stations and radio stations are owned, by and large, by people with money, and they have a particular economic interest which often represents a political interest. It is an interest which may or may not agree with my own. Sometimes I agree enthusiastically. Sometimes I disagree.

At any rate, my experience in my own state is that the preponderance of television and radio station owners in my judgment disagree with me rather often. The only protection I have had is the protection written into the law. I recognize the difficulty, and I recognize that the law should be changed. But I think we should do everything we can, not only to protect individual persons, but, far more important, to protect ideas which contradict the preponderant opinion of television and radio station owners throughout the country. That is why I say to the Senator from Rhode Island that later I shall offer an amendment which I have previously shown him.[29]

In the debate Proxmire told his colleague Pastore and the rest of the Senate that he was "pleading for more controversy, not less," but he was concerned that if left to their own devices, some broadcasters would "present one viewpoint and one viewpoint only."

As the debate neared its climax, Pastore tried to summarize his Wisconsin colleague's position:

> What the Senator from Wisconsin is doing, as I understand, is appending to the Amendment a statement of the philosophy that these media are in the public domain, and that, where it is practically possible, all sides shall be given a fair opportunity of exposure to the public.

Proxmire answered, "The Senator is correct."[30]

The Proxmire amendment was reluctantly accepted by Pastore, who considered it superfluous and said so. The House and Senate wanted to make it clear that nothing in the amendment of the Section 315, equal-time rule could be construed as impinging upon and in any way softening the Fairness Doctrine. Accordingly, the specific language of the Fairness Doctrine was incorporated into Section 315(a) of the Communications Act:

> Nothing in the foregoing sentence shall be construed as relieving broadcasters in connection with the presentation of newscasts, news interviews, news documentaries and on-the-spot coverage of news events from the obligation imposed upon them under this act to operate in the public interest and *to afford reasonable opportunity for the discussion of conflicting views on issues of public importance* [emphasis added].[31]

Inadvertently, therefore, Senator Proxmire caused Congress to accord legislative recognition of the Doctrine's existence, a fact that Senator Pastore never lets him forget. Ironically, in 1975 Proxmire was stunned to be reminded of his role in the 1959 legislation. In the ensuing years a long series of FCC findings and court rulings have reiterated the fairness concept, which was now etched in the marble of congressional recognition. Henceforth the lawyers' argument that Congress had never passed Fairness Doctrine legislation would be hard to justify.

With the growth of the television documentary in the fifties and sixties—*See It Now, CBS Reports,* NBC's *White Paper*—combined with the advent of the *Today* show, the development of the half-hour network evening news on all three networks, and the fading of such barons as Richards, Shepard and Crosley, the Fairness Doctrine began to function more as the spirit of responsible broadcasting than as the letter of the law. The Commission kept its promise to stay out of program content, refusing to substitute its "rigid" judgment of fairness for that of the licensee. Indeed, the licensees enjoyed wide discretion in fulfilling their fairness obligations. The history of that period is certainly on the FCC's side. After virtually every controversial program—"Harvest of Shame," "Battle of Newburgh," "Biography of a Bookie Joint" and "Hunger in America"—fairness complaints were filed, and the FCC rejected them all. As FCC general counsel Henry Geller put it, "We just weren't going to get trapped into determining journalistic judgments."

In the sixties, Fairness Doctrine controversies continued, but most of the Commission's rulings adverse to the licensee—all but one of them—involved local stations, usually obscure ones. Nevertheless, some of the cases proved to be handy tools for refining and further shaping the intent of the Doctrine. For example, in 1963 the Cullman Broadcasting Company transmitted a one-sided program opposing the nuclear test-ban treaty. Station WKUL of Cullman, Alabama, subsequently refused air time for the opposing viewpoint, claiming that it could not obtain sponsorship for such a rebuttal. The Commission stepped in to rule that the absence of paid sponsorship could not negate the station's duties as a public trustee, nor "the public's paramount right to hear contrasting views on controversial issues of public importance."[32]

However, WKUL continued its defense by arguing that it had presented contrasting views on the treaty in other programing. The FCC agreed, noting that "It would appear that your obligation . . . to the 'fairness doctrine' has been met."[33] The Commission permitted WKUL a wide range of forums acceptable for the presentation of opposing viewpoints, and rejected the claim made by the Citizens Committee for a Nuclear Test Ban Treaty (a newly formed organization which had been encouraged by the Kennedy Administration to counteract anti-treaty propaganda) that it had a right to air time to answer criticism of the treaty. WKUL's "own good-faith judgment" that it had presented contrasting arguments was sufficient.

Although Cullman Broadcasting won its case, the FCC's ruling is significant for its principles—that the Fairness Doctrine is applicable to *all* issues, not just local controversies, as asserted by Cullman, and that the right of the public to hear both sides is paramount. The potential impact of this ruling did not go unnoticed by some Washington politicians.

Despite scores of complaints through the years, a network was not found in violation of the Fairness Doctrine until 1968, when a Chet Huntley radio news analysis on meat inspection was judged to have contained "personal attacks" and no contrasting viewpoints. The violation was particularly disturbing because this otherwise responsible and honored journalist neglected to advise listeners that he owned a cattle ranch in New Jersey. The penalty imposed by the FCC merely afforded some minutes of radio time for spokesmen of the meat inspectors; NBC licensees were never jeopardized.[34] (Technically, networks as such are not licensed by the FCC. However, the close to two hundred stations that are affiliated with each network are subject to regulation. In addition, since each of the three commercial networks owns the legal limit of five VHF television stations and up to seven AM and seven FM radio stations, the FCC does have direct enforcement power.)

In another ruling, in 1970, NBC won a significant case before the FCC. In a report about air safety and private planes, Commission staff members had found a lack of fairness, and requested NBC to provide time to the private-aircraft owners. Reversing its staff, the Commission held that the Fairness Doctrine did not apply "to so brief, peripheral or subsidiary a reference to controversial matter." The Fairness Doctrine, the FCC ruled, was not applicable because it believed that a contrary course would interfere greatly with broadcast journalism and thus run counter to the goal of promoting robust, wide-open debate.[35]

A year later the FCC once again found that a network had contravened the general intent of the Fairness Doctrine. In 1971, in spite of all the attacks by Vice-President Spiro Agnew and others that the networks had been unfair to President Nixon's Vietnam war policies, the FCC and its Nixon-appointed chairman ruled that the three commercial networks had televised the President in five major speeches on the war, with no similar opportunity for a speech by those who opposed the war. Thereupon the networks were directed to provide time for at least one such speech, and they all complied.

But in the crazy-quilt pattern of the refining of the Fairness

Doctrine, it was not the lofty problems of presidential access or of a network documentary seen by a large audience that put the FCC on a collision course with the First Amendment. Instead, it was a personal attack over a small station in Red Lion, Pennsylvania, in 1964. Even prior to that, a series of alleged abuses by radio stations in Florida and Montana in the early sixties provoked the FCC into extending its still vaguely defined Fairness Doctrine into a rigid primer of standards.

The Mapoles case of station WEBY in Milton, Florida, involved charges of misuse of daily newscasts to transmit "false and malicious statements that attacked the personal character"[36] of public officials. The petition to revoke its license was denied by the Commission "because [the persons] knew of the attacks, were appraised of their nature, and were aware of the opportunities afforded them to respond."[37] But what emerged from the "victory" for the licensee was a headnote which to anyone who read it left no doubt as to what the FCC demanded:

> A broadcast licensee has an affirmative obligation to broadcast programs devoted to discussion and consideration of public issues, and may engage in editorializing. However, the licensee also has an obligation to see that persons holding opposing viewpoints are afforded a reasonable opportunity for the presentation of their views. Where attacks of a highly personal nature have been made on local political officials, the licensee has an affirmative duty to take all appropriate steps to see to it that the persons attacked are afforded the fullest opportunity to respond.[38]

In the KBMY case, the station in Billings, Montana, allegedly tried to "discredit and vilify"[39] the general manager of the National Rural Electric Cooperative by broadcasting editorials at least five times daily which opposed the creation of public-utility districts in Montana. Here the FCC, under Chairman Newton Minow, held that the station had erred, and once again the Fairness Doctrine was spelled out for all stations to obey:

> We conclude that in failing to supply copies of the editorial promptly to Mr. Ellis [general manager of NREC] and delaying in affording him the opportunity to reply . . . you have not fully met the requirements of the Commission's fairness doctrine.[40]

Again no disciplinary action was taken, but the findings in the Montana and Mapoles cases became cornerstones of what the FCC termed its Fairness Primer.[41] It was adopted by the FCC on July 1, 1964, and offered a clear warning to the broadcast industry.

When Reverend John M. Norris of Red Lion, Pennsylvania, the owner of radio station WGCB, received a letter from Fred J. Cook five months later, the enshrinement of the Fairness Doctrine was about to begin. Nowhere in the massive legal record, with all its citations and historic precedents, is there evidence of the political origins and motivations of this case. What the thirteen jurists on three separate high courts were unaware of at the time of the *Red Lion* decision was that a year earlier, in a climate of hysteria and backlash, a small group of well-intentioned men near the seat of national power had set in motion these forces and events by their determination to utilize the Fairness Doctrine and the FCC's regulatory arsenal to obtain free time, and to inhibit and keep off the air what they considered to be noxious and dangerous views.

3

RED LION:
Conversation
in the Fish Room

~~~~~~~~~~~~~~~~~~~~~~~~~~~~~~~

The constant flow of letters from the Committee to the stations may have inhibited the stations in their broadcast of more radical and politically partisan programs.

SPECIAL COUNSEL MARTIN E. FIRESTONE
IN A CONFIDENTIAL MEMORANDUM,
DEMOCRATIC NATIONAL COMMITTEE, 1964

Kenneth O'Donnell, the trusted friend and appointment secretary of President Kennedy, had never heard of Red Lion. In the autumn of 1963 the President's policies were being bombarded by a coast-to-coast battery of such right-wing commentators as the Reverends Carl McIntire and Billy James Hargis. Both were particularly damaging to the Kennedy Administration when the nuclear test-ban treaty with the Soviet Union was up for Senate ratification. Faced with the strong possibility that Senator Barry Goldwater would be the Republican nominee in 1964, members of the Kennedy Administration were concerned that the hundreds of ultra-right-wing radio stations could be a decisive factor in the election a year hence.

On October 17, 1963, O'Donnell summoned to the White House Wayne Phillips, a former reporter for the *New York Times* and the Denver *Post* and at that time special assistant to the Administrator of the Housing Administration. A skilled publicist, Phillips had helped run several Administration conferences on urban problems.

"O'Donnell met me in the Fish Room," Phillips recalls, "and we talked in a corner while the President was escorting Marshal Tito of Yugoslavia through the room. O'Donnell told me that the FCC had recently ruled that radio stations must air both sides of controversial issues, and asked me to meet with Nick Zapple, counsel to the Senate Communications Subcommittee, to see if this could be used to provide support for the President's programs."

O'Donnell remembers his meeting and conversation with Phillips, and has the impression that earlier, President Kennedy had told him about a conversation he'd had on the Fairness Doctrine with Senator Pastore, Zapple's boss. Pastore has no memory of such a conversation, but his concern about right-wing zealots is a matter of record. On August 27, 1963, he had written to the FCC about fairness and the growth of certain groups "who are anxious to impose a particular point of view or oppose propositions and saturate the airways with only one point of view by buying time and syndicating programs favoring only one side of an issue." The senator left no doubt that he expected the FCC to prevent this dangerous trend from "becoming a reality."[1]

President Kennedy's preoccupation with this trend was no secret. Only a few days before O'Donnell enlisted Phillips in the cause, Marquis Childs had reported in the St. Louis *Post-Dispatch* that Kennedy had unburdened himself with considerable bitterness to a friend and long-time associate on the subject of top-bracket taxpayers and the tax exemption they used to spread right-wing propaganda. Kennedy wanted this loophole closed, but he also wanted the FCC and his friends on the "proper" Senate committees to act.[2] Hence, O'Donnell chose Wayne Phillips to take a look at the radio programs and to protect the Administration's interests.

After his meeting with O'Donnell, Phillips says he met with Zapple in the Senate Building, and that the committee counsel "briefly outlined to me the Fairness Doctrine and gave me the mimeographed ruling by the FCC dated July 26, 1963, outlining the Doctrine and another ruling relating to the Cullman case." Zapple recalls the meeting and says that "Phillips and the Democratic National Committee were determined to use the Fairness Doctrine to counter the radical right." As noted earlier, the Doctrine had been made the basis of a claim for time in support of the

President's bid to win Senate ratification of the nuclear test-ban treaty with Russia.

The test-ban treaty was one of the noble goals of the Kennedy Administration, but at the time of Senate ratification in September, there had been serious concern that pressure from the right might cause a sufficient number of "military-industrial" senators to kill it. Norman Cousins, publisher of the *Saturday Review*, who had played a key role in sensitizing Chairman Khrushchev and President Kennedy to the need for such a treaty, played an even more important part in mobilizing public opinion. It was decided that SANE, the National Committee for a Sane Nuclear Policy, of which Cousins was the founder and co-chairman, was too identified with world federalism and more comprehensive disarmament, and that a Citizens Committee for a Nuclear Test Ban Treaty be founded at the specific request of the President. James J. Wadsworth, former U.S. Ambassador to the United Nations and a Republican, was named chairman, and Cousins, in one of the most generous acts of its kind in American history, contributed $400,000 of his own. "I had to sell the *Saturday Review* to do it," says Cousins. Fifty thousand dollars of this money was earmarked to counteract the ultra-right radio attacks; Lenore Marshall, a New York poet, also contributed $50,000. Ruder & Finn, a well-known public-relations firm serving the Democratic National Committee, handled the publicity for the bipartisan committee, which had a blue-ribbon board of distinguished Americans. Virtually every time a Hargis or a McIntire denounced the test-ban treaty, a letter was sent out demanding reply time under the Fairness Doctrine. Special programs were taped for this purpose, and the success of the campaign, especially in certain "unsure states," was credited with mobilizing public opinion in favor of the treaty. On September 24, 1963, the Senate ratified the treaty by a vote of 80 to 19, far more than the required two-thirds majority.

The success of this experience taught the Kennedy Administration how the Fairness Doctrine could be employed for high-priority legislation, and in Phillips' briefings by O'Donnell, Zapple and others, it was mentioned at length. There is no doubt that O'Donnell and the Democratic National Committee expected him to "see if it [the Fairness Doctrine] could be used to provide support for the President's programs."

Phillips learned more about the nature of his assignment from

Wesley McCune, a long-time Democratic party aide who operated Group Research, Inc., a Washington organization which ran a clipping and research service on right-wing publications and broadcasters. McCune provided Phillips with his extensive files on right-wing broadcasters, but could supply no recordings because of the cost.

Alerted to the need for these, Phillips purchased some primitive equipment and began monitoring radio broadcasts in the basement of his home in Bethesda, Maryland, tape-recording them and requesting transcripts and station lists. "It soon became apparent to me," he said, "that extreme right-wing broadcasting was exceptionally heavy on particular stations and in particular areas of the country, and that the content of these broadcasts was irrationally hostile to the President and his programs."

In January 1964, after President Kennedy's assassination, Phillips officially joined the staff of the Democratic National Committee as Director of News and Information. He had been recommended for his new post by Kenneth O'Donnell. Phillips soon realized that he couldn't run a professional listening post in his home at night and commissioned McCune to set up a monitoring service. "The Democrats gave me a large bundle, about ten thousand dollars. I had to buy all the equipment," McCune recalls.

The Democrats continued to develop techniques to combat right-wing radio propaganda, and in May prepared a kit explaining "how to demand time under the Fairness Doctrine" for a women's conference. The idea was simply to harass radio stations by getting officials and organizations that had been attacked by extremist radio commentators to request reply time, citing the Fairness Doctrine. When political friends and organizations such as the National Housing Conference were under attack, Phillips himself requested and sometimes received reply time. "All told," he recalls, "this volunteer effort resulted in rebuttals on over five hundred radio programs." Phillips also began working with Fred J. Cook, a friend from New York newspaper days. It was out of this association that the Goldwater book and the *Nation* article grew.

What has never been reported was that Cook's book, whose original title had been *Goldwater: Fanatic of the Right,* was inspired by and might not have been published without the guaranteed purchase of 50,000 copies by the Democratic National

Committee. This support was not as extensive as Laurance Rockefeller's financing of the Victor Lasky book critical of former Supreme Court Justice Arthur Goldberg during the 1970 Rockefeller-Goldberg gubernatorial race, but the purpose was similar: to circulate a partisan biography which was admittedly harshly critical of a political foe.

Cook started the research and writing of the book in May, and when no major publisher could be found by late July, his agent offered it to Grove Press with the advice that the Democratic National Committee was interested in it and was prepared to buy thousands of advance copies. Several days later Wayne Phillips thanked Grove Press for "letting me know in advance of the book you plan to publish about Senator Goldwater," encouraging them to publish this "important book," and promising to purchase 50,000 copies of the book at 12 cents each. A week after the offer from the Democratic National Committee, the publisher had galley proofs.[3]

Grove Press says it printed 250,000 copies but sold only 44,000 copies other than the 72,000 finally ordered by the Democratic National Committee. This order, which virtually guaranteed the cost of printing and of Cook's $1,000 advance, obviously helped convince Grove to publish the book. As part of the arrangement between Cook and Grove, the author received a penny for every copy of the Goldwater book sold at cost to "special groups" such as the Democratic National Committee. Cook's total royalties from the book were between $1,800 and $2,000.

Richard Seaver, managing editor of Grove Press at the time of the Goldwater book, rejects the notion that the book was subsidized by the Democrats: "We would have published it because we thought it an important book." In retrospect Seaver comments, "Grove Press lost money on the deal. I guess you could say we acted as the printing house for the Democrats, which really hurt the sales because anyone who wanted the book could get it from the Democrats for nothing."

This episode has a bizarre epilogue. Grove Press had difficulty in collecting the $8,640 it was owed by the Democratic National Committee, and had to turn the matter over to lawyers for collection.

Cook readily acknowledges his close working relationship with the Democratic National Committee and says, "It was only natural that while I was working on the Goldwater book, Phillips would suggest the 'Hate Clubs of the Air' piece."

Phillips says he began talking with Cook in May of 1964 about writing a critical article on right-wing broadcasters. Cook's recollection is slightly different; he contends that Phillips contacted Carey McWilliams, editor of *The Nation,* and suggested that Cook be commissioned to put such an article together. As Cook recalls it, "I was already writing my book about Goldwater, and was working with Phillips and the DNC, who provided me with most of my material from their vast files . . ." McWilliams has confirmed that the idea came from Phillips, but he is not certain whether Phillips first contacted *The Nation* or Cook.* McWilliams certainly made the final decision to publish the article, but Phillips and McCune provided Cook with much of the research material and a master tape of the most virulent broadcasts. Cook acknowledges that Phillips gave him the idea for "Hate Clubs of the Air," but rejects the suggestion that the article was all but written by the Democratic National Committee.

Cook admits that he made no effort to interview Hargis, McIntire or other "right-wing fanatics" described in his exposé. He carefully attributed quotes to their proper authors, i.e., "Wesley McCune . . . Director of Group Research, Inc. . . . estimated last year that the airwave propaganda budget was close to $20 million." As part of his *Nation* article, Cook offered his readers "a compilation made about the first of the year of the major propagandists and their audiences." This information was compiled sev-

---

* After a condensation of this chapter in the *New York Times Magazine* ("What's Fair on the Air," March 30, 1975), McWilliams publicly disavowed the reference to Wayne Phillips as initiator of the *Nation* article. In a letter to the editor (April 27, 1975) McWilliams wrote: "It is not true that Wayne Phillips suggested the idea for the article on the so-called 'Hate Clubs of the Air' which Fred J. Cook wrote, and *The Nation* published. It was my idea." He also denied that the article had been in any way arranged by the Democratic National Committee.

Despite McWilliams' objections, I stand by my original statement. McWilliams himself, on two separate occasions in October 1974, told me that Phillips, not Cook or he, first proposed the story and made major contributions to its content. Until then, I had never heard of Phillips' relationship to the *Nation* article, and it was McWilliams' unexpected revelation that caused me to seek out Phillips, who confirmed his role in the article, as did Cook and several others.

eral months before Phillips alerted Cook to the story, and it is reasonable to assume that it came from Phillips. McCune did the accompanying map of the propaganda net, an illustration which neither Cook nor *The Nation* chose to identify as the product of the research arm of a major political party.

In the wake of Cook's article, Phillips, McCune, the Democratic National Committee and their allied organizations accelerated their campaign to mute right-wing radio broadcasters. "Thousands of copies of Cook's article were sent to state Democratic leaders and to every radio station in the country known to carry right-wing broadcasts," Phillips recalls, "together with a letter from Sam Brightman of the DNC pointing out that claims for time would be made in the event of attacks on Democratic candidates or their programs."

In July of 1964, in response to this activity, Reverend Carl McIntire, "outraged by the letter," unleashed a series of personal attacks on Brightman. The deputy chairman of the staff of the Democratic National Committee demanded reply time, and as a result was given free time on some six hundred stations. Nevertheless, the right-wing barrage continued unabated. McIntire aimed a broadcast at Carl Rowan, the respected black journalist who had succeeded Edward R. Murrow as Director of the United States Information Agency, charging that Rowan was unfit for the office. Radio commentator Dan Smoot, a former FBI agent, compared the 1964 Democratic National Convention that nominated Lyndon Johnson to a "Munich beer-hall coup." Again the committee demanded reply time, and some thirty stations complied.

Not content merely to respond to the attacks, the committee went on the offensive. Phillips enlarged his staff, adding Martin E. Firestone, an attorney and former staff member of the FCC with an insider's sophistication in the intricacies of the Fairness Doctrine, who became the volunteer staff adviser to the Democratic committee. Firestone escalated and professionalized the committee's broadcasting campaign.

Then an event on the night of July 16 further stimulated the Democrats to intensify their battle against the right wing. At the Cow Palace in San Francisco, Senator Barry Goldwater stood before an emotional Republican convention to accept the presidential nomination with the now famous battle cry: "Extremism in the defense of liberty is no vice . . . Moderation in the pursuit of justice is no virtue." Stunned by the shrillness of the rhetoric and the roar of the crowd, Wayne Phillips called an account executive at Ruder & Finn, and they both agreed that the DNC's radio project had to be accelerated.

The strategy designed by Phillips and Ruder & Finn prescribed a low profile. The Democratic National Committee organized a bipartisan front organization, the National Council for Civic Responsibility, and Arthur Larson, a prominent liberal Eisenhower Republican and once Director of the United States Information Agency, was recruited to head it. Funds for the council were solicited with full-page newspaper advertisements signed by a broad range of moderate and liberal intellectuals in the country who shared a deep concern over the growth of the John Birch Society and other right-wing extremist groups. The advertisement alerted readers to the fact that "$10 million is spent on weekly radio and television broadcasts in all fifty states by extremist groups."[4] More than $21,000 in contributions were received in response, but more than half of the money Larson set as his fund-raising goal came from major Democratic party contributors at the behest of the DNC. "We created the client," says a former account executive at Ruder & Finn, "and then the client retained and paid us with funds we channeled to them." Bill Ruder, an Assistant Secretary of Commerce in the Kennedy years and an acknowledged leader in public relations, says frankly, "Our massive strategy was to use the Fairness Doctrine to challenge and harass right-wing broadcasters and hope that the challenges would be so costly to them that they would be inhibited and decide it was too expensive to continue."

The National Council for Civic Responsibility relied heavily on material supplied by McCune's Group Research organization, and Fred Cook was paid $1,500 to write anti-extremist material for the council. But even the NCCR façade required a front to qualify as a tax-exempt shell. More important, the Democratic National Committee wanted to camouflage its direct contributions to the council. The Institute for Public Affairs, a defunct Washington "citizens lobby" group originally funded in 1948 by several labor unions, was disinterred. Phillips says he found the IPA in the phone book, but Dewey Anderson, executive director of the moribund institute and a cattle rancher then living at Lake Tahoe, claimed that James H. Rowe, a prestigious Washington lawyer and close adviser to President Johnson, called him to learn whether its tax-exempt status was still in effect. Rowe then asked Anderson to fly to Washington the next day.

Anderson, then sixty-seven, later recalled being escorted by Rowe through the side door of the Democratic National Committee office to meet National Chairman John Bailey and Treasurer Dick McGuire. He was told by Rowe and Bailey, "We've got the money, you've got the exemption and we need you to fight these right-wing radio extremists." Thus did the National Council for Civic Responsibility become the National Council for Civic Responsibility of the Public Affairs Institute. Its initial funding of $25,000 came directly from the Democratic National Committee "book fund," with the assurance that there would be other contributions from the party and from major Democratic contributors making tax-free gifts. Anderson was also introduced to Phillips and the executives of Ruder & Finn, and was told he would work with them and with Arthur Larson, whose appointment as chairman of the NCCR was soon to be announced.

A sum of some $250,000 was used to produce and sponsor anti-right-wing broadcasts, and to print and distribute literature exposing the John Birch Society and other extremist groups. The radio shows, as shrill and one-sided as what they were fighting, were called "Spotlight" and ran on some sixty stations. They were narrated by "commentator" William Dennis, the pseudonym of an actor employed by Ruder & Finn. Larson, who had publicly opposed the election of Goldwater, repeatedly stressed the fact that the National Council for Civic Responsibility was nonpolitical. At a news conference in New York's Overseas Press Club, he told skeptical reporters that "the council's formation had nothing to do with the presidential campaign or with the right-wing views of Republican candidate, Senator Barry Goldwater . . . Our group was in the making for nearly two years." [5] In the audience at the time, Anderson said that he almost stood up to contradict this.

Because of the close association of James Rowe with President Johnson, and also because of John Bailey's standing as chairman of the Democratic National Committee, there is little doubt that this contrived scheme had White House approval. Ruder & Finn officials say that the President was constantly kept informed by Treasurer McGuire. Today Phillips recalls the affair with both remorse and humor: "I don't think we'd do it that way today, but the embarrassing thing was that the day after the Johnson landslide, Anderson took off with fifty thousand dollars that we hadn't spent. I guess you can figure out why we were in no position to sue him." Anderson vehemently denied this allegation: "There was less than thirty-five thousand dollars left, and I had vouchers to prove we had debts for all of it." Anderson and his 1964 comrades share considerable acrimony. "It was a seamy, sleazy operation, and they made me a patsy," he says. A Ruder & Finn executive comments, "It took a Washington bureaucrat from North Dakota to take us." Looking back on it, another Ruder & Finn executive said, "If we did in 1974 what we did in 1964, we'd be answering questions before some congressional committee."

Larson, who had long been a target of the radical right, recalls his role in the NCCR with embarrassment. "The whole thing was not my idea," he says, "but let's face it, we decided to use the Fairness Doctrine to harass the extreme right. In the light of Watergate, it was wrong. We felt the ends justified the means. They never do." Then he adds sadly, "I guess I was a babe in the woods. As soon as I knew the Democrats were putting money into it, I wanted out."

In retrospect, Firestone, now a prominent Washington communications lawyer representing station owners—a number of whom would want him to help repeal the Fairness Doctrine—admits, "Perhaps in the light of Watergate, our tactics were too aggressive, but we were up against ultra-right preachers who were saying vicious things about Kennedy and Johnson." Then, with a smile that reflected a period of youth that seems to have a moral statute of limitations, Firestone said jokingly, "I guess I could have become the Donald Segretti of those years, but Wayne Phillips always kept me from going too far."

Whatever lessons hindsight has taught, this campaign in 1964 against right-wing broadcasts was at the time considered a success by its creators. In a summary written during the closing days of the presidential election, Firestone pointed with pride to 1,035 letters to stations that produced a total of 1,678 hours of free time from stations carrying McIntire, Dean Manion and Smoot. Both he and Phillips felt a genuine sense of accomplishment. In a report to the Democratic National Committee, Phillips wrote: "Even more important than the free radio time was the effectiveness of this operation in inhibiting the political activity of these right-wing broadcasts . . ." In a confidential report to Phillips and the DNC, Firestone stressed the nature of the campaign that "may have inhibited the stations in their broadcast of more radical and politically partisan programs."[6] He concluded that most of the stations are "small rural stations . . . in desperate need of broadcast revenues . . . The right-wingers operate on a strictly cash basis and it is for this reason that they are carried by so many small stations. Were our efforts to be continued on a year-round basis, we would find that many of these stations would consider the broadcasts of these programs bothersome and burdensome (especially if they are ultimately required to give us free time) and would start dropping the programs from their broadcast schedule."[7]

During this period after the elections, the Democratic National Committee was considering future use of the Fairness Doctrine. As Phillips recounts it, "Sometime during this period Fred Cook asked for help in requesting time under the Fairness Doctrine to reply to a personal attack broadcast by Billy James Hargis. The help was given, and he sent letters to radio stations asking for time following the general format the committee had been using. It was this request which precipitated the Red Lion case."

It may well be that KXEN in St. Louis was the first to notify Cook that he had been the subject of an attack, but among the persons who heard the broadcast were the monitors at McCune's listening post. "What's wrong with Cook being told by the Democratic National Committee or anyone else of the broadcast that mentioned him," says McCune, "and getting help from the Democratic National Committee in phrasing his demand for a reply?" They also provided him with a list of the stations which normally broadcast Hargis. When some of those stations agreed to broadcast his reply, both Cook and Phillips remember that the Democratic National Committee helped the journalist to make copies of his response. Firestone continued to counsel Phillips, who in turn advised Cook on his right to reply time under the personal-attack rule, and instructed him on how to petition the FCC to obtain free time if a station refused. Cook says he sought advice from his own local attorney.

Perhaps Cook was not aware that he was being used in this campaign of inhibition; he may have been unwittingly manipulated in a sequence that began in the Fish Room of the White House and ended four years later in the Supreme Court. Perhaps he was only a citizen who wanted to defend his good name, even in Red Lion, Pennsylvania.

4

RED LION:
The Race
to the Circuits

*" 'Destroy thou them, O God, let them fall
by their own counsels.' "*

PSALMS 5:10, QUOTED BY
REVEREND JOHN M. NORRIS

Of the two hundred stations to which Cook sent his mimeographed letter, most responded, but rejected his request for reply
time. WJBS in De Land, Florida, answered: "We are happy to
make equal time available to you on the exact same basis as was
made to the Christian Crusade program . . . If you will forward
a tape of your reply, accompanied by a check for $5, we will
be glad to schedule it for broadcast."[1] KNOT in Prescott, Arizona, wrote: "I totally reject your demand for time at our expense. Nowhere in the FCC regulations is there such a clause."[2]

In all, fewer than fifty stations offered Cook the right of rebuttal. To these he sent an audio tape which he had made at an
Asbury Park station, or one re-recorded in Washington by the
Democratic National Committee. In his three-minute reply he
said that Hargis, whom he called "a demagogue," had every right
to criticize his book on Goldwater, but that his "vicious attack on
me was . . . smear, innuendo, the discrediting of a man by libel."
In arguing his innocence, Cook read excerpts of a letter to him
from Manhattan District Attorney Frank Hogan which exonerated him of any responsibility for his former newspaper colleague Eugene Gleason's false accusations. Hogan's letter read in
part: "Mr. Gleason not only admitted in our office that the charge

was untrue, but also completely exonerated you [Cook] of all responsibility . . ."[3]

The Red Lion station's uncompromising response to Cook's letter stated: "Our rate card is enclosed. Your prompt reply will enable us to arrange for the time you may wish to purchase." "Owner" Norris, as he signed his mail, also enclosed similar letters he had recently sent to the Democratic National Committee and the American Civil Liberties Union, denying them air time they had requested to answer attacks by Dan Smoot against President Johnson, the social security program and the civil rights movement. In response to all this "harassment,"[4] religious and political pressure and persecution, as he termed it, Norris sent his rate card as a solicitation for business.

Because of what he considered to be the strident tone of Norris' answer, although others were equally hostile, Fred Cook wrote him a second letter: "Your letter of December 28 . . . does not answer the first question I asked you: 'Did you or did you not broadcast the attack that Reverend Hargis made upon me in late November? . . . if you did," Cook went on, "I submit that the least of your obligation in this matter is to grant me free time for a brief reply. Otherwise, it is conceivable that radio stations might be able to drum up a fairly good business by selling time to persons who have been slandered."[5]

Reverend Norris' response was swift and to the point: ". . . we are at a loss to understand your statement that we ought *not* to 'drum-up' business—we could ask 'How else may we be expected to stay in business?' " Then Norris asked a question which, in its naïveté and bluntness, cut to the heart of a question which some sophisticated licensees thousands of times bigger have never dared ask: ". . . what would happen if General Motors advertised the 'best car' and Ford demanded 'free time' to inform our listeners that they had been slandered? This would remove all broadcasting from the realm of free enterprise, leaving only government subsidized and controlled radio. I am sure, Mr. Cook, that you would not wish this to happen."[6]

Cook now turned to the FCC for redress, just as his *Nation* article and Phillips and Firestone had suggested, and asked that the Commission order Norris and WGCB to grant him reply time. But Red Lion's position continued to be uncompromising. ". . . WGCB will give Mr. Cook an appropriate amount of time to answer the alleged attack upon him in the Hargis program if he advises us that he is financially unable to 'sponsor' or pay for such a broadcast. We are quite certain that it would be impossible for us to obtain other sponsorship of such a broadcast."[7]

However, the Democratic National Committee, along with its chairman and counsel, kept the heat on Red Lion. On February 4, just as Cook was going before the Commission, the Democratic National Committee cited: Red Lion and nine other stations which had steadfastly refused to grant time, requested during the 1964 campaign, to answer a Dan Smoot broadcast charging that President Johnson "would do anything to help his election this fall—even contrive a war if necessary"; a McIntire-Walker attack on Carl Rowan; and an attack on the State Department by the "Manion Forum," a right-wing radio show. The election was long since over, and Johnson had scored a massive landslide, but the Democratic National Committee wanted to keep the pressure on, and to put teeth in the Fairness Doctrine for future elections. The committee charged Red Lion and the other nine stations with "a flagrant disregard of the terms of the Fairness Doctrine," and asked the FCC "to take action against these licensees which it finds to have been in violation of . . . its regulations."[8]

Norris felt that his station was being harassed because of its closeness to Carl McIntire, who with the younger Norris was about to apply for a station in Media, Pennsylvania. The reverend firmly believed that the Democratic National Committee, Cook and the FCC were all conspiring against him and his fellow religious broadcasters. Rallying those stations being attacked for their "pro-American" broadcasts, Norris exhorted them to "Resist the devil and he will flee from you."[9]

But Norris was not content merely to inspire the morale of his fellow broadcasters. On the same day, February 12, 1965, he replied to the FCC. Rejecting the criticism of his "tormentors," Norris wrote: "Now well into my 82nd year, I have never before been subjected to such religious and political persecution." The government's attack on his station would not bother him, he went on; citing the gospel according to Matthew, he proclaimed that God was on his side: " 'Blessed are ye, when men shall revile you, and persecute you, and shall say all manner of evil against you falsely, for my sake.' "[10]

In addition to his firm rejection, Norris attempted to short-circuit the controversy and the whole regulatory process by having the Fairness Doctrine declared unconstitutional. On September 21, 1965, he sought a sweeping declaration from a specially consti- tuted three-judge District Court in Washington. This tactic was immediately blocked by Chief Judge David Bazelon's refusal to appoint such a panel. In a terse order that now appears startling in view of Bazelon's latter-day flight from the Fairness Doctrine, the court called Red Lion's request "frivolous."[11]

The FCC did not regard the Hargis broadcast as frivolous. On October 6, almost eleven months after the attack, following a lengthy study by its examiners, the FCC determined that "ele- mental fairness"[12] required that Mr. Cook be notified of the at- tack and given a comparable right to reply, whether he was able or willing to purchase time or not.

Ordered to obey the dictates of the Fairness Doctrine, Norris ironically sought tactical refuge in its intent. In effect, WGCB claimed that Cook had started it all with his article in *The Nation*. It requested reconsideration of the decision by the FCC on the grounds that the journalist's original attack in the "Hate Clubs of the Air" absolved the Red Lion station of responsibility to grant comparable use of the station's facilities for reply time. However, the claim that Cook and *The Nation* were the original attackers was quickly rejected by the Commission, which of course had no knowledge of the origins of the article. The Commission even echoed Cook by going so far as to suggest that if spon- sorship of air time was the only method to respond to personal attack, "under such a construction, personal attacks might even be resorted to as an opportunity to obtain additional revenues."[13]

At this point in the skirmish, the normal procedure would have been for Norris to accept the FCC order and write Cook to sug- gest that he send WGCB a reply tape. The records of the case would have been closed and would have joined the files of the other 356 Fairness Doctrine complaints lodged with the FCC that year. (The Commission requested additional information on only 169 such complaints in 1965. Since there are 8,500 licensees, this means that only one out of 47 stations received such inquiries.)

But the low growl from Red Lion was about to become a mighty roar. Norris refused to accept the FCC finding that he was the public trustee and proxy of the public's interest rather than the owner of the franchise. The FCC's scolding so bristled the octogenarian that he sarcastically began signing his letters to the Commission "John M. Norris, Proxy." Spurred on by Reverend Carl McIntire, who seems to have had some kind of spiritual interest in WGCB, just as the Norris family did in his station in Media, Pennsylvania, Norris vowed to fight on: "The bigger they come the harder they fall." Portraying the FCC as Goliath, he invoked David: " 'Destroy thou them, O God, let them fall by their own counsels.' "[14]

Red Lion Broadcasting Company's attorney, Benedict Cottone, a former general counsel to the FCC and a communications veteran who specializes in protecting stations with "delicate" FCC renewal problems, insists he urged Norris not to sue in the Court of Appeals. But by now Norris saw himself as a martyr representing not just his fellow Christian warriors, but the entire broadcast industry.

Still, the commitment for a tiny radio station with gross revenues of less than $90,000 a year in taking on the FCC in costly litigation was not one that the Norris family alone could undertake. Victor Parker, a true believer in the McIntire-Norris gospel, and as he describes his duties, "bodyguard, chauffeur and management engineer for Reverend Norris," urged his employer to sue. "I wanted us to take on the bigots of the FCC and keep an open mike for those who preached against the godless enemy Communism."

Parker turned to Robert Manuel, an attorney who had helped him organize the Taxpayer's Alliance in Fairfax, Virginia. "I had never heard of the Fairness Doctrine," says Manuel, "until that day in 1965 when Parker introduced me to Norris."

At one time Manuel had been a lawyer for the National Labor Relations Board and thereafter the Republican counsel for the McClellan Government Operations Committee. In 1962 he gained brief national fame when he was fired as minority counsel to a House committee after leaking to the New York *Herald Tribune* a secret report allegedly linking Billy Sol Estes and Vice-President Lyndon Johnson. As an attorney practicing law in Alexandria, Virginia, he hardly qualified as a communications specialist or a constitutional authority, so to assist him, he recruited Thomas B. Sweeney, with whom he had worked on the NLRB and who was "an expert with the conservative Jeffersonian view of the Constitution."

While Sweeney went to the law books, Manuel's first assignment was to visit "the religious-broadcast fat cats" and find some partners to share the estimated $40,000 cost of the lawsuit. "Hargis promised five thousand dollars, McIntire ten thousand. Walter Knott of the Berry Farm in Orange County, California, gave a thousand dollars; a station in Ohio gave five hundred; and Colonel Hunt, after talking to us for twenty-four hours, said he'd think about it," recounts Manuel. "But he never came through with anything but a few of his books."

Norris, his son John and Parker were impressed with Manuel and Sweeney, who were convinced that the National Association of Broadcasters would become partners in the suit against the FCC. This influential trade association, representing 3,500 radio and television stations, did join with Red Lion Broadcasting Company, but with considerable reluctance. It is true that for more than a decade the powerful NAB and other industry lobbyists had been waiting for the right test case to challenge the FCC's "growing appetite to regulate fairness," but even the broadcasters most militantly opposed to government regulation wanted no part of Reverend Norris' crusade. "We had waited fifteen long years to challenge the Fairness Doctrine," said one prominent member of the communications bar, "and we didn't want to walk into court with a right-wing radical any more than we did some left-wing nut."

The National Association of Broadcasters feared that any attempt by Norris to challenge the FCC ruling in the Court of Appeals was bound to lose—that the weak facts in the Red Lion case would result in the court's sanctioning of a strong Fairness Doctrine. Vincent Wasilewski, president of the broadcasters' association and once its general counsel, says candidly that he always had misgivings about it and believed it to be "a bizarre case not worthy of the aims and image of the broadcast industry." NAB officials tried desperately to persuade Norris to drop his appeal, and even offered to reimburse the station for all legal costs. Because of similar misgivings, W. Theodore Pierson, a commanding figure among Washington communications lawyers, a political conservative and a fundamentalist on First Amendment issues who would later play a major role in this drama, also attempted to discourage Norris from pursuing the case. But the reverend was not to be persuaded; he was now convinced that "the devil was loose in the FCC corridors," and that it was his godly mission to drive him out.

Only when it became obvious that Norris would not back down, says Wasilewski, did the NAB reluctantly agree to give him financial support so that this "fragile and unattractive case" would have proper counsel and funds for the expenses of such litigation. *Broadcasting* magazine reported that at its June 1966 meeting the NAB board appropriated up to $10,000 to help defray Red Lion Broadcasting's legal fees. Wasilewski says the board, which had experienced legal counsel on its staff, and others available to it, stopped short of demanding that Norris retain NAB's choice of lawyers "because it might be viewed as improper."

But Red Lion Broadcasting Company's entry into the appellate arena was almost blocked a second time. The three-man Court of Appeals for the District of Columbia heard arguments on September 26, 1966, by Robert Manuel and Tom Sweeney for WGCB and by Henry Geller for the FCC. Manuel and Sweeney were veterans of the Washington political wars, but their advocacy was hampered by the seemingly brutal facts of *Red Lion*, and they were overwhelmed by the expertness of Geller. A specialist in communications law, Geller said that arguing *Red Lion* was "like shooting fish in a barrel." With one dissent the court dismissed Red Lion's actions on the grounds "that the declaratory rulings contained in the Commission's letters are not orders from which an appeal may be taken or judicial review sought."[15] Translated, this means that technically the FCC action against WGCB was only advisory and could not be tested in court.

The FCC, however, was not content with a victory on technical grounds; it believed that its fairness orders should be subject to immediate and full review, and wanted a constitutional knock-out based on the tailor-made facts of *Red Lion*. As general counsel Henry Geller put it, "It was a thing of beauty and we wanted to go all the way." Therefore the Commission and the government petitioned for rehearing en banc (before the full court), and this ten-man court then directed that the Red Lion case should be decided on its merits. Both the FCC and Norris wanted to go all the way to the Supreme Court, even if the National Association of Broadcasters and the giants of the industry did not.

In June 1967 the Court of Appeals decided that "the American people own the broadcast frequencies,"[16] that Norris and his station's constitutional rights had not been abridged in this application of the Fairness Doctrine, and that Fred Cook was entitled to suitable reply time. "The Fairness Doctrine," wrote Judge Edward A. Tamm in his opinion, "is not unconstitutionally vague, indefinite or uncertain . . ."[17] Further, Red Lion's broadcast did "constitute a serious abridgement" of Cook's free-speech rights. "I find in the Fairness Doctrine a vehicle completely legal in its origin which implements by the use of modern technology the 'free and general discussion of public matters [which] seems absolutely essential to prepare the people for an intelligent exercise of their rights as citizens.' "[18] In a concurring opinion, Judge Charles Fahy expressed some doubts about parts of Judge Tamm's reasoning but agreed that "a reply to a personal attack is not conditioned upon the ability of the licensee to obtain paid sponsorship for the reply."[19]

Those forces which had dreaded Red Lion as a "miserable case at the fastidiously wrong time" now sensed that their worst fears would become a reality if their crusade against the Fairness Doctrine were to march into the Supreme Court under the mangy banner of *Red Lion* and Reverend John M. Norris. The industry, and especially Ted Pierson, searched for a second front, and inadvertently the FCC provided that vulnerable opening, as one high official of the Commission admitted.

On April 6, 1966, as it was becoming obvious that the Red Lion case would be fought out in the courts, the FCC, confident of being upheld, had issued a "Notice of Proposed Rule Making" to promote the Fairness Doctrine, and "to clarify and make more precise the obligations of broadcast licensees where they have aired personal attacks and editorials regarding political candidates."[20]

What this ritual meant was that the Commission's finding in the Red Lion case was still a loosely woven concept and could not become wholly effective until new rules had been proposed and adopted. Without such rules, a station could flagrantly violate the Fairness Doctrine. Thus, if WGCB in Red Lion or another station with a similar infraction disobeyed the FCC's decision, such refusal could be considered at license renewal time, but traditionally the Commission has been reluctant to impose the death-penalty sanction of license revocation. To be effective, the FCC needed an enforcement tool "somewhere between nothing and death," and it was anxious to promulgate its new rules because it was convinced that they would be sustained in the Court of Appeals and wanted them to be ready for adoption when the decision was handed down.

The Commission asked for comments on its proposed rules, and received twenty-six replies. Eighteen broadcast stations or group owners were opposed to the new rules, charging violation of the First Amendment, while eight organizations, ranging from the National Council of Churches of Christ to the American Civil Liberties Union, supported the Fairness Doctrine as within the spirit of the First Amendment. It would take the FCC fourteen months to adopt the proposed rules; the tactical delay was to give the Court of Appeals time to decide *Red Lion*.

Thus, after the Tamm opinion on *Red Lion* was handed down on June 13, 1967, the FCC, their actions in the Red Lion case confirmed, adopted new rules on personal attack only twenty-two days later. But the commissioners and staff admit that they were not prepared for what happened next. The broadcast industry was now more fearful than ever about *Red Lion*'s chances in the Supreme Court, where Norris was determined to seek a final review, so Ted Pierson, representing the Radio-Television News Directors Association (RTNDA), worked out a plan that caught the FCC off-guard: an attack on the Fairness Doctrine purposely separated from the weaknesses of *Red Lion* and designed to steal the spotlight from it. His plan was to keep what he calls "the fat cats" out and to appeal the FCC's ruling in the name of individual professional broadcast journalists who were being inhibited by the fairness rules.

The National Association of Broadcasters also preferred Pierson's plan because it attacked the legality of the personal-attack rules, and "affords a more appropriate vehicle than does the Red Lion case, . . . particularly in the Supreme Court." In a letter to Manuel and his Red Lion client, the NAB alluded to the prospects of moving the Pierson appeal to Chicago. "There is a wide choice of circuits available for such an appeal, thereby affording the broadcasters a second bite at the apple, perhaps in a more sympathetic forum than in the District of Columbia." Norris still would not be deterred, but the NAB decided to bet on Pierson.

The Pierson plan was designed as a non-network effort, but the occupants of two mid-Manhattan executive suites were not about to yield their championing of broadcasters' rights to anyone, "even to Ted Pierson."

Actually, three suits were brought within four days. If Pierson had prevailed, CBS and NBC might have stayed out. For years Pierson had been the *pro bono* legal counsel for the Radio-Television News Directors Association. The members of this unincorporated group of a thousand managers and editors of radio and television stations knew very little about *Red Lion* and the Fairness Doctrine, and depended on their honorary life member, Ted Pierson, for most of their legal philosophy. Pierson convinced RTNDA's board that a suit against the FCC and its new rules was the right suit at the right time, and if he had his way, in the right place—Chicago, whose Seventh Circuit Court of Appeals, with its reputed anti-Washington bias, might provide a more salubrious atmosphere. With a total annual budget of less than $50,000, the RTNDA had no resources for such a contest, but Pierson volunteered to obtain the financial cooperation of some of the large station and group owners, whom his firm represented, to help defray the costs.

However, Pierson and the RTNDA were destined to have some competitors and/or partners in the litigation whether they wanted them or not. The law firm representing at least one of the networks had no enthusiasm for anything remotely connected with *Red Lion* and advised against litigation, but the top managements of both CBS and NBC were determined that if there was to be a crusade against the Fairness Doctrine, they were going to be in the vanguard. As Frank Stanton, then president of CBS, recounted recently, "We had stayed out of several other unpopular cases involving the First Amendment, and we felt that we wanted to lend our moral suasion and the record of CBS News to any such litigation."

Pierson tried to dissuade the two networks on the grounds that they would appear to the courts as big business resisting regulation; he wanted the case to focus on the First Amendment rights of "a poor evangelical preacher from Pennsylvania and the professional newsmen simply trying to report the news, rather than on a lot of 'fat cats.' "

There were other points of contention. While Pierson wanted the case tried in Chicago, CBS and NBC preferred New York and the Second Circuit Court because of the sympathetic presence of the *New York Times*. Not only were CBS's attorneys and its Washington law firm, Wilmer, Cutler & Pickering, nervous about *Red Lion* but they feared that Pierson's "fundamentalist" rejection of the Fairness Doctrine would offend the judiciary, particularly the Supreme Court; the network believed a more moderate position would fare better. CBS felt that the respected record in news and public affairs of a network news department made it a sympathetic candidate for the protections of press freedom.

Therefore the three law suits proceeded on three different tracks, and when Pierson's firm heard that CBS was about to file in New York, "the race to the Circuits was on."

A few minutes before noon Central standard time, on July 27, 1967, the Radio-Television News Directors Association filed suit in the Seventh Circuit Court of Appeals in Chicago. (The RTNDA was allowed standing in the Seventh Circuit because its president for that year worked for radio station WGN, which provided the organization with a Chicago mailing address.) The RTNDA's position, as stated by Pierson in the petition to review, was that "the Commission's rules, by providing for economic, administrative and other burdens as a condition to voicing personal attacks, serve to penalize broadcasters for, and thus to deter them from, sharply criticizing public officials and public figures."[21] The RTNDA claimed that not only were specific new rules unconstitutional but the Fairness Doctrine itself was in violation of the First Amendment.

At 4:50 Eastern standard time on the same day CBS, Inc., filed its challenge in the Second Circuit Court in New York. NBC, four days behind, filed its attack on the last day of July 1967.

Jarred by these three fresh suits, the Federal Communications Commission reacted with a speed not usually associated with Washington's regulatory agencies. Just one week after the last of the industry challenges, and only a month after the adoption of its new rules, the FCC suddenly amended its regulations. Aware of criticism that it was unduly interfering with news operations, it attempted to counter that charge by exempting "bona fide newscasts or on-the-spot coverage of a bona fide news event"[22] from the new rules. But this patchwork didn't satisfy the broadcasters. In stinging briefs, both networks called for further revisions. In a brief with an appendix which was in itself a documentary history of broadcast journalism from Murrow to Sevareid to *CBS Reports,* CBS contended that the new rules weakened the First Amendment far more than the single order in the Red Lion case, which "was unaccompanied by any enforcement sanction and concerned only a single past broadcast by a single station."[23] Citing its own traditions of fairness, CBS attempted to separate its position of responsibility from the Red Lion case, which it believed to be "plainly distinguishable . . . , the station involved in *Red Lion* has made no effort to comply with the general fairness doctrine in its treatment of Mr. Cook's book . . ."[24] More temperately, CBS accepted "the traditional Fairness Doctrine [which] treats the licensee as mature and responsible; it does not arrogate to the Commission an assumed omniscience." The network opposed the new personal-attack rules as improperly interfering with licensee discretion. "It is but a short step from these requirements to other commands . . ."[25]

As an example, the CBS objections focused on Eric Sevareid's nightly commentary, and protested that in a normal year application of the personal-attack rule would force CBS to "issue more than 50 invitations to identified individuals or groups . . . The amount of time that would have to be offered would be substantially greater than the time required to broadcast the [original] commentaries."[26]

The networks were not the only ones that were unhappy. The Justice Department, specifically Assistant Attorney General Donald Turner under Ramsey Clark, had no appetite to commit government attorneys to a series of courtroom confrontations in defense of rules with such assailable flaws. But its brief was softer: "We are fully prepared to support the Commission's position that the Fairness Doctrine is constitutional . . . however, we have some concern that the rule, as drafted, raises problems that might be minimized by appropriate revisions . . ."[27] In other words, the FCC should soften its position before the Justice Department agreed to take on the broadcast news media.

In the face of this opposition, and with the permission of the Court of Appeals in Washington, the Commission amended the rule further "to exempt bona fide news interviews" (e.g., *Meet the Press* and *Face the Nation*) and "commentary or analysis in the course of bona fide newscasts."[28] Sevareid, Howard K. Smith and David Brinkley were now in the clear.

But Lee Loevinger, one of the most articulate and acerbic members of the FCC, objected to what he called the "Eric Sevareid Rule": ". . . the Commission cannot draft or apply rules that operate on the basis of its attitude toward particular individuals. If the commentaries of Eric Sevareid are entitled to exemption from the rules, then so are the commentaries of Richard Cotton,* Carl McIntire and a host of other commentators."[29]

Expressing his own respect for Sevareid, Loevinger dissented from the exemption amendments as much as he did the "tortuous" new personal-attack rules because they have been "inadequately considered and badly drafted" and "are unreasonably and unconstitutionally vague . . . I have come to doubt the competence of a government agency such as the Commission to promulgate rules such as these in the area of speech."[30]

In spite of Loevinger's dissent, the proposed rules were adopted by the FCC with clearly defined protections for the broadcast journalist as opposed to the religious or political crusader. There were certain other inconsistencies in the exemption; Sevareid or Harry Reasoner, for example, was not obligated, when providing commentary as part of a bona-fide news program, to inform the object of his critical analysis; however, the same commentary excerpted from the original and broadcast by itself on radio in a program bearing only the commentator's name was subject to all the personal-attack obligations.

Despite such concessions in the new rules on personal attack, none of the four separate but concurrent lawsuits against the FCC were withdrawn. Norris had already asked the Supreme Court to grant certiorari.** Supporting the RTNDA brief, some

---

* Cotton, a far-right commentator, had been charged with broadcasting anti-Semitic views.

** A "Writ of Certiorari (Latin)," according to Black's *Law Dictionary*, is "an appellate proceeding for reexamination of action of inferior tribunal"—meaning that the higher court is willing to consider the case of the losing side in a criminal or civil litigation.

The Supreme Court of the United States receives more than 4,000 requests for certiorari each year and accepts some 175 cases. Often the justification for certiorari is the persuasion of at least four Justices that the point at issue is ripe for constitutional review. Sometimes it is to resolve a conflict between two or more lower courts.

of Pierson's major clients (Time-Life Broadcast, RKO General and six other television and radio group owners) wanted to test the Fairness Doctrine; so did CBS and NBC.

The NBC brief, more like RTNDA's than CBS's, did not concede the constitutionality of the Fairness Doctrine and blasted the personal-attack and editorializing rules as interference with the right of free speech. "The rule has the effect," said NBC, "of discouraging broadcasters from taking stands on public issues. It requires them to censor carefully discussion and other programs. . . . It places in the hands of the Commission the power, by its day-to-day interpretations of a vaguely worded rule, to affect in more subtle ways the content of what is broadcast . . ."[31] In addition, NBC leaned on Benjamin Franklin, who was reported to have said that his "newspaper was not a stage coach with seats for everyone." The network's position was that the Constitution guaranteed "a free press, not free access to the press. The guarantee of free press has never meant . . . that it is the province of government to secure for every individual or group, or point of view free and equal access to the press."[32]

The next move was up to the Court of Appeals, and it acted by consolidating the three cases into one, which on October 24, 1967, became known as *RTNDA et al.* v. *the FCC.* The Seventh Circuit was awarded jurisdiction, just as Pierson had planned it, simply because the RTNDA suit had been filed and stamped in the Federal Court House in Chicago three hours and fifty-five minutes before the CBS lawyers reached the courthouse in Foley Square. Since the government was not seeking the appeal, there was no reason for the Washington court to take the case.

Almost unheard amid the nominating convention's din and turmoil of that 1968 spring and summer in Chicago, the RTNDA, CBS, NBC and their corps of attorneys—the names of the list read like those receiving honorary degrees at a prestigious law school—descended on the Seventh Circuit Court in Chicago. Because three well-known and highly competitive Washington law firms were involved, and each was jealous of according anyone else the star role, Pierson recruited, and the others accepted, Archibald Cox of Harvard Law School, the Solicitor General in the Kennedy-Johnson years. Cox, who had argued some ninety cases before the Supreme Court, gave the petitioning team clout and "a touch of class." He was opposed in court by Daniel R.

Ohlbaum, deputy general counsel for the FCC, who knew the intricacies of the case but who was no match for his opponent, a skillful debator and constitutional scholar.

The broadcaster's strategy worked—at least in Chicago. In a unanimous opinion, the court struck down the FCC's rules on right of reply to personal attack as colliding "with free speech and free press guarantees contained in the First Amendment . . ."[33] Judge Luther M. Swygert, speaking for the unanimous Seventh Circuit Court, was not prepared to go so far as to disagree categorically with his brethren on the District of Columbia Circuit Court's holding in Red Lion, referring to that decision as "one ad hoc order," but he and his colleagues left no doubt as to where they stood on the broad implications of the issue:

> First . . . we are not prepared to hold that the Fairness Doctrine is unconstitutional. Moreover, we do not believe that it is necessary to decide that question in this review. Second, we are in disagreement with the District of Columbia Circuit's holding in Red Lion, sustaining the Commission's order, inasmuch as we think that the order was essentially an anticipation of an aspect of the personal attack rules which are here being challenged.[34]

Most rewarding to the broadcast petitioners was the Seventh Circuit Court's rejection of the Commission's reliance on "the alleged difference between the broadcast press and the printed press to sustain its position that the rules are constitutional":[35]

> The characteristic most frequently advanced by the Commission to distinguish the printed press from the broadcast press is that radio and television broadcasting frequencies are not available to all. Data comparing the broadcast press and the printed press, however, shows that there are more commercial radio and television stations in this country than there are general circulation daily newspapers. In most major metropolitan areas there are several times as many radio and television stations as there are newspapers.[36]

When WGCB petitioned for judicial review of Red Lion immediately after it lost its case in Judge Tamm's court in June of 1967, the Supreme Court had granted certiorari and then postponed it, pending the decision in the Seventh Circuit Court of Appeals, which was handed down on September 10, 1968.

As the Supreme Court had anticipated, the FCC appealed the Seventh Circuit decision, and on January 13, 1969, the Court granted a writ of certiorari. Actually, as insurance, the RTNDA had requested such a writ by the Supreme Court even before judgment in Chicago, but it had been denied. Red Lion Broadcasting and the RTNDA, whose strained relationship had taken their cases on separate but equal routes, were now a single proceeding, with a date in the highest court in the land.

If Reverend Norris and the journalists of the RTNDA were strange bedfellows, their battery of distinguished lawyers were no more compatible. "They were all prima donnas," says one of their junior colleagues, "but some were more prima than others."

Enter a new star. Reverend Norris, "more gung ho than ever about his chances of winning in the Supreme Court," as one of their colleagues phrased it, decided that he needed a prestigious advocate with more experience trying cases in the Supreme Court. He felt, as did his counsel, Robert Manuel, that Manuel would be no match for Solicitor General Erwin N. Griswold, who would be representing the FCC and the government. Tom Sweeney and others convinced Reverend Norris and his son John that they needed an outstanding conservative lawyer. Their first recommendation was former Supreme Court Justice Charles E. Whittaker, but he felt that it would be inappropriate to try a case before his recent colleagues. "We wanted a true believer in our conservative crusade," Sweeney recalls. "We didn't want some fancy liberal from Harvard who would look on Norris as some right-wing kook who was also entitled to the protections of the First Amendment." They finally settled on Roger Robb, whose ideological credentials were a matter of record.

Robb had won national fame in the nineteen-fifties as the "prosecutor" of atomic physicist J. Robert Oppenheimer (his official title was Counsel for the Atomic Energy Commission), and later as the defender of Otto Otepka, a right-wing activist who had leaked State Department secrets. He was also the attorney for Fulton Lewis, Jr., whose nightly commentaries on the Mutual Broadcasting System won him wide acclaim among ultra-conservatives. Robb had also defended Earl Browder, the Communist party leader, and is as proud of that victory as he is of the libel suit he won for Senator Barry Goldwater against magazine publisher Ralph Ginzburg. The attorney hesitated taking the Red Lion case because it was rumored that if Richard Nixon was elected President, he would nominate his friend Robb to a high federal bench, and the lawyer was concerned that his appointment might come just before or during the Supreme Court argument and cause embarrassment. Nevertheless, at the pleading of McIntire and others, Robb reluctantly agreed to take on the case, even though he had no special expertise in the vagaries of broadcast law.

Once again the National Association of Broadcasters tried to persuade Norris to drop the case; they were leery of Robb and the effect of an archconservative on the liberal Warren court. Norris' unwillingness to reconsider his choice of counsel was the final straw in convincing the NAB to terminate its financial support.

Normally each side is permitted only one hour in oral arguments, but because two cases were involved (Red Lion and RTNDA-NBC-CBS), the time was extended. Nonetheless, a pretrial arbitration panel had to be convened to designate the stars and assign their time. As Red Lion counsel, Robb was automatically entitled to half the broadcasters' time.

Because of his standing and success in the Seventh Circuit arguments, Archibald Cox was designated as the chief spokesman for NBC, CBS and the RTNDA, but others wanted to be heard. (Cox was very much at home before the Supreme Court, but like Robb, he was not a communications lawyer.) At one point, when the three major law firms in the case asked to share the argument and/or rebuttal time, Cox is reported to have said, "If that's the way you feel, I'll take my marbles and go home."

For the FCC, the case would be argued by the Solicitor General. Griswold was a First Amendment authority who as dean of Harvard Law School had stood firm against Senator Joseph McCarthy in the fifties, but like his opponents, he was not a specialist in communications law.

At long last, on April 2, 1969, Reverend Norris and his son John drove the ninety miles from Red Lion, Pennsylvania, to Washington to sit in their reserved seats in the jammed hearing room of the Supreme Court. Meanwhile, Fred Cook was home in

New Jersey writing a book on McCarthyism, *The Nightmare Decade,* oblivious to the fact that the form letter he had mailed to Red Lion, Pennsylvania, more than four years before had stimulated a constitutional confrontation.

5

RED LION:
Judgment Day
in the Supreme Court

~~~~~~~~~~~~~~~~~~~~~~~~~~~~~~~~~~

JUSTICE BYRON WHITE: *And you say the public has no right . . . to say t̓o the licensee
that here is some material that you must
broadcast, at some point in your operation?*
ROGER ROBB: *Your honor says the public has
a right to hear it. I would say the government has no right to dictate to the broadcaster that he must present it to the public
in a certain way in a certain time through a
certain person.*

ORAL ARGUMENT IN RED LION
APRIL 2, 1969

Like a wild-card team in the Super Bowl, *Red Lion* reached the
Supreme Court via a series of flukes and misplays, but the final
twist was the single empty seat in the jammed chamber. It was
not in the spectators' section or at counsels' table, but at the long
bench where the senior Justice's chair remained empty; Justice
William O. Douglas was recovering from an appendectomy. The
vacant chair was an omen; Ted Pierson remembers looking at it
and saying to a colleague, "That's bad for our side. Now, if Hugo
Black doesn't ask the right questions, we're lost."

Roger Robb began by telling the Court that he would focus
on the constitutional issue, while Cox would concentrate on the
statutory questions raised by the personal-attack rules. Like his

adversary, Solicitor General Griswold, Robb relied heavily on First Amendment rhetoric. He posed the pivotal point: "whether or not the order of the Federal Communications Commission to Red Lion imposes a burden of previous restraint upon free speech and the press which is forbidden by the First Amendment."[1] He reminded the Justices that even the lower court and the Commission had conceded that such a burden was imposed on the broadcaster, but they had asserted that it was not an undue burden. "We submit," continued Red Lion's counsel, "that the commandment of the First Amendment is simply: Thou shalt not abridge. And it is not 'you may abridge, but please try to keep it reasonable.' "[2] Robb described Red Lion's modest circumstances and explained that for a small station "facing such competition, any donation of free time . . . is not a trivial concern, and might very well drive the station out of existence."

Justice John M. Harlan asked Robb if the financial aspects were all that bothered his client. "What about the interruption of programs?"

"Yes, indeed," Robb responded.

Harlan seemed to feel he had detected an inconsistency. "But initially you [Red Lion] started out to comply with the Commission's regulation on condition that [Cook] would pay you or prove indigency."

"Yes sir, but . . . we have to consider the entire impact."[3] Robb said that the burden of disruption, like the threat of a fine, could "have a chilling and deterrent effect upon . . . Red Lion's First Amendment right."[4]

Justice Thurgood Marshall then inquired about the prospects of offering "public time" to someone like Cook, and Robb pointed out that WGCB had one hour a day called "Free Time" and that anyone who wished might appear. Then, aware of the geography involved, he added, "I don't know whether Mr. Cook would insist that the station pay his expenses to get there or not."[5]

Freely acknowledging that Reverend Hargis had attacked Cook, Robb warned that if the Supreme Court gave approval to the Commission's rules, "Red Lion in the future will tread more cautiously." The end result, he argued, would amount to censorship "nonetheless virulent for being self-imposed."[6]

Justice Byron R. White, who during the hearing asked more

questions than any of his colleagues, wanted to know if Red Lion's objections extended to attacks made on its news shows. "Would there have to be a . . . right of reply . . . ?"

Robb's answer was as ingenuous as the Justice's question. "I read those new rules, and to tell the truth, I am not sure what the answer would be because I know those new rules exclude regular news programs from the personal-attack doctrine, but whether this [the Hargis broadcast] could be construed as a news program I really don't know, sir."[7] (The next day Robb asked the Court's permission to reanswer White's question, "which I failed to understand fully."[8] Red Lion's attorney admitted that "under no stretch of the imagination could [Hargis' attack] be considered a bona-fide news broadcast." But he recovered some lost ground by pointing out that at the time of the Hargis program "there was no exemption for a personal attack carried in a news broadcast."[9])

Whenever his name or Red Lion was mentioned, the elder Norris would turn to his son and ask in a loud whisper, "What'd he say, what'd he say?" and each time a Supreme Court guard, unaware of who the old man was, would lean over and threaten to eject him if he continued to disturb the Court.

Solicitor General Griswold, representing the government of the United States, had two foes to face—Robb in *Red Lion* and Cox in *RTNDA*. He began the first case by reviewing the long history of FCC regulations ("Congress, the Federal Communications Commission and . . . the broadcast industry have been groping for a sound and workable solution"[10]), then by addressing the broadcaster's right to speak freely and the public's right to hear more than one voice.

Griswold rejected Robb's defense of Norris on grounds of partial ignorance of the Fairness Doctrine. He cited the Fairness Primer which the FCC had distributed to all stations prior to the Hargis broadcast of 1964. He also chronicled the development of the personal-attack rules. Looking toward his adversary, Archibald Cox, who would be representing the networks in the next case, he said, "There is little trouble under the Fairness Doctrine . . . with the great networks and the stations which they control. The problem arises mostly with the small independent stations, as in the present case."[11]

The Solicitor General explained that like a moderator in a

New England town meeting, the FCC was less concerned with Fred Cook's personal right of reply than it was with insuring that the public have an opportunity to hear "robust debate."[12] The spectrum should not be viewed "merely as the exclusive, private fief of the broadcaster."[13]

Scoffing at Red Lion's charge that it had been "chilled" by the Fairness Doctrine and inhibited by the FCC rules, Griswold argued that the station "went ahead and broadcast the attack on Cook after the Commission had published the fairness primer in 1964, when it knew just what was expected of it by the Commission." Red Lion Broadcasting had arrogantly ignored the policy, assuming that "every minute of the time available to a broadcast licensee is his to use as [he] sees fit for [his] own . . . financial profit."[14]

Ignorance of the law would obviously be a better defense than simply ignoring it, and Robb in his rebuttal returned to Griswold's accusation that Reverend Norris had defied the FCC: ". . . I am advised that there was nothing clearly stated prior to this ruling which put Red Lion on notice that it must give this free time."[15]

Justice White then compared the air to a public street or a park, and pointed out that even when the government grants "certain selected people the exclusive right to use the parks . . . they must let somebody else use them, too, sometimes."[16]

Robb declared that he had trouble with the analogy of broadcasting and public parks: "Everybody can't have a license for a radio station because there aren't enough frequencies to go around."[17]

White granted this, but asked if the government awarding these radio franchises ought not "to be able to require that they let somebody else into the facility now and then when there is good reason to do so."

"That might be taken care of by the general Fairness Doctrine," Robb replied, which he said he didn't want to deal with. Still, there was a sharp distinction between a general requirement that a radio station must observe general fairness or else risk losing its license and "[this situation], where the government undertakes to tell a broadcaster what it must broadcast and who it must put on the air."[18]

Justice White pressed Robb further. "I ask you again: would

you say that the Government would be disentitled . . . to require that the licensee allow certain specific material to go on the air, rather than just leaving it up to him?"

"I would answer no," Robb replied, then quickly added, "That is what they are doing in this case."

White wasn't satisfied. "And you say the public has no right . . . to say to the licensee that here is some material that you must broadcast, at some point in your operation?"[19]

Robb rejected this, as he did the government's right to dictate *anything* to broadcasters: "Your honor says the public has a right to hear it. I would say the government has no right to dictate to the broadcaster that he must present it to the public in a certain way in a certain time through a certain person."[20]

Chief Justice Earl Warren continued this line of questioning, asking Robb about the difference between requiring a radio station to give free time to answer attacks and the FCC's refusal to renew licenses on the basis of broadcast records. Robb answered that it was more a question of principle than degree, suggesting that the FCC's dictation of programing would amount to censorship.

But Warren, who had been on the liberal side of most First Amendment cases, would not accept the word "censorship" here. "Certainly it doesn't mean to require an answer is censorship . . . ?" Robb seemed puzzled over where the Chief Justice was heading. "Isn't it something else?"[21] asked Warren. Robb reluctantly agreed that perhaps it was different, but insisted that any free-time requirement to answer a personal attack was, if not direct censorship, at least a crack-in-the-door encroachment of free speech.

When the Court turned from *Red Lion* to *RTNDA,* Griswold switched from his role as defender of the District of Columbia Circuit's opinion to that of critic of the decision by the Seventh Circuit in Chicago. Now his opponent was Archibald Cox. Spectators in the chamber sensed a special chemistry between these two stars of the Harvard faculty. One was distinguished professor; one had been dean. One had been Solicitor General; one was currently Solicitor General.

In *Red Lion,* Griswold and Robb had argued facts about the admitted attack on Fred Cook, but in *RTNDA,* Griswold complained, there were no facts. "The whole proceeding puzzles me. No one has yet been ordered to do anything. No penalties or forfeitures have been imposed; there are no specific concrete facts before the Court. The facts just float around . . ."[22]

Griswold claimed that in their briefs, Cox and his clients had fired on the personal-attack regulations "with a widely scattering shotgun."[23] Aware that the broadcast industry had little appetite for *Red Lion,* the Solicitor General wondered why they didn't wait for a legitimate test case by which to challenge the Fairness Doctrine, rather than conjuring up "what somebody might suppose could happen . . ."[24] He argued that the FCC's valid exercise of its regulatory responsibilities was being challenged not by actual grievances but rather by law professors' favorite teaching tool—hypotheticals, "a parade of horrors."

Archibald Cox was faced with a difficult tactical position. The networks and the RTNDA had rushed to place their challenge to the new fairness rules in the Court alongside the *Red Lion* litigation. Because of this necessary speed, the case had been brought as a test of the proposed rules before the FCC had issued any specific judgments based on the rules. As a result, Cox was open to this criticism that the RTNDA case was before the Court on a hypothetical basis.

To counter Griswold's point, Cox centered part of his argument on "a real hypothetical." Still, though the example was a real broadcast, he could only offer the Justices his prediction of the effect of the new rules, since they had not yet been applied. The illustration was a commentary by Eric Sevareid that marked the death of *Time* publisher Henry R. Luce. After describing Luce's career, Sevareid had turned his attention to the newsmagazine: "*Time* strained in every sentence to avoid dullness, which often meant straining the truth. . . . Many journalists have always distrusted it, nearly all have always read it.[25]

Cox argued that the Sevareid broadcast attacked a particular group, the editors of *Time,* and hypothesized that since Sevareid's commentary had attacked the personal integrity of *Time*'s editors, who he claimed constituted an identified group, they had a right to reply under the new personal-attack regulations. Then he painted a portrait of a journalist under fire. Facing a deadline, Cox told the Court, Sevareid would have to turn to someone for advice about whether commentary violated the rigid strictures of the personal-attack rules. And where would he turn? Most likely, Cox said wryly, "to lawyers."

Speaking to the nation's highest forum of lawyers, Cox argued that it would be easy to predict the advice Sevareid would receive: ". . . the result all too often is likely to be that Mr. Sevareid will decide, 'Well, I had better not say what I think.' " Moreover, said Cox, perhaps the effect of the fairness rules would be even more severe than forcing a commentator to tiptoe through his commentaries. Forced to be "a little more bland . . . he [Sevareid] might decide to transfer it to a medium where he could not be subject to this kind of inhibition."[26]

Questioned by Justice Hugo L. Black, Cox said that his thesis was that Sevareid might be "put under pressure to trim"[27] his journalistic sails. The mere possibility of such untoward pressure should be enough to void the new fairness rules, he argued; this "pressure to trim" put the Fairness Doctrine on a collision course with the First Amendment.

But Cox's choice of Henry Luce as a test case left him open to sallies by the Court. Justice Potter Stewart wondered if the Sevareid commentary might not be exempt from the Fairness Doctrine. "There is nothing controversial about the death of Henry Luce,"[28] he stated. The laughter that accompanied Stewart's comment did not derail Cox, who was long accustomed to the repartee of Supreme Court argument. The lawyer simply noted that the key issue of his example was the personal attack against the editors of *Time*. Some Justices pointed out that a *Time* editor didn't exactly face an access problem.

Impatient to finish with the Sevareid example, Justice Black asked Cox if this was the core of his argument. When the attorney indicated that it was, Black turned his attention from the specific example to the legal principles involved. Zeroing in on Cox's view of the fairness rules, he began a dialogue with the former Solicitor General that was not quite the exchange that the industry's allies—the RTNDA, CBS and NBC—had hoped to hear on argument day. RTNDA's guiding force, Ted Pierson, whispered to a young colleague, "I'm afraid these questions tell us exactly where Black stands."

Justice Black asked Cox if he was arguing that the Congress or "its acting subsidiary," the FCC, did not have the power to protect those subjected to personal attacks broadcast over stations licensed by the FCC. In a two-part reply, Cox answered that not only is the fairness "regulation . . . beyond the power of Congress," but even if Congress *did* have such authority, it had not been delegated to the FCC.

Was this, Black asked, "the real basis" of Cox's argument?

"Yes," the former Solicitor General replied.

Was Cox saying, Black asked, that there would be no relief for a man who had been personally attacked by a radio station or broadcast?

On shaky ground, with the weakest aspect of his case exposed, Cox tried to counter the question. He didn't want to imply that there was no remedy; after all, the situation would be "entirely different" if the personal attack was "willfully false."[29]

Cox then tried to direct the Court's attention to another example of how the Fairness Doctrine would hamper journalists, but before he could say anything more than "Let me give you another illustration," Black cut him off. If a man was subject to a personal attack, the Justice asked, how could he communicate to the public about its falsity or truth?

Cox replied quickly. If the aggrieved party was a public figure, he argued, he would have "access to a number of media" and would have the chance to "present his views . . . in all kinds of ways."[30]

With Cox already on the defensive, Justice White continued the assault. Referring back to the Sevareid example, he noted that it was obvious that an editor of *Time* had access to rebut a personal attack. Cox said he understood White's comment, but noted that "in nearly all these cases," the party attacked had "ample opportunity" to present his view. Nevertheless, "the Commission automatically comes along and applies this requirement."[31]

Cox's role was hampered by the fact that he was advocating different arguments for different clients: "To be quite candid, Mr. Chief Justice, I am speaking for a number of parties here."[32] The RTNDA, NBC and CBS shared only Cox's legal fees; their views on the Fairness Doctrine and the new rules had less in common. CBS was willing to accept the Fairness Doctrine, but not the new rules, while NBC and the RTNDA wanted Cox to argue against the mere idea of fairness regulation.

The hard-line attitude of the RTNDA and NBC was based, Cox argued, on the concept that a "Government notion of fairness" violates the First Amendment, and that while there might be some "circumstances that [could] be conjured up" justifying federal fairness regulations, "no such condition [exists] in the broadcast industry today." In NBC and the RTNDA's view, the vision of "the insulated listener that the Commission hypothesizes" had been proved unrealistic. Broadcasting, Cox noted, with its multitude of outlets and its complementary role with other media, had given the public greater means to communicate, not less.

His obligation to NBC and the RTNDA satisfied, Cox turned to the more moderate position taken by CBS. This network argued that "even if we suppose" there is some justification for the Fairness Doctrine, the new personal-attack rules should be voided because "they impose much heavier and more burdensome restrictions than are necessary."[33]

Chief Justice Warren asked if Cox could distinguish between the hard-line and moderate positions "in principle, not in degree."

Demonstrating his skill as a Supreme Court tactician, Cox told the Chief Justice that as Justice Oliver Wendell Holmes had once said, "all constitutional differences in the end come down to differences in degree."[34] The Fairness Doctrine, he went on, left the broadcasters some discretion "as to whether a reply is needed," while the personal-attack rule called for virtual "line-by-line, item-by-item" scrutiny of broadcasts by the government; moreover, he added, the new rules specified that "you must give [time] to a particular individual."[35]

By the end of the oral arguments, the task of the Justices was clear. In hours of argument during the past two days, they had heard the First Amendment invoked sixty-two times by the three advocates. The Court was faced with conflicting definitions of the Constitution and contrasting views on the vital question of the degree of government involvement in the most powerful system of communications in history.

The Court could decide, as Roger Robb argued for Red Lion and John Norris in his summation, that the First Amendment rejects *any* government regulation of broadcasting:

> The Government argues that the personal-attack rule is necessary in order that the public may have both sides of controversial issues, and specifically so the public may hear both the attack and

the answer. The argument, we suggest, overlooks the fact that if
the personal-attack rule is sustained, the public is likely to hear
neither the attack nor the answer, for the reason that the attack
may never be broadcast at all. Instead of stimulating wide-open,
robust, and uninhibited debate, the rule will tend to choke it
off . . . to dry it up at its source.

My personal opinion, Your Honor, is that you don't balance
First Amendment rights. You either have them or you do not. As
I say, I don't think the First Amendment says you can abridge
just a little bit, or reasonably. I think the First Amendment says
you can't abridge, and I think that this is an attempt to
abridge. . .[36]

Or the Justices could agree with Archibald Cox and his diverse
clients. To them the danger was not only indirect government
pressure forcing broadcasters to exercise self-censorship; just as
important, Cox pointed out to the Justices, was that electronic
speech controlled by the state was a fundamental breach of the
First Amendment.

. . . I would point out that the challenged regulations lay hold of
speech itself. This is a fact which distinguishes every other case
involving broadcasting that has come before this Court because
they all had to do with the economic regulation of the industry.
We are not talking about fair labor standards or labor relations
or the anti-trust laws here. We are talking about a regulation
which says, as I indicated earlier, that if you express ideas [of a]
certain character, ideas which can be described as an attack on
somebody's integrity or honesty or other personal qualities, or if
you put someone on the air who may engage in those attacks,
then you run the risk of having to carry certain obligations which
are onerous. But if you steer clear of those ideas, if you prefer
blandness to biting criticism of the shabbier self-seeking, then you
are safe, you don't have to worry. We think that this is fairly
characterized as a regulation of speech itself.[37]

On argument day the First Amendment banner had stretched
far enough to encompass all the crusaders. Robb and Cox emphasized the need to keep the industry free of government interference. On the other side Solicitor General Griswold argued that
the government had a prime concern in protecting the public's
right to the airwaves, and that it was not willing to leave this
guardianship exclusively to commercial broadcasters.

. . . As I contended in the argument in the Red Lion case, our opponents in these cases seek to put us in opposition to the First Amendment, and we do not accept that position. I suggest that on analysis it is the Government and the Federal Communications Commission which are the real champions of the First Amendment here. The Commission's regulations serve to foster important First Amendment values which our opponents would have the Court sacrifice in the guise of upholding the narrow and financially motivated claim to unfettered control of air waves that had been licensed to their custody.[38]

In the days between argument and judgment, several dramatic events occurred in the Court. Justice Abe Fortas, whom President Johnson had nominated to succeed Earl Warren as Chief Justice, had departed, reducing the number of participating Justices to seven.* Justice Douglas had returned to the bench after his illness, but because he had missed the oral arguments he did not participate in the Justices' conference on the case, or in the decision.

On May 6 President Nixon appointed Roger Robb to the District of Columbia Court of Appeals, and on May 9 Judge Robb asked the Supreme Court to remove his name from the pleading. This, of course, was only a technicality.

Lastly, President Nixon had nominated Warren E. Burger to succeed Chief Justice Warren and the Senate confirmed him as Chief Justice on June 9, the same Monday that the Red Lion–RTNDA decision was announced.

Justice Byron White, who had dominated the questioning on the argument days, was appointed by the Chief Justice to write the unanimous opinion of the seven participating judges. After Black's intense questioning of Cox, none of the broadcast lawyers were optimistic about the outcome, but few anticipated a unanimous rejection of their arguments.

Not only was the District of Columbia Court of Appeals upheld

* Under pressure because of a questionable financial link to a Nevada foundation and financier Louis Wolfson, Fortas resigned from the Court on May 14. The Court record indicates that he missed the second day of argument. He says that the first day's arguments suggested that he or his former law firm, which specialized in communications law, might have a conflict of interest, so "I recused myself."

in its decision that the FCC had the right to order Red Lion
Broadcasting to grant Fred Cook reply time, but the Supreme
Court also reversed the Chicago Seventh Circuit opinion that the
personal-attack rules were a violation of the First Amendment.
Just as the National Association of Broadcasters and most com-
munications lawyers feared, Red Lion had pulled down the
RTNDA, CBS and NBC with it. Some would argue that the
RTNDA case was doomed to fail in the high court on its own,
but it might never have reached the Court had the industry not
sensed the possibility of the disastrous defeat of Red Lion.

The Court rejected Robb's contention that the personal-attack
rules were "not precise" and that the new regulations were so
vague that they were impossible for a station like Red Lion to
discern. Wrote White:

> . . . we cannot conclude that the FCC has been left a free hand
> to vindicate its own idiosyncratic conception of the public inter-
> est or of the requirement of free speech. . . . There was nothing
> vague about the FCC's specific ruling in *Red Lion* that Fred
> Cook should be provided an opportunity to reply. The regula-
> tions at issue in RTNDA could be employed in precisely the
> same way as the fairness doctrine was in *Red Lion*.[39]

The Court also rejected the First Amendment arguments of
Cox and Robb and supported Solicitor General Griswold's reasoning:

> We need not and do not now ratify every past and future
> decision by the FCC with regard to programming. There is no
> question here of the Commission's refusal to permit the broad-
> caster to carry a particular program or to publish [his] own views.
> . . . Such questions would raise more serious First Amendment
> issues. But we do hold that Congress and the Commission do not
> violate the First Amendment when they require a radio or tele-
> vision station to give reply time to answer personal attacks and
> political editorials.[40]

Justice White's opinion used Congress' will and the FCC almost
interchangeably. In rejecting the RTNDA's claim that the Commission had misinterpreted the intent of the Senate and House
in their 1959 amendments to Section 315 by applying the amend-

ments to the Fairness Doctrine, White quoted the manager of that bill, Senator John Pastore:

> We insisted that the provision [of presenting important public questions fairly and without bias] remain in the bill, to be a continuing reminder and admonition to the Federal Communications Commission and to the broadcasters alike, that we were not abandoning the philosophy that gave birth to Section 315, in giving the people the right to have a full and complete disclosure of conflicting views on news of interest to the people of the country.[41]

As further proof of the Senate's intent, Justice White quoted another manager of the bill, Senator Hugh Scott: "It is intended to encompass all legitimate areas of public importance which are controversial, not just politics."[42]

The Supreme Court also rejected the broadcasters' arguments that the increase in the availability of broadcast frequencies, compared to the declining number of daily newspapers, no longer justified FCC regulation and control. Justice White wrote: "Scarcity is not entirely a thing of the past. Advances in technology . . . have led to more efficient utilization of the frequency spectrum, but uses of that spectrum have also grown apace."[43] As long as "it was essential for the Government to tell some applicants that they could not broadcast because there was room for only a few," the FCC had a responsibility to ensure fairness:

> When there are substantially more individuals who want to broadcast than there are frequencies to allocate, it is idle to posit an unabridgeable First Amendment right to broadcast comparable to the right of every individual to speak, write or publish.[44]

The White opinion also agreed with the FCC on the proxy argument that Norris had found so offensive:

> By the same token, as far as the First Amendment is concerned those who are licensed stand no better than those to whom licenses are refused. A license permits broadcasting, but the licensee has no constitutional right to be the one who holds the license or to monopolize a radio frequency to the exclusion of his fellow citizens. There is nothing in the First Amendment which prevents the Government from requiring a licensee to share his frequency with others and to conduct himself as a proxy or fiduciary with

obligations to present those views and voices which are representative of his community and which would otherwise, by necessity, be barred from the airwaves.[45]

The opinion did acknowledge that the First Amendment was not "irrelevant to public broadcasting" (its term for commercial and noncommercial radio and television), and noted that "Congress itself recognized in §326, which forbids FCC interference with 'the right of free speech by means of radio communication.'" But it also stated that "it is the right of the viewers and listeners, not the right of the broadcasters, which is paramount."[46]

There was only one slight ray of encouragement for Reverend Norris and the giant industry which had once envisioned this litigation as a rare opportunity to nullify the Fairness Doctrine: "And if experience with the administration of these doctrines indicates that they have had the net effect of reducing rather than enhancing the volume and quality of coverage, there will be time enough to reconsider the constitutional implications. The fairness doctrine in the past has had no such overall effect."[47]

The decision concluded: "The judgment of the Court of Appeals in *Red Lion* is affirmed and that in *RTNDA* reversed and the causes remanded for proceedings consistent with this opinion. It is so ordered."[48]

Of the huge legal bills, some were never paid. John H. Norris claims that the National Association of Broadcasters still owes him half of the $10,000 they "promised my father," and Robb's firm was never fully compensated for its work. The NAB clearly lost interest in Red Lion Broadcasting when Norris refused to drop the case after the RTNDA action was begun.

All that remained to be done was for Reverend Norris to get in touch with Fred Cook. (Curiously, Cook says that he did not even know that his complaint had ended up in the Supreme Court, and he learned about the decision from the Asbury Park *Press*.) Eleven days after the decision Reverend John M. Norris yielded to the law of the land and wrote:

Dear Mr. Cook:

This communication is in regard to a recent decision by the Supreme Court of the United States. In line with that decision we are offering you fifteen minutes of air time on Friday, July 4,

1969, on WGCB at no cost to you, in place of the regularly scheduled broadcast by Christian Crusade. This time has been made possible by contributions we have received from "friends of WGCB."

We will accept your taped broadcast or you may appear in person if you so desire. Please indicate your preference. If you desire to have us send you a blank tape, let us know and we will send it to you. Kindly let us know no later than July 1 whether this offer is acceptable or indicate whether you have any preferred date in order that we may give you the usual advance notices on our station.

> Yours in His service,
> WGCB Radio Stations
>
> (signed) Rev. John M. Norris, Owner

Whereupon Cook, who had inaugurated the correspondence with Norris in November of 1964, wrote the final communiqué in what had become the monumental *Red Lion* file:

June 26, 1969

Dear Reverend Norris:

I have your letter of June 19 with your offer of 15 minutes of free radio time to answer the 1964 attack made on me by the Rev. Billy James Hargis of the Christian Crusade. I want to thank you for responding so quickly to the U.S. Supreme Court decision in this case and for offering me far more time than I had sought originally.

However, some four and a half years have now passed since the Hargis broadcast of late November, 1964. To be of any effect, an answer to a personal attack such as this should be made as soon as possible. I cannot see much point at this late date in raking up and rehashing the entire episode, the details of which have probably been forgotten by most listeners.

Naturally, I was happy about the Supreme Court decision, which I feel was a healthy one and decidedly necessary. It should do much good in the future. For your information, most of the radio stations around the nation which carried the original Hargis program concerning me complied immediately with the FCC guidelines in existence at that time and granted me the few minutes of free time that I asked to reply. Others, who at first resisted, followed suit after the FCC issued a specific order in the case; and, in the end, as you are doubtless aware, only your own Red Lion station was left. In these circumstances, since I feel that I had my say on the other stations across the nation, and since so much time has elapsed that little I could say now would have much pertinence or meaning, I feel it best to decline your offer of free time on WGCB.

Thanks again for making the offer. I will send a carbon of this letter to the FCC in Washington so that the agency may know of your action and my response.

Yours truly,

(signed) Fred J. Cook

The file on Case 600 was officially closed, but *Red Lion* had become part of the language. The argument would go on and on, long after Reverend Norris' death at the age of ninety-one.

Years later, after his experience as Watergate prosecutor had made him a national hero, Archibald Cox would look back on this case as one that might have fared better "if we'd had only one client."

"You mean just the RTNDA?"

"No, I mean Red Lion," replied Cox. "In freedom-of-speech cases, the most effective kind of client is an unpopular cause, or just some S.O.B. who has a right to be heard."

Reverend Billy James Hargis agrees. He is still bitter about *Red Lion* and Cook: "If he was such a great journalist and loved freedom so much, how come he started something which limited freedom of speech and set back freedom of the press two hundred years?" Hargis, now fifty-one, is a "frustrated and ailing" preacher who has suffered several strokes and is desperately trying to get his weight down from 280 to 200 pounds. In the Tulsa Cathedral headquarters of his "Christian Crusade," he is surrounded by spectacular religious Renaissance art, juxtaposed with photographs of his crusades with Senator McCarthy, General Walker and Governor Wallace. He is now philosophical about his reverses: "I just never had the stuff to make it on television, and many radio stations are now afraid to run me." He still believed that Reverend Norris was "the only honest hero in *Red Lion*. I was just a pamphleteer with a message which I was willing to pay his station to run, and the old man believed that anyone else who wanted time on his air had to pay for it too."

Hargis was also bitter toward Nixon "for putting me on the IRS most-wanted surveillance list while writing me nice letters." He was angry with the courts for taking away the tax-exempt status of his "Christian Crusade." Mostly he blamed "Walter Reuther, who spelled it all out in a secret letter to the Kennedys in 1960," Fred Cook, the FCC, and the Johnson crowd for "trying to shut me up during the Goldwater campaign." He said, "What are we left with? The Fairness Doctrine, which the left-inclined use to keep the right wing off the air, and which the right wing uses to silence the left. What good is that? It can be used to keep everybody off the air." He pointed to the "twenty-three books liberals have written against me . . . I can handle those," he added, "but the fallout from *Red Lion* hurt everyone. Just to knock me off."

Reverend Hargis had made a persuasive case so far, but then, like a star witness who is unable to resist making one final point, he plunged on, his voice rising. "The trouble with our side is that there's no common bond among conservatives like McIntire, Hunt and me. Too much competition and free enterprise, I guess. Look at H. L. Hunt, who claimed that he made a million dollars a day in oil—the only thing he ever gave me was a steak dinner. With all his money, why didn't Hunt buy our side a television network, or at least try to buy the Dallas *Times-Herald* when it was up for sale? He wouldn't even do that."

6

WXUR:
Killing Gnats with a Sledgehammer

~~~~~~~~~~~~~~~~~~~~~~~~~~~~~

But if we are to go after gnats with a sledge-hammer like the Fairness Doctrine, we ought to at least look at what else is smashed beneath our blow.

CHIEF JUDGE DAVID L. BAZELON,
DISSENTING IN <u>BRANDYWINE</u>, 1972

Carl McIntire is no gnat. He is nearly six feet two, handsome and electric, and though at sixty-nine some of the fire and brimstone has been banked, his evangelical voice is still capable of instant persuasion. He has been known to rally an audience on a single radio station to send in $50,000 to rescue his church or keep the "Twentieth Century Reformation Hour" on the air. During the Six-Day War in the Middle East he raised $5,000 for Israel, though many Jewish leaders consider McIntire to be anti-Semitic. His religious conglomerate, with headquarters in Collingswood, New Jersey, owns the Faith Theological Seminary, a publishing company, hotels, colleges in New Jersey and Cape Canaveral, Florida—and for a few short years, radio stations WXUR and WXUR-FM in Media, Pennsylvania.

In 1936 McIntire was suspended from the Presbyterian Church or, in his version, left it "because I must obey God rather than the General Assembly where their orders conflict with my conscience." Resigned or defrocked, McIntire soon founded the Bible Presbyterian Church, in Collingswood, but enjoyed scant success until the nineteen-sixties when Reverend Norris converted him to radio. Overnight the "Twentieth Century Reformation Hour" became a daily ritual on six hundred small radio stations. As Mc-Intire tells it, "We found a way we could reach the public under the liberty we have in our Constitution. I found we could not get our story before the public through the networks, and the press was generally blocked against us." Convinced that most Americans were "prisoners of the left-wing media," McIntire determined "that by the use of little radio stations spread around the country, we could get on and talk about those matters in the free exercise of religion . . . and reach millions of people . . ."

McIntire and his seminary never seriously considered owning a radio station of their own until 1964, when a few stations, under growing pressure from the FCC to observe the Fairness Doctrine, began canceling his program. The decisive blow came when WVCH in Chester, Pennsylvania, after being told by its Washington counsel that carrying McIntire might jeopardize its license, terminated its contract. This meant that McIntire's voice was blacked out in his home territory. The Philadelphia area and southern New Jersey were fertile McIntire country, and a new outlet was desperately needed.

The Norris family provided the answer. Reverend Norris' son John, who was busy fighting Red Lion's battles with the FCC, heard that station WXUR was having financial difficulties, and that its owners might sell. His father confided to McIntire that he wanted to buy WXUR as an extension of the Red Lion group, but lacked the required cash. "Why not purchase it with funds from the seminary," suggested the reverend, "and you run it." He believed the station could make money for the seminary and provide McIntire with an outlet on his home ground.

Media is a Philadelphia suburb between Bryn Mawr and Swarthmore with a population of 7,000. In 1964 McIntire and Norris requested permission from the FCC to transfer ownership to them from Brandywine-Main Line Radio, Inc. The price was $450,000; $25,000 was paid in cash, the Faith Theological Seminary placed a mortgage on its property for $425,000, and an insurance policy of $100,000 on McIntire's life was used as collateral.

In their petition for transfer, McIntire and Norris promised, as do most radio and television applicants, to operate in accordance with the National Association of Broadcasters code, though they never were members of that organization. But of more consequence to their future confrontations, the new owners promised to comply with the Fairness Doctrine.

WXUR was not without its enemies even in 1964–65. Eighteen prominent Philadelphia organizations, offended by McIntire's "notorious" broadcasts on the Chester station, intervened and urged the FCC to oppose the transfer. The National Council of Churches, the Urban League, the Anti-Defamation League of B'nai B'rith, and prominent Baptist, Presbyterian and Catholic organizations, among others, implored the Commission to deny the transfer because of McIntire's history of "intemperate attacks on other religious denominations, various organizations and government agencies, and political figures." McIntire was using the public air to "help create a climate of fear, prejudice and distrust of democratic institutions."[1]

The protest was not heeded. On March 17, 1965, just as WGCB in Red Lion was moving toward its historic confrontation with the FCC, the Commission approved the sale of WXUR-AM and WXUR-FM to the Faith Theological Seminary, on the grounds that a McIntire-Norris radio station guaranteed that it would "afford reasonable opportunity for the presentation of contrasting viewpoints on any controversial issue . . ."[2] Commissioner Kenneth Cox voted against it because he doubted McIntire's qualifications, but the majority of the Commission voted approval on the grounds of diversity and because of McIntire's promise to uphold the Fairness Doctrine.

But the FCC's approval was short-lived. One year later the new owners filed for a routine three-year license renewal. Once again those eighteen Philadelphia organizations protested, this time with a series of specifics, charging that WXUR had been "one-sided, unbalanced, and weighted on the side of extreme right-wing radicalism" in its first year of new ownership. The protesters had monitored WXUR and cited numerous examples of anti-Semitic remarks and one-sided attacks on the Supreme Court, on the United Nations and on major news media.[3]

Much of the most offensive material occurred during WXUR's call-in shows, presided over by Tom Livezey, a man with a special talent for attracting those citizens of the City of Brotherly Love who stayed up late worrying about Jews, blacks, radicals and Billy Graham. Some examples:

WOMAN LISTENER: About this B'nai B'rith Anti-Defamation League . . .
why don't they get upset at all these smut and filth that's going
through the mails?
LIVEZEY: And who do you think is behind all this obscenity that daily
floods our mails, my dear?
LISTENER: Well, frankly, Tom, I think it is the Jewish people.
LIVEZEY: You bet your life it is.[4]

On another occasion Livezey encouraged a listener to read a
poem about his desire to be a dog so that he could desecrate the
graves of such people as Franklin D. Roosevelt and Martin Luther King, Jr.

McIntire's own programs on WXUR, which he broadcast from
his offices in Collingswood and Cape May, New Jersey (he has
only been in Media a few times), were also controversial. He
continuously praised Reverend Ian Paisley, firebrand of the Evangelical Irish Protestant Movement who understands that "Ro-
manism breeds Communism," and denounced Billy Graham and
his followers as "cowardly appeasers, liberal teasers and Communist pleasers."

A Unitarian minister in Delaware County (of which Media is
the county seat), Reverend David Kibby, attacked McIntire for
creating "a community of hate" and for being "a Christian fright-
peddler, a prophet for profit and a merchant of hate." The following Sunday, Kirby retracted his remarks about profit ("I simply
have no way of knowing that he does profit"), but he reiterated
that the hate was real enough, as well as "the tendency to retreat
to tribalism of many different kinds." The Pennsylvania House
of Representatives passed a resolution calling for an FCC investigation of WXUR for its "extremist views,"[5] and a similar demand was urged by the Media Borough Council. McIntire is not
a popular figure in Media, which happens to have a large minority
population, and sponsors were urged to cancel their advertising
on the station. McIntire and Norris claimed that there was an
organized boycott, but religious groups in opposition denied this.
In any case, local advertising stopped completely, but as Norris
says, "We more than made up the slack with paid religious programs and were virtually sold out."

After intense scrutiny, the FCC examiner determined that in
spite of such criticisms, WXUR should be allowed to keep its license. The examiner cited that the Faith Theological Seminary

had acquired WXUR because the management claimed "that religion was underserved in the area . . . especially . . . conservative fundamentalist religion."[6] He also noted that "the entire broadcasting format over the license period and since has been one which welcomed all opposing viewpoints."[7]

But when the full Commission reviewed the record, it reversed the examiner and ordered that the renewal application be denied. There were several reasons for this drastic sanction. The FCC closed its opinion by stating "that Brandywine failed to provide reasonable opportunities for the presentation of contrasting views on controversial issues of public importance, that it ignored the personal-attack principle of the Fairness Doctrine, that the applicant's representations as to the manner in which the station would be operated were not adhered to . . ."[8] FCC Commissioner Robert E. Lee called it "a landmark case." He said it was the first time that the FCC had refused to review a station's license because of Fairness Doctrine violations.[9]

On August 6, 1970, Brandywine filed a motion to reconsider with the Commission on the basis that the Commission's July decision extended the concept of the Fairness Doctrine to an unconstitutional brink. However, the Commission denied the request.[10]

What angered McIntire and Norris most was that the chairman of the FCC, Dean Burch, had voted against them. They remembered him as the campaign manager of Senator Goldwater's 1964 crusade to rescue America from the welfare state and international Communism. The Red Lion and Media stations were part of a conservative network "to give our side a voice, and now the man that Richard Nixon sent to the FCC was closing us down," said Norris. Dr. McIntire believes that the move was the President's retribution for his broadcast commentaries against Nixon's attempt to get America out of Vietnam and into Red China. "It was just another one of those dirty tricks from that Watergate gang," McIntire says. "That fellow Colson [was] the one who delivered the message to Burch to close us down." Burch, now a Washington communications lawyer, denies that Colson or anyone at the White House ever discussed the WXUR case with him.

WXUR and its attorney, Ben Cottone, who had declined to participate in the Red Lion case, were anxious to appeal the Commission's decision. "The FCC was not just asking a station to grant reply time, but was issuing a lethal order to put a station off the air forever," said Cottone.

Cottone also cited the chilling effect of the Fairness Doctrine on other stations carrying McIntire broadcasts, many of which had canceled the series or required that he change his style. WRIB in Providence, Rhode Island, told the preacher that he must not mention any names on future broadcasts because, according to the Fairness Doctrine, "I must notify all those who are attacked on your program within seven days following the broadcast and allow them time . . . Failure to comply is subject to a $1,000 fine." WMEN in Tallahassee, Florida, canceled, "afraid to do anything to offend the FCC." WVNS in nearby Lewisburg wrote: "Our relationship has continued amiably for nearly six years and we are sorry to terminate your broadcasts." Dozens of other stations across America canceled McIntire's broadcasts because of their reading of the personal-attack rules, while others waited for the outcome of the WXUR case.

"I was muffled by the Fairness Doctrine," says McIntire. "I was crushed by it. I used to have six hundred stations, but it has dwindled to only a couple of hundred or so now."

On September 25, 1972, the Court of Appeals in Washington unanimously affirmed the Commission's right to terminate WXUR's permit to broadcast. But the same court had an undetected time bomb in store, and forty days later, it dealt the Fairness Doctrine its most devastating blow.

Judge Edward A. Tamm, who had written the opinion in the original Red Lion case, said: "The record of Brandywine-Main Line Radio is bleak in the area of good faith. At best, Brandywine's record is indicative of a lack of regard for fairness principles; at worst, it shows an utter disdain for Commission rulings and ignores its own responsibilities as a broadcaster and its representations to the Commission . . . During the entire license period Brandywine willfully chose to disregard the Commission mandate."[11]

Referring to Brandywine's initial license application, Tamm said: "These men, with their hearts bent toward deliberate and premeditated deception, cannot be said to have dealt fairly with the Commission or the people of the Philadelphia area. Their statements constitute a series of heinous misrepresentations which,

even without the other factors in the case, would be ample justification for the Commission to refuse to renew the broadcast license."[12] But tucked into the opinion of the three-judge panel
were two bland sentences. Chief Judge David L. Bazelon also concurred "in affirming the decision of the FCC, solely on the ground
that the licensee deliberately withheld information about its programming plans." Bazelon added that a "full statement of his
[Bazelon's] views will issue at a later date."[13]

. When this full statement was released, it turned out to be a
complete reversal. Paraphrasing Supreme Court Justice Robert
H. Jackson, who in another famous decision had paraphrased the
British jurist Baron Bramwell, Bazelon wrote: " 'The matter does
not appear to me now as it appears to have appeared to me
then.' "[14]

The date of Chief Judge Bazelon's dissent—November 4, 1972—
was the eve of Richard Nixon's sweeping second-term election
to the Presidency. It was a period when the press, both print and
electronic, was under siege from Nixon, Agnew and other powerful members of the Administration, and Watergate was still a
"caper" to most Americans. There is reason to believe that Bazelon sensed that an entire Administration was attempting to use
its awesome power to nullify vital parts of the Constitution—
specifically the First Amendment—and that his carefully couched
dissent was one judge's way of making a statement:

> In this case I am faced with a prima facie violation of the First
> Amendment. The Federal Communications Commission has sub-
> jected Brandywine to the supreme penalty: it may no longer
> operate as a radio broadcast station. In silencing WXUR, the
> Commission has dealt a death blow to the licensee's freedom of
> speech and press. Furthermore, it has denied the listening public
> access to the expression of many controversial views. Yet the
> Commission would have us approve this action in the name of the
> fairness doctrine, the constitutional validity of which is premised
> on the argument that its enforcement will *enhance* public access
> to a marketplace of ideas without serious infringement of the First
> Amendment rights of individual broadcasters.[15]

Bazelon told his colleagues that the Fairness Doctrine was applying a double standard to broadcast and print journalism, and
that the WXUR attacks in question did not focus on inaccuracies,
but on the "bias" or lack of "fairness" in the presentation. He

maintained that "the great weight of First Amendment considerations cannot rest on so narrow a ledge . . ."[16] as Brandywine's misrepresentations. Bazelon warned: "In the context of broadcasting today, our democratic reliance on a truly informed American public is threatened if the overall effect of the fairness doctrine is the very censorship of controversy which it was promulgated to overcome."[17] A liberal, Bazelon left no doubt about his distaste for the offensive and disruptive nature of WXUR's brand of programs, but he feared such material far less than the strangulation of the public's right to hear McIntire's type of robust debate. "It is beyond dispute that the public has *lost* access to information and ideas . . . as a result of a single blow of this doctrinal sledgehammer."[18] Bazelon concluded: "I would remand the entire case to be reviewed in light of the matters discussed in this opinion."[19] He was suggesting that the FCC should take another look at their decision to terminate WXUR's license.

In defending the majority decision from Bazelon's broadside, Judge J. Skelly Wright explained that proof of abuse of the Fairness Doctrine was not a necessary justification for removing WXUR's license. That had not been his reason. Deception, he told Bazelon, and the voiding of the license were ample grounds and not too narrow a ledge for such drastic action. But Wright admitted that the Fairness Doctrine was creating a "constitutional 'thicket' "[20] that was being restudied by the Commission.

In writing separate opinions, the three judges of *Brandywine* did little to disentangle that thicket. Judge Tamm accepted the Commission's action and upheld the FCC's reliance on the Fairness Doctrine as a regulatory tool. He was joined by Judge Wright, who, finding enough ground to support the Commission on the charge of deception, left the fairness issue unresolved. Tamm and Wright outvoted Chief Judge Bazelon, who, switching sides, took the Fairness Doctrine to task and found it constitutionally lacking. To Reverend McIntire, Bazelon was suddenly a hero. "In WXUR," he recalls, "we had a beautiful case until Tamm and Wright sabotaged me by elevating charges of deception to major claims of misrepresentation."

All legal remedies exhausted, the order for WXUR to cease operations became effective on midnight, July 5, 1973. Over the air McIntire predicted that "WXUR will become the number-one Christian martyr in the nation."

The last night on the air was one to remember—a combination

of a wake and a New Year's Eve countdown as the band played and McIntire called out the hours and then minutes to the government-ordered shutdown. As one listens to the tapes of that final hour today, there is the feeling of a ghost station. McIntire's last message to his loyal flock pleaded with God and the FCC for time: "Our Father and God, we thank Thee that this station . . . has rebuked the devil and exposed wickedness . . . Lord, grant our great petition and, Oh God, tomorrow night, if it is Thy will, put us back on the air. Make that judge give the restraining order necessary that the people may hear, that they may be able to enjoy those blessings of liberty and, the free exercise of religion." As "Onward, Christian Soldiers" ended, he cried, "Good night and goodbye for a few days." But WXUR would be back: "Remember, when the rapture comes, the FCC cannot stop us from talking. We will be with Christ." Then "Nearer, My God, to Thee" rang out—the hymn the *Titanic*'s orchestra is supposed to have played when that great ship went down.

Even some who hated everything McIntire stood for were troubled by the specter of this one small station being snuffed out by a federal order. "We haven't heard the Rev. McIntire say anything yet that we agree with," wrote the *News of Delaware County*, "but our racists, bigots and 13th Century minds should be encouraged to speak out at every opportunity." The newspaper was wary of the federal government, and particularly of its Presidents "deciding who is prejudiced and who isn't and duly licensing only those it judges to be without prejudice." The editorial warned against silencing those who spout hate: ". . . we'd rather have them all out in the open and up on their soapboxes every day. That way we can keep an eye on them."[21]

The next day McIntire and Norris cannibalized parts of WXUR's transmitter and transferred operations to a "pirate ship," Radio Free America, off the Jersey coast. For ten hours McIntire beamed his Christian, pro-Vietnam, now anti-Nixon messages to his devoted listeners until a court order threatened to send the Coast Guard. ("The big mistake Carl made was to outfit a ship of U.S. registry," said one of his associates.) "We were willing to give everyone access to Radio Free America," says McIntire. "I even sent a telegram to Jane Fonda inviting her to join our broadcast." The floating transmitter was an international sensation and made McIntire a kind of folk hero to many who denounce his views.

McIntire acknowledges his error on the registry with a wink
and a prophecy that "Radio Free America has not made its last
voyage and may yet sail under a foreign flag." Then he asks, "Have
you heard my hymn, 'The Song of the Fairness Doctrine'?" With
slight urging, Brian King, staff organist and a business associate of
John Norris, goes to the upright piano in McIntire's headquarters
and obliges:

> Have you heard of the Fairness Doctrine
> The Song of the FCC?
> It's designed to protect opposing views
> To prove that speech is free
> But the song of the Fairness Doctrine
> We regretfully construe
> Is out of tune entirely
> With the Christian point of view
>
> In the Song of the Fairness Doctrine
> Discordant notes are heard
> Because of raucous foreign sounds
> Our heritage is blurred
> Yes this Song of the Fairness Doctrine
> Is pitched in a minor key
> It gives full voice to the liberals
> But leaves out you and me
>
> Oh fellow Christian patriots
> Let's raise our voice in song
> Let's herald forth the word of God
> And thus correct the wrong
> We have a song of victory
> To broadcast far and wide
> Come on you Christian warriors
> And join the winning side.

For all the desperate pleadings of WXUR's last days on land,
on sea, and on the air, Bazelon's opinion in McIntire's defense
endures as the most quoted denunciation by an independent and
respected mind of the FCC's attempt to ensure fairness. In subsequent decisions, Bazelon continued to raise his voice against
"pouring concrete around [the] foundation of a doctrine which
enhances the public's right of access in some circumstances but
abridges that right in others."[22] He urged the FCC and the courts
to "take our blinders off and look further toward First Amend-

ment goals than the next regulatory step which the FCC urges us to take in the name of fairness . . ." We cannot "simply hang our hats on *Red Lion* and relax."[23]

Other constitutionalists came to McIntire's defense. Senator Sam Ervin rose in the U.S. Senate to state: "When all the legal mumbo-jumbo is cleared away, the fact remains that the FCC chose to apply highly technical rules to this single station, having been forced by outside political pressure to do so."[24]

Encouraged by the Bazelon and Ervin positions and their impact on both the legal and communications professions, WXUR asked the Supreme Court for a writ of certiorari. "This time we thought we had a chance," says lawyer Ben Cottone. "We had Bazelon's dissent, and we had the facts that in this case the Commission had departed from its promise to the Congress and the Supreme Court that it would not apply the ultimate sanction of taking away licenses without due warning." But on May 29, 1973, the Supreme Court turned down WXUR's plea for review, though not unanimously, for there was one aye vote. Only Mr. Justice Douglas urged the Court to take a second look at the Fairness Doctrine.

Almost three years later, the blinking lights on WXUR's transmitter towers still dominate the night sky over Media, and Carl McIntire waits for the renewal of the license that may never come.

7

WLBT:
Line Trouble in Mississippi

~~~~~~~~~~~~~~~~~~~~~~~~~~~~~~~~~~

"The word of the hour, of the day,
of the year, is 'never.' "

FRED BEARD, GENERAL MANAGER,
WLBT, JACKSON, MISSISSIPPI, 1962

Thurgood Marshall is the first black man to sit on the Supreme Court of the United States. But long before his appointment, as director of the Legal Defense Fund of the National Association for the Advancement of Colored People, on September 7, 1955, he was a guest on the NBC *World At Home* television broadcast. During the interview he discussed the ramifications of the 1954 landmark decision *Brown* v. *Board of Education*, which he had successfully argued before the Supreme Court. "I don't know how many years desegregation will take," said Marshall, "but it won't take as long as many die-hard Southern government officials hope." As he explained to millions of Americans how the Court had ruled that the "separate but equal" standard was unconstitutional, an interruption slide flashed on the television line of Channel 3, station WLBT in Jackson, Mississippi. The slide read: "SORRY, CABLE TROUBLE FROM NEW YORK."*

---

* This incident was reported in the Jackson *State Times* of October 17, 1955. The *Times* said that WLBT's general manager, Fred Beard, had told an audience that "recently when a Negro attorney was speaking on TV, he had cut the program off and substituted a 'Sorry, Cable Trouble' sign." Beard later claimed that he had been misquoted about the sign, but affirmed that he had cut off Thurgood Marshall "because the TV networks were overloading the circuits with Negro propaganda."

Two years later the same station broadcast a program called "The Little Rock Crisis," and all the participants were white segregationists and officials of the state of Mississippi: Senator James O. Eastland, Congressman John Bell Williams and Governor James P. Coleman. When Medgar Evers, NAACP field secretary for the state of Mississippi, sought response time to present his organization's position on integration, he was refused. WLBT's owners did not consider their presentation of the Little Rock crisis controversial; rather, they explained, it was "a report from our duly elected officials to the people of Mississippi." WLBT also stated that it had a policy of "not presenting local programs dealing with the issue" of racial integration because they might prove "inflammatory."[1]

In 1962, when James Meredith and other civil rights activists were attempting to integrate the University of Mississippi at Oxford, and the state was in near-rebellion over his pending admission, WLBT's general manager went on the air to rally white supremacists, urging them "go out to Oxford and stand shoulder to shoulder with Governor Barnett and keep that nigra out of Ole Miss." Moreover, a WLBT editorial broadcast on September 14 informed viewers that "Governor Barnett has said 'Never' and he means 'never' . . . The word of the hour, of the day, of the year, is 'never.' "

Also in September of 1962, WLBT broadcast a series of spot announcements paid for by the Jackson (White) Citizens Council, urging resistance to integration because Communists were behind the "racial agitation" resulting from the U.S. government's attempt to integrate schools. Although 45 percent of its listening public were black and there were only two television stations in town, the station made no attempt to present opposing views. In fact, WLBT's general manager was a prominent member of the Citizens Council.

In 1963 a three-hour NBC documentary called "American Revolution," a milestone that marked the first time a network devoted an entire evening to a single issue, was interrupted with another "SORRY, CABLE TROUBLE" slide. The "line failure" from New York came at the exact moment when the program was reporting a sit-in at the Woolworth store in Jackson, and failure was "repaired" soon after this sequence ended. (At a subsequent FCC hearing the station's general manager submitted an unsigned letter from the local telephone company certifying that the interruption was unavoidable.) The Huntley-Brinkley Nightly News program was reportedly occasionally interrupted when it was covering civil rights, and sometimes, prior to news reports on the *Today* show, a WLBT announcer would warn, "What you are about to see is an example of biased, managed, Northern news. Be sure to stay tuned at seven twenty-five to hear your local newscast."[2]

WLBT constantly attacked Tougaloo, the prominent black college near Jackson, and permitted white political leaders to denounce it with such invectives as "We are nursing a viper to our breast—Communists are teeming up there at Tougaloo." The president of the college was never permitted to respond.

When famous black athletes such as Bill Russell and Jackie Robinson came to Mississippi, WLBT refused to interview them on the grounds that they were there as civil rights advocates, not as athletes. There is no record that during the civil rights struggle any black was ever invited to appear in a discussion on a controversial issue. Segregationist practices also pervaded other programing during this period. On a series of children's programs, *Youth Speaks, Teen Tempos* and *Romper Room,* no black child was ever seen. WLBT provided time to one white church for religious services every Sunday and allotted ten minutes every day to other churches, but never did a black church get its turn, even though blacks represented half the number of churches and church members in the area. (There was one fifteen-minute program at 6:45 A.M. on Sunday that featured a black minister.) News programs, such as they were, consistently mocked blacks. Phrases such as "nigger" and "nigra" were standard WLBT vocabulary. Manager Beard operated the Freedom Bookstore, a white-supremacy propaganda library, as an agency of and at the station, and used WLBT's air to promote pro-segregation books.

The other television station in Jackson, WJTV, was almost as insensitive to black aspirations, and both of them were warned by the FCC to honor the Fairness Doctrine and to inform black leaders when they or their causes were attacked. Such cautions were ignored by the WLBT licensee, the Lamar Life Broadcasting Company, an obscure subsidiary of the Lamar Life Insurance Company owned by the millionaire Murchison family of Texas.

By the early sixties Mississippi had become a battleground of the civil rights epoch, but the national media did not illuminate the front-line struggles being waged by such emerging black leaders as Medgar Evers and Dr. Aaron Henry, who risked his small business and his personal safety to lead the Mississippi NAACP chapter. Many of these black activists received more television exposure and were better known in Washington, New York and Los Angeles than in Jackson, where the NAACP and Evers had been filing complaints with the FCC against the two Jackson television stations.

The legend that no black citizen of Mississippi was ever permitted to be seen on local television in the context of a public issue was not strictly accurate. There were two momentary exceptions. In 1962 Reverend Robert L. T. Smith ran against Representative John Bell Williams. With some pressure from the FCC, led by its chairman, Newton N. Minow, Smith finally won a battle for the right to purchase one half-hour of television time. Minow remembers he was first alerted to the problem by a phone call from Eleanor Roosevelt.

On another occasion Medgar Evers was given his only scheduled appearance on a locally originated program. In May of 1963, with black boycotts and sit-ins at their height, Jackson's Mayor Allen Thompson, who had nightly access to all television and radio stations, attacked the NAACP and "other outside troublemakers," and accused Medgar Evers of being one of the chief agitators. Backed by seventy-five of Jackson's leading businessmen, the mayor rejected Evers' recommendation that a biracial committee be appointed to help solve Jackson's problems. On behalf of the NAACP, Evers demanded reply time, and to his surprise was informed by the management of WLBT that he could have half an hour on May 20. At the time, there were reports that White House and FCC concern may have prompted this sudden change in policy. "It was a call from 'Big Jim' that did it," according to someone close to the situation—"Big Jim" being Senator Eastland. According to this source, the senator had been on the telephone with a high official in the Justice Department.

Tension in Jackson was at such a high pitch and the scheduling of Evers' broadcast was announced in such charged terms and so angrily received that a live appearance at a designated time and studio might have precipitated violence, so secret arrangements had to be made to video-tape his remarks prior to the broadcast. Evers' quiet speech called for unity and conciliation with the mayor and the white community, and he concluded by asking the white people of Jackson to put themselves in black peoples' shoes: "If you suffered those deprivations and were often called by your first name, or 'boy,' 'girl,' 'auntie' and 'uncle,' would you not be discontent?" For the first time Mississippi blacks watched a calm, forceful native son explain the goals of the civil rights movement and the need for peaceful demonstrations and voter registration.

Twenty-three days later Medgar Evers was assassinated. In a bar on the edge of Jackson, a white man was reported muttering, "Maybe this will slow the niggers down."

The day before, Governor George Wallace had stood before Deputy Attorney General Nicholas deB. Katzenbach in front of the doors of the University of Alabama in a final vain attempt to block integration.[3]

The death of Medgar Evers did not slow down Reverend Everett Parker, a minister of the United Church of Christ in New York City. Parker's friends in Mississippi called to tell him of the assassination, and warned him to postpone his search for a test case that would force access to broadcasting for the blacks of the Deep South. Undeterred, Parker flew to Jackson the next week.

Everett Parker is a maverick who has been harassed by influential forces in the broadcast industry and by Mississippi sheriffs who once followed him and his wife from Jackson to Vicksburg to Clarksdale. Born in Chicago in 1913, he began his career there as a radio announcer and advertising executive, and was briefly on the public-affairs staff of NBC. At the age of twenty-seven he switched to the divinity school at the University of Chicago and became an ordained minister of the Congregational Christian Church. Thereafter he spent a few years at Yale teaching and researching broadcasting, and in 1954 founded the Office of Communication under the auspices of the United Church of Christ. The New York–based organization was originally funded by the church and the Marshall Field Foundation, and in recent years grants have also been made by the Ford, Markle and AFL-CIO foundations.

As Parker had been looking for a segregated city in which to make his move on behalf of minority access, the Evers assassination and the blatant abuse of the minimal standards of fairness by general manager Beard and WLBT helped him to settle on Jackson. Like most television stations, WLBT keeps few video tapes or program transcripts, so when Parker was ready to collect facts on which to base his case, he monitored the station for a week, from March 1 through March 7, 1964. The volunteer staff of monitors came from Millsaps College, a segregated white institution in Jackson, and the team was coordinated by Professor Gordon Henderson, whose wife had once been employed by the A. C. Nielsen Company and who understood the techniques. Convinced that the study showed discrimination by the station, Parker swiftly filed a petition to have WLBT's license renewal denied.

There was one member of WLBT's staff whom Parker was not willing to condemn. In fact, news director Dick Sanders* was the only member of WLBT's staff who attempted to maintain any communication with the black community. Sanders recalls that most of his conversations with Medgar Evers, Robert L. T. Smith and other NAACP leaders were monitored and reported to Fred Beard, who saw the black leaders as "the enemy." Sanders, who admits that discrimination was practiced by WLBT, nevertheless believes that it was no worse than many other stations in the Deep South, especially after Beard was replaced a year later. "The community was inflamed. I never understood the Civil War until then . . . If we had put any more blacks on the air, the hotheads from Rankin County would have bombed the station." Sanders also says that if any black children had appeared on the segregated *Romper Room*, the white kids on the program would have been threatened. He views the situation as a tragedy, but doubts that Northerners in 1975 can "imagine what it was like in Mississippi in 1963 . . . People would call my wife and say, 'You get that nigger-lover off the air or he won't be coming home again.' " Fear of reprisal may be little excuse for the policies of the Jackson stations, but the fact that it existed provides a clue to the explosiveness of the times.

When Parker reviewed his strategy informally with FCC Chairman E. William Henry, he was advised of the importance of

---

* Dick Sanders is now an editor for ABC News, Washington.

participation by local citizens in any FCC petition. In other words, he had to persuade Mississippi residents to sign the documents. Even in hindsight, the attempt to secure those signatures sounds like something from *Mission: Impossible*, and it was. Moving by night in unlit cars, Parker and Professor Henderson sought out Aaron Henry and Robert L. T. Smith, the Methodist minister who had run for Congress and who was an organizer of the Mississippi Freedom Democratic Party. At first Henry resisted because his attorney advised him that he was taking his life into his hands, but he finally signed because he realized that Parker was going to proceed with or without him and because he was convinced that the petition had a better chance of succeeding with some local blacks backing it. Reverend Smith, also aware of the risks, signed because of his own encounter with the Mississippi media in 1962.

Thus, in 1964, when WLBT filed its routine license-renewal application, Parker and the United Church of Christ, which was to spend $240,000 on the litigation before it was over, together with Dr. Aaron Henry and Robert L. T. Smith, intervened on behalf of all other television viewers in the state of Mississippi. Their petition claimed that WLBT discriminated by failing to have a proportionate amount of blacks in commercials and entertainment, and was unfair in its presentation of controversial issues, especially those involving blacks. They also claimed that WLBT discriminated against the local Catholic church.

In order to establish "standing"—the legal term which defines the parties who have a right to participate because they are or could be adversely affected by the outcome of a proceeding—Smith and Henry claimed that they represented individuals and organizations that, in violation of the Fairness Doctrine, were denied a reasonable opportunity to answer criticism. These Mississippi groups, they stated, represented almost one half of the WLBT listening audience, which was denied an opportunity to be heard and was generally ignored and discriminated against by the station's programing.

The Commission held that Smith, Henry and the United Church of Christ had no legal standing to intervene. However, it recognized that it ought to consider the substantial issues brought to its attention, and it acknowledged many of the allegations. Therefore, the FCC agreed that "serious questions are

presented whether [or not] the licensee's operations have fully
met the public interest,"[4] and that it was "a close question
whether [or not] to designate for hearing these applications for
renewal of license."[5] Nevertheless, the Commission concluded—
without any hearing to resolve these serious questions—that
WLBTs' license should be given a one-year renewal:

. . . this particular area is entering a critical period in race relations, and that the broadcast stations, such as here involved, can
make a most worthwhile contribution to the resolution of problems arising in this respect. That contribution is needed now—and
should not be put off for the future. We believe that the licensee,
operating in strict accordance with the representations made and
other conditions specified herein, can make that needed contribution, and thus that its renewal would be in the public interest.[6]

This one-year probation period was granted on the condition
"that the licensee comply strictly with the established requirements of the fairness doctrine," and that "the licensee immediately
cease discriminatory programing patterns."[7]

Of the seven Commission members, only Chairman William
Henry and Kenneth Cox protested the decision to renew WLBT's
license for a year without holding hearings. They cited such
abuses as the blackouts, distortions and flagrant discrimination,
and protested that the five-man majority did not attempt to
answer the charges of "lack of good faith in this area of programing, or . . . of using the station's facilities for personal ends."
Such alleged abuses, the two dissenters claimed, "cannot properly
be sloughed aside—without resolution or, indeed, even mention."[8]
They also pointed out that though WLBT had stated several times
that it did not present local programing dealing with segrega-
tion to avoid being "inflammatory,"[9] it had not hesitated to
broadcast a series of local programs espousing the segregationist
viewpoint. And when the station had been queried about its
editorials declaring "Never" to James Meredith's admission to
Ole Miss, its answer was that this programing did not deal with
racial integration as such but rather with states' rights in a
constitutional crisis. Such misrepresentation, said Henry and
Cox, was a most serious offense; indeed, in the past the FCC
had denied renewal on this ground alone, so how could the other
commissioners ignore it here? In his dissent Chairman Henry
stated:

These petitions contain most serious allegations which, if true, would indicate that the station has made misrepresentations to the Commission, deceived the public, violated Commission policy, broken Federal and State laws, and ignored the needs of a substantial portion of the community it has pledged to serve. The Commission, in my opinion, should resolve these important issues in an evidentiary hearing. The licensee is entitled to such a hearing as a matter of right on the question of license renewal; to deny the same right to complaining members of the public is, in this instance, a clear abuse of discretion.[10]

Witnesses to the FCC debate recall the rage with which Henry and Cox faced the leader of the majority opinion, Lee Loevinger. Four-letter epithets were hurled across the Commission chamber. As the outcome became clear, a senior staff official stalked out, declaring, "This is evil, this is evil . . ."

Reverend Parker and his attorneys, Orrin Judd and Earle K. Moore, asked the Court of Appeals to overturn the FCC's probational ruling, and the case was argued on December 23, 1965, in Washington, D.C., before Judges Warren E. Burger, Carl McGowan and Edward Tamm. Their decision three and a half months later was devastatingly critical both of the Commission's conclusion and of its method of reaching it. "The Commission seems to have based its 'political decision' on a blend of what the Appellants alleged, what its own investigation revealed, its hope that WLBT would improve, and its view that the station was needed,"[11] the Court of Appeals stated. In the court's unanimous judgment, Burger readily dismissed the FCC's finding that the appellants had no proper standing simply because "economic injury and electrical interference"[12] were not involved. The court differed with the Commission's "traditional position that members of the listening public do not suffer any injury peculiar to them and that allowing them standing would pose great administrative burdens."[13] Rather, the petitioners had standing, Burger wrote, because they were consumers "with a genuine and legitimate interest . . . we can see no reason to exclude those with such an obvious and acute concern as the listening audience."[14] Quoting the legal scholar Edmond Cahn, Burger declared further: " 'Some consumers need bread; others need Shakespeare; others need their rightful place in the national society—what they all need is processors of law who will consider the people's needs more significant than administrative convenience.' "[15]

This decision of the court on "standing" was of significance far beyond Jackson. It opened the door to a new era in which blacks, Chicanos, women's groups and all organizations interested in improving television had standing to petition the Commission, and if dissatisfied with its ruling, to seek review in the courts. This meant that the public could no longer be ignored, either by the broadcaster or the FCC—that if one member of the public raised a substantial issue, the FCC must hold a hearing and resolve it in fair and reasoned fashion. For the first time the public could make the broadcaster account directly for his stewardship of the airwaves; no longer did it have to rely solely on the Commission or on sporadic congressional attention. Never before had so few—the five-man FCC majority—unintentionally done so much for the public interest than when they set the stage for Burger's historic opinion. Without this decision, public-interest law in the broadcast field would never have emerged.

Having granted standing to the appellants, the Court of Appeals proceeded to come out against the renewal of WLBT's license. "The Commission argues in this Court," wrote Burger, "that it accepted all Appellants' allegations of WLBT's misconduct, and that for this reason no hearing was necessary." But the judge pointed out that this was not justification for renewal: "When past performance is in conflict with the public interest, a very heavy burden rests on the renewal applicant to show how a renewal can be reconciled with the public interest."[16]

The court seemed to mock the FCC's rationale for the one-year renewal. Burger compared this to posting "the wolf to guard the sheep in the hope that the wolf would mend his way because some protection was needed at once and none but the wolf was handy." Since the station had stoutly denied all the charges against it, the three judges saw in WLBT no "capacity or willingness to change"; therefore the FCC's "pious hope" was no "substitute for evidence and finding."[17]

Aware of the Commission's fear that removal of WLBT's license might leave Jackson temporarily with only one station, Burger wrote: "It is open to question whether the public interest would not be as well if not better served with one TV outlet acutely conscious that adherence to the Fairness Doctrine is a *sine qua non* of every licensee."[18] He concluded: "We hold that the grant of a renewal of WLBT's license for one year was erroneous. The Commission is directed to conduct hearings on WLBT's renewal

application, allowing public intervention, pursuant to this holding," and the FCC's ruling was "reversed and remanded."[19]
What this meant was that the FCC should reconsider the wisdom
of permitting Lamar Life to continue the operation of WLBT,
and that final jurisdiction to review was retained by the Court of
Appeals.

The serious look took the FCC two more years, and while it
was looking, WLBT began improving its record.

Paul Porter, WLBT counsel and himself a former FCC chairman, told the FCC on June 4, 1968, that WLBT had made substantial strides to correct some of the charges against it. "A Negro
Student Apprentice Program has been implemented," said Porter.
". . . Mid-day devotional services are being rotated amongst
both Negro and white ministers, and representatives of Protestant,
Catholic and Jewish faiths. Integrated local and network programs
are and have for some time been the policy of this station . . . In
brief, the station is doing everything and we think more than this
Commission has the right . . . or duty to expect from its
licensees."[20]

In his argument Porter also claimed that the charges brought
by the United Church were for the most part unsubstantiated.
Speaking of the "Sorry, Cable Trouble" charge, Porter said:
"That is a myth that will haunt this station for the rest of its
electronic life."[21] Further, he pointed out that the monitoring
study had been characterized as "worthless" by the FCC examiner.[22] In concluding, he argued that "I am not claiming that this
station was a paragon of perfection during the '61–'64 period.
What I am claiming is that it did in the environment of its own
community do a sensible, responsible job."[23]

Apparently Porter's argument convinced some of the commissioners, because on June 27 WLBT's license was renewed for a
full term of three years. As five of the seven commissioners put it,
"We caution, however, against any conclusion that WLBT's performance . . . was spotless, or a model of perfection to be emulated
by other stations . . . We only conclude that the intervenors have
failed to prove their charges and that the preponderance of the
evidence before us establishes that station WLBT has afforded
reasonable opportunity for the use of its facilities by the significant community groups comprising its service area."[24] The majority further held that the intervenors (Smith and Henry and
United Church of Christ) had not met their burden of proof on

several issues like "Sorry, Cable Trouble," and that recent "marked improvements" in WLBT's local programing had been a positive factor.[25] However, one staff member did not agree; he called the decision a "white mouse."

William Henry was no longer chairman of the FCC, and his successor, Rosel H. Hyde, voted with the majority for renewal. Kenneth Cox and Nicholas Johnson, a newly appointed commissioner, were outraged, and filed a 32-page dissent calling the decision "a classic caricature of the FCC at its worst."[26] The final paragraph of their dissent is a sad denunciation of their fellow commissioners for their willingness "to go to such great lengths to protect a license with a very bad record," and for ignoring "what we believe the court of appeals directed us to do . . . Indeed, it would appear that the only way in which members of the public can prevent renewal of an unworthy station's license is to steal the document from the wall of the station's studio in the dead of night, or hope that the courts will do more than review and remand cases to the FCC with instructions that may be ignored."[27]

Twelve months later Judge Warren Burger, in his last opinion on the Court of Appeals, sent a loud and clear signal that the court did not expect regulatory agencies to ignore its directions. If the FCC was too timid to act, he and his two associates, McGowan and Tamm, would. The decision read, in part:

. . . the Commission exhibited at best a reluctant tolerance of this court's mandate and at worst a profound hostility to the participation of the Public Intervenors and their efforts . . .

The Commission itself, with more specific documentation of the licensee's shortcomings than it had in 1965 has now found virtues in the licensee which it was unable to perceive in 1965 and now finds the grant of a full three-year license to be in the public interest.

We are compelled to hold, on the whole record, that the Commission's conclusion is not supported by substantial evidence. For this reason the grant of a license must be vacated forthwith and the Commission is directed to invite applications to be filed for the license.[28]

This would appear to be the first time in history that a U.S. court had in effect ordered a license in any of the regulated fields—railroads, airlines, telephone service, public utilities and the like—to be terminated. (Two years later it was the FCC that took away Brandywine-Main Line Radio's license to operate station WXUR).

The case was remanded to the FCC, and in June 1971 Lamar Life lost its license to broadcast over station WLBT. In its stead, a temporary license was awarded Communications Improvement, Inc. Although Lamar Life did not appeal the decision of the Circuit Court which vacated the renewal, it did appeal to the Supreme Court to grant certiorari on the FCC decision which gave a temporary license to Communications Improvement. The newly appointed Chief Justice, Warren Burger, did not participate, but certiorari was denied, and the FCC decision was allowed to stand.

Burger's 1969 decision was hurriedly written, making it possible for legal purists to fault it in some technical respects, although from a practical standpoint it was a brilliant solution. For example, the FCC clearly was wrong in basing its decision on WLBT's recent "marked improvement" in local programing for the black community; Burger had declared in his 1966 opinion that a station must run on its record, but in his 1969 opinion he refrained "from holding that the licensee be declared disqualified from filing a new application . . ."[29] In other words, WLBT was allowed to participate in the new hearing, despite the fact that without its post-1964 improvements, the station would not have been able to stay in the running for the license renewal.

But this is mild criticism of a bold action by the Court of Appeals. If the FCC lacked the courage to uphold the public interest, the court did not falter in discharging its responsibility that the "rule of law" be followed. And the practical consequence, when coupled with the earlier decision on "standing," was profound: a powerful television station had lost its license for failure to serve the public interest. The message that Burger had tried to deliver in his 1966 opinion was driven home with a vengeance: "After nearly five decades of operation the broadcast industry does not seem to have grasped the simple fact that a broadcast license is a public trust subject to termination for breach of duty."[30]

Technically, WLBT never went off the air, and its signal still dominates the Jackson area, but for the past six years its voice and image have been remarkably different. It is still Channel 3, but it is unlike any other television station in the Deep South or in the nation. The present general manager, William Dilday, Jr., is black and a first-rate administrator, recruited from Boston. The president and chairman are white; and the board is integrated and represents both Mississippi and the national community. The six o'clock news has a black anchorman, while the ten o'clock news is presided over by a white reporter. The new WLBT schedules more news and public affairs than most stations, and a 1974 documentary on Mississippi poverty attracted national recognition. The station continues to have larger audiences than its CBS competitor on Channel 12, particularly in the news and public-affairs area.

As one citizen of the Old South who lived through the trauma of the sixties put it, "I never thought I'd see the day that a Negro could teach me anything, but it's just a more interesting station than it used to be."

Communications Improvement, Inc., is still considered an interim management. Several Jackson groups, including Lamar Life, have applied for the permanent license, and it is generally anticipated that a coalition of the most responsible applicants will win the franchise, which is now more valuable than ever. The fate of WLBT is still unclear, but the face of Channel 3 has changed dramatically since the day when station manager Fred Beard said "Never!"

8

UNPROTECTED SPEECH:
Some Commercials May Be Hazardous to Your Health

~~~~~~~~~~~~~~~~~~~~~~~~~~~~~~~~~~~~~

Whatever else it may mean, we think the public interest means the public health.

BANZHAF V. FCC, U.S. COURT OF APPEALS
FOR THE DISTRICT OF COLUMBIA, 1968

"The greatest cigarette vending machine ever devised . . ."

CBS ADVERTISEMENT, 1962

Just as *Red Lion* demonstrates the dilemmas of the personal-attack provisions of the Fairness Doctrine, *Banzhaf* v. *FCC* tests the use of the Doctrine as an instrument of public policy. The Banzhaf cigarette-advertising case involved millions of dollars and some of the nation's most powerful lobbies and influential law firms in a bitter debate to determine whether the public interest embraces the public health. Does the state have the power to protect the health of its citizens, even if it means violating freedom of speech and "the sanctity of the First Amendment," as the broadcast industry put it?

Banzhaf must be viewed against the perspective of the sixties, when cigarette advertising was the most pervasive single message on television and radio. Children learned the Kent jingle and all about "Marlboro Country" before they could recite the ABCs or the pledge of allegiance. What they should have learned, as one judge noted, was that "the Salem girl was in fact a seductive merchant of death—that the real 'Marlboro Country' is the grave-yard."[1] Some $300 million were spent each year on radio and television spots. In 1962 CBS bought seven-column advertisements in leading newspapers showing a cigarette vending machine combined with a television set; the caption read: "The greatest cigarette vending machine ever devised . . ."[2] Several members of the staff of CBS News suggested to management that since a number of documentaries had examined the relationship between smoking and lung cancer, the advertisement might prove an embarrassment, and the campaign was killed in those newspapers where it had not yet run.

The debate over cigarettes and health came to a climax in 1964 when the long-awaited Surgeon General's report and the subsequent Federal Cigarette Labeling and Advertising Act of 1965[3] made it clear that "normal use of this product can be a hazard to the health of millions of persons."[4]

Despite the growing volume of medically accepted evidence, the broadcast industry proclaimed that the proof was only circumstantial, and continued to accept lucrative contracts from the tobacco industry. Broadcasters argued that a government prohibition of cigarette commercials would be in violation of the First Amendment, at least as long as the sale of the product was still considered legal. Though Frank Stanton, president of CBS, suggested privately that television voluntarily ban cigarette advertising, the proposals never got very far in an industry which believed that such a move would cause serious damage to its financing, and that the loss of revenue would mean that the level of spending for news and public-affairs programs might have to be reduced. Ironically, cigarette advertisers seemed to have an affinity for the nightly news programs because according to the advertising agencies' motivational researchers, the public believed that any product identified with persons of the quality and integrity of Chet Huntley, David Brinkley and Walter Cronkite couldn't be harmful to anyone.

Such was the industry and regulatory climate on December 1, 1966, when John F. Banzhaf III, aged twenty-three and just out of Columbia Law School, wrote his now-famous letter to the management of WCBS-TV, the network's flagship station in New York City. Banzhaf argued that the "portrayals of youthful or virile-looking or sophisticated persons enjoying cigarettes in . . . exciting situations . . . create[s] the impression that smoking . . . is a necessary part of a rich full life." These commercials presented one side of a "controversial issue of public importance," and he asserted that under the Fairness Doctrine, WCBS-TV was obligated to "affirmatively endeavor to make its . . . facilities available [free] for the expression of contrasting viewpoints . . ."[5]

In his response, WCBS-TV's general manager Clark George rejected Banzhaf's demand, noting that the station had broadcast several news and information programs on the health-smoking controversy, as well as five public-service announcements of the American Cancer Society. Furthermore, CBS doubted that "the fairness doctrine can properly be applied to commercial announcements solely and clearly aimed at selling products and services."[6]

Banzhaf proceeded to forward his complaint and the George reply to the FCC, charging that the station was violating the Fairness Doctrine. Six months later, in a historic decision, the Commission agreed with Banzhaf, stating: ". . . a station which presents such advertisement has the duty of informing its audience of the other side of this controversial issue . . . that, however enjoyable, such smoking may be a hazard to the smoker's health."[7] Even Lee Loevinger, the commissioner most fearful of government interference with free speech, reluctantly went along with the majority "because of a strong feeling that suggesting smoking to young people, in the light of present knowledge, is something very close to wickedness." The fact that Commissioner Rosel Hyde, a cautious, caretaker chairman, favored such drastic action is generally attributed to his strong Mormon beliefs.

Still, the Commission stopped short of upholding Banzhaf's demand for equal time, emphasizing that "the amount and nature of time to be afforded is a matter of good faith . . ."[8] In effect, the FCC was directing stations which carried cigarette commercials to provide a significant amount of time each week for such public-service announcements as those produced by the American Cancer Society.

The FCC ruling became a major news story across the nation and stimulated frantic demands for clarification and a rehearing. The Commission emphasized that the Banzhaf ruling applied only to cigarette commercials, and denied any intention of encouraging or allowing other vocal minorities to be awarded free announcements to counter other alleged controversial products.[9] In response to another request for clarification, the Commission ruled that stations which carried cigarette advertising were under no obligation to provide the cigarette companies free time in which to refute broadcast claims that smoking endangers health.[10]

The ruling provoked a series of legal challenges to the FCC and appeals to the federal courts by an ever-widening spectrum of litigants. The National Association of Broadcasters felt that it would fare better if its appeal was heard in tobacco country, so it and its allies filed for review in the Richmond-based Court of Appeals. Once again the race to the Circuits was on. Banzhaf had anticipated this maneuver, and appealed the FCC's decision in the District of Columbia Court of Appeals on the grounds that although he had won "significant" time to rebut cigarette commercials, he had not been accorded equal time. Banzhaf's legal maneuverings worked: the cases were joined and heard before the Washington court. Broadcast stations, networks and the tobacco industry were all arrayed against the FCC. Nevertheless, the case became known as *Banzhaf et al. v. FCC*, even though the two litigants were on the same side of the issue except on the matter of equal time versus "significant" time. Meanwhile, pending the appeal, the FCC ruling went into effect. A barrage of cigarette commercials was answered by a smaller but persuasive salvo of anti-cigarette commercials, at a ratio of about 5 to 1.

Twenty-three months after citizen Banzhaf wrote his letter to WCBS-TV, the United States Court of Appeals, with Chief Judge David L. Bazelon presiding, heard the case argued by a battery of Washington lawyers. Once again Paul Porter, this time representing the tobacco interests, found himself arguing against the Fairness Doctrine, which he had once believed in. In fees and expenses the public-interest side of the case was outspent by at least 30 to 1. Banzhaf was represented by Earle K. Moore and also appeared himself.

The tobacco and broadcast industries' arguments were based on narrow interpretations of the Cigarette Labeling Act and of the Bill of Rights, "because the First Amendment permits no regulation of program content" and because "the cigarette ruling in particular violates the First Amendment."[11] They claimed that when the Congress had passed the Labeling Act of 1965 warning ("Caution: Cigarette Smoking May Be Hazardous to Your Health"[12]), it meant to forbid any other regulation addressed to the problem except for the Federal Trade Commission's expressly exempted power to police false and misleading advertising. The industry lawyers argued that if the Senate and House had wished to do any more than simply provide ample warning, they would have specifically passed such laws. Since there had been no other cigarette legislation, they reasoned that the FCC had no authority to order free time for anti-smoking messages.

This complex legal reasoning received little support from the Court of Appeals, which gave its approval to the FCC's ruling:

> A man who hears a hundred "yeses" for each "no" when the actual odds lie heavily the other way, cannot be realistically deemed adequately informed. Moreover, since cigarette smoking is psychologically addicting, the confirmed smoker is likely to be relatively unreceptive to information about its dangers; his hearing is dulled by his appetite. And since it is so much harder to stop than not to start, it is crucial that an accurate picture be communicated to those who have not yet begun.[13]

The court also rejected the industry's claim that the FCC's cigarette ruling violated the First Amendment: "[It] does not convert the Commission into either a censor or Big Brother."[14] Chief Judge Bazelon's opinion went on:

> The Cigarette ruling does not ban any speech. In traditional doctrinal terms, the constitutional argument against it is only that it may have a "chilling effect" on the exercise of First Amendment freedom by making broadcasting more reluctant to carry advertising.
>
> The speech which might conceivably be "chilled" by this ruling barely qualifies as constitutionally protected "speech." It is established that some utterances fall outside the pale of First Amendment concern . . . Promoting the sale of a product is not ordinarily associated with any of the interests the First Amendment seeks to protect . . .[15]

But the court rejected Banzhaf's claim that anti-smokers should be granted equal time. "Such a specific requirement," it ruled, would be "an unnecessary intrusion upon the licensee's discretion."[16] In the same vein, the court turned down the cigarette manufacturers' request for rebuttal time to answer the anti-smoking messages ordered by the FCC.

In his majority decision, Bazelon was clearly aware of the

"First Amendment issues lurking in the near background."[17] But he noted that more than First Amendment issues were at stake here. On the key question of "public interest versus public health" Bazelon was unequivocal: "Whatever else it may mean, however, we think the public interest indisputably means the public health . . . The power to protect the public health lies at the heart of the State's political power . . . The public health has in effect become a kind of basic law."[18]

Staggered by the decision, the cigarette and broadcast industries asked the Supreme Court to review the lower court's holding. But certiorari was denied, which meant, in effect, that the Court, without revealing its reasons, had decided that the Bazelon decision would prevail.[19]

The final chapter was written on April 1, 1969, when the Congress passed legislation which prohibited all cigarette advertising on radio and television after December 31, 1970. Actually this law emerged from a wild series of hearings, lobbying and filibustering during which the tobacco interests attempted to block tougher labeling regulations. Senator Frank Moss of Utah led the battle, but the spark that had started it all was Banzhaf's original letter.

Typically, the cigarette-advertising blackout on radio and television was delayed from December 31, 1970, to midnight, January 1, 1971, so that the revenues from the last spate of one-minute commercials during the football bowl games would not be lost. In the waning moments of the Orange Bowl game, as the Marlboro man galloped across the screen for the last time, an era which had begun on radio with "Reach for a Lucky instead of a sweet" and "Not a cough in a carload" ended—save for the lawsuits.

Curiously, not everyone who agreed that cigarette smoking was harmful or who saw the constitutional validity in the Banzhaf judgment approved of the congressional banning of cigarette advertising on the broadcast media. Some of these doubts were soon voiced in a case involving Capital Broadcasting, Inc., whose stations in Mississippi and Colorado had sought a court ruling on the constitutionality of the Public Health Cigarette Smoking Act of 1969. Unlike the Banzhaf First Amendment arguments, Capital Broadcasting raised Fifth Amendment due-process objections. The company argued that while the ban on cigarette advertising did not violate Fifth Amendment rights per se, the legislation had singled out one of the media—broadcasting—and excluded print from the ban. This double standard, they argued, was unconstitutional, an "arbitrary and invidious" distinction. The majority of the special three-judge court denied the claim, stating that the Fifth Amendment did not compel legislators to prohibit all like evils or none: "A legislature may hit at an abuse which it has found, even though it has failed to strike at another."[20]

Judge Wright disagreed with the majority of the court, not because he agreed with the broadcasters' due-process argument or because his opinion was intended "as a Magna Carta for Madison Avenue," but simply because he believed that "the Banzhaf decision was correct and that [the Public Health Cigarette Smoking Law] is unconstitutional."[21] He was convinced that airing cigarette commercials and anti-smoking announcements was a better solution to the issues raised by Banzhaf and the Surgeon General's report than the total ban passed by the Congress, since, as he noted, "when people are given both sides of the cigarette controversy, they will make the correct decision . . . That is, after all, what the First Amendment is all about."[22]

Wright's bristling dissent was not based on the legal implications of the broadcasters' claim as much as on the practical impact of the legislation, which he termed a political deal:

> The history of cigarette advertising since *Banzhaf* has been a sad tale of well meaning but misguided paternalism, cynical bargaining and lost opportunity. In the immediate wake of *Banzhaf*, the broadcast media were flooded with exceedingly effective anti-smoking commercials. For the first time in years, the statistics began to show a sustained trend toward lesser cigarette consumption.[23]

Citing U.S. Department of Agriculture statistics to prove his point, Wright contended:

> The *Banzhaf* ruling . . . clearly made the electronic media advertising a losing proposition for the industry . . . The result of the legislation was that both cigarette advertisements and most anti-smoking messages left the air, the tobacco companies trans-

ferred their advertising budgets to other forms of advertising such as newspapers and magazines where there was no Fairness Doctrine to require a response.[24]

The passage of the Public Health Cigarette Smoking Act did herald a dramatic legislative coup for the tobacco industry. With the cigarette-smoking controversy removed from the air, the decline in cigarette sales halted and almost immediately consumption increased.

As Judge Wright's worst fears came to pass, and as smoking increased despite the lack of commercials, the broadcast industry's warnings that the blackout on cigarette advertising might be dangerous to their economic health were exaggerated, to say the least. (Leonard Goldenson, president of ABC, testified during the congressional debate over the Cigarette Act that withdrawal of cigarette commercials "could well mean a substantial cutback in our news and public affairs operations. . . . We do not believe that Congress would look with favor on any such forced curtailment of network service to the American public."[25] Four years later the industry's profits were higher than ever and ABC's financial commitment to news and public affairs had finally given the network parity with its two rivals.)

In his dissent Judge Wright also raised a worthwhile point about political deals. If Congress found cigarette smoking hazardous to the public's health, why did it not ban its being advertised in *all* media? Surely the logical response to such a hazard should be to increase efforts to educate citizens and to end all promotion? Congress' job was the public interest, not that of the tobacco industry, which had sought the ban in broadcasting in order to end the controversy and free millions of dollars for diversification.

In *Banzhaf* the Court of Appeals and the FCC had a relatively easy job. The government had found that cigarette smoking was a serious potential hazard to public health; broadcasters were promoting use of this product; therefore broadcasters, as public trustees, had the obligation to inform their listeners about the hazard. As both the court and the FCC stressed, "This obligation stems not from some esoteric requirements of a particular doctrine [Fairness] but from the simple fact that the public interest means nothing if it does not include such a responsibility."[26] But what about countercommercials for products and services that fall into the gray area—where an advertised product is clearly useful and beneficial to individual consumers, yet creates hazards to the environment and the nation's "quality of life"? Detergents, high-lead-content gasolines and even automobiles fall into this category. Those arguing against *Banzhaf* warned that because of the way the problem of cigarette commercials had been handled, there would soon be a regulatory nightmare of similar demands for government intervention by a variety of public-interest groups.

It was a prediction that almost immediately proved correct. Even before the last cigarette commercial was off the air, a public-interest group had trained its sights on automobile advertisements, charging that motorcar emissions could be dangerous to one's health. The suit, brought by an environmental group, Friends of the Earth, was specifically aimed at WNBC-TV in New York City, but the target of the plaintiffs was every radio and television station that carried product advertising.

Friends of the Earth, which described itself as a national organization dedicated to the protection and preservation of the environment, had monitored the schedule of WNBC-TV, the network's owned-and-operated station in New York City. Their first letter to WNBC in early February 1970 cited five "abuses":

(1) January 26, 1970, 8:15 P.M., 30 sec., an advertisement for Ford Mustang, picturing the car on a lonely beach, and stressing its "performance" (large engine displacement);

(2) Same date, 8:15 P.M., 30 sec., an advertisement for Ford Torino stressing size;

(3) January 22, 1970, 6:15 P.M., 30 sec., an advertisement for Chevrolet Impala stressing the great value of its size ("you don't have to be a big spender to be a big rider"), including the standard 250-horsepower V-8 engine;

(4) January 5, 1970, 8:05 P.M., 30 sec., an advertisement for Ford Mustang and Torino GT, again stressing size ("4-barrel, V-8" and "up to 429 cubic inches") and advocating "moving up to" a larger car;

(5) December 10, 1969, 11:15 P.M., encouraging the use of high-test leaded gasoline for cold-weather starting ("the cold-weather gasoline").[27]

Friends of the Earth and its advocate Geoffrey Cowan, a leader in public-interest law, asserted that these products were especially heavy contributors to the city's "oppressive and dangerous" air pollution, and asked that WNBC-TV "promptly make known the ways in which it intends to discharge its responsibility to inform the public of the other side of this critical controversy." Friends of the Earth stated that it could not afford to purchase air time but offered to produce broadcast spots "presenting the anti-auto-pollution case."[28]

WNBC's management swiftly turned down the demand, citing that the FCC's decision in the Banzhaf case was limited by its terms to cigarette advertising. The network noted that the decision, in the Commission's own words, did not impose any Fairness Doctrine obligation on broadcasters "with respect to other product advertising."[29] WNBC also referred to a number of its programs which had dealt with automobile pollution and contended that its viewers had been informed about both sides of the controversy.[30]

Unsatisfied by the station's response, Friends of the Earth complained formally to the FCC, charging WNBC-TV with "failure to fulfill its 'fairness doctrine' and 'public interest' obligations"[31] and asking the Commission to investigate and take appropriate action to make NBC comply. Letters supporting the complainant were filed by the Environmental Protection Administration of New York and by Citizens for Clean Air, Inc.

WNBC-TV remained adamant,[32] aware that compliance with these demands would open the floodgates to hundreds of similar complaints and create a situation in which almost every commercial minute might carry with it a responsibility to grant an unpaid counterannouncement. The potential financial stakes in this confrontation were far higher than in the cigarette controversy.

Still startled by the effectiveness of its dramatic remedy in the cigarette ruling, the FCC was determined not to venture into this uncharted new field. While recognizing that automobiles "result in many deaths each year . . . because their gasoline engines constitute the main source of air pollution,"[33] the Commission held that resolution of the air-pollution problem caused by the gasoline engine was a complex one and called for congressional evaluation of many factors. Congress had not urged that people should now stop using automobiles, as it had in the case of cigarettes. "We decline . . . to extend the cigarette advertising ruling to other products," the FCC informed Friends of the Earth. "We should adhere to our previous judgment that cigarettes are a unique product permitting the simplistic approach adopted in that field."[34]

The FCC was making the point that while the environmentalists might have a complaint against certain automobile and gasoline commercials, any controls on advertising were the business of Congress, and in the absence of action by Congress, the Commission should stay its hand. Significantly, the Court of Appeals had stated in *Banzhaf*: ". . . our cautious approval of this particular decision does not license the Commission to scan the airwaves for offensive materials with no more discrimination than the 'public interest' or even the 'public health.' "[35]

When Friends of the Earth appealed the FCC's ruling, the Court of Appeals of the District of Columbia held that there was no plausible difference between the gasoline and automobile commercials cited by Friends of the Earth and the cigarette advertisements of *Banzhaf*. Both types of commercials urged the use of products that had substantial built-in health hazards. "The distinction," wrote Judge Carl McGowan for the majority, "is not apparent to us, any more than we suppose it is to the asthmatic in New York City for whom increasing air pollution is a mortal danger. Neither are we impressed by the Commission's assertion that, because no governmental agency has as yet urged the complete abandonment of the use of automobiles, the commercials in question do not touch upon a controversial issue of public importance."[36]

The court reminded the FCC that at the time of its *Banzhaf* ruling it had gone to "great pains to warn that it did not contemplate its extension to product advertising generally,"[37] but McGowan implied that the Commission was taking this self-imposed restraint too literally. In other cases the regulatory agency had already been obliged to moderate its view that "commercial advertising, apart from cigarettes, is immune from the fairness doctrine."[38]

Judge McGowan pointed out that in its *Chevron* ruling the FCC stated that if a sponsor used his commercial time to debate a controversial issue to the community—such as whether strip mining had harmful effects or a factory should be closed for emitting noxious fumes—"the fairness obligations would ensue."[39] And while this was just a dictum in the Chevron case, in the Esso case the FCC had ruled that a commercial message had been used "to discuss one side of controversial issues . . . namely (1) the need of developing Alaska oil reserves quickly and (2) the capability of the oil companies to develop and transport that oil without environmental damage."[40] (The Alaska pipeline was not specifically mentioned, but it was clearly the subject of the message.) In that decision the Commission had held that Alaska oil commercials were subject to Fairness Doctrine rules, and WNBC, which coincidentally was the target station in the Esso case as well, was given ten days to inform the Commission of what additional material it intended to broadcast to satisfy its Fairness Doctrine obligations.

The Court of Appeals recognized that the FCC faced "great difficulties in tracing a coherent pattern for the accommodation of product advertising to the fairness doctrine," and that it was for this reason that the Commission was commencing a broad inquiry to examine the issues. "Pending, however, a reformulation of its position," the court concluded that the Friends of the Earth complaint was indistinguishable from the Banzhaf case in terms of the reach of the Fairness Doctrine.[41] Accordingly, "the Commission erred in concluding that the advertising in question did not present one side of a controversial issue of public importance," and the case was remanded to the FCC "to determine whether the licensee had been adequately discharging its public service obligations . . . to achieve the balance contemplated in the Fairness Doctrine."[42]

Despite the potential, the Court of Appeals judgment had minimal impact, perhaps because the majority opinion was not unanimous, or because the "further action" on remand took the form of a secret agreement between the two parties. Part of the secret settlement between WNBC-TV and Friends of the Earth included a proviso that there would be no formal public announcement of the details of the station's remedial action to satisfy the Fairness Doctrine. The station agreed to broadcast a series of one-minute anti–automobile-pollution announcements; these would appear twice a day, one in the morning during the Today show, and one in the evening during prime time. These countercommercials, some narrated by Eli Wallach, would run for one month, then skip a month and resume for another thirty days.

This formula provided Friends of the Earth with approximately 120 minutes of free air time in return for a promise not to continue its petition to deny WNBC-TV its license. Other television stations in New York heard the message, and some, though not all, agreed to carry these countercommercials.

There were other reasons for the modest impact of the Friends of the Earth ruling. The FCC won two other cases that involved an analogous issue. Public-interest petitioners sought time to present an opposing view to military-recruitment announcements sponsored by the U.S. Armed Services on radio. The petitioners argued that these announcements endorsed the desirability of volunteering for military service without regard for the role of the U.S. military in Vietnam. The FCC held that the recruitment announcements raised no controversial issue within the Fairness Doctrine,[43] and two courts—the D.C. Circuit and the Ninth Circuit—affirmed this decision.[44] In another case, the D.C. Circuit affirmed the FCC's judgment that product commercials urging the use of Chevron F-310 to combat air pollution were not an issue within the bounds of the Fairness Doctrine. The narrow question, the court held, was the product efficacy of F-310, and this was not a controversial issue of public importance.[45]

Finally, the FCC was allowed in the Friends of the Earth case to rethink and reformulate its position. The other shoe didn't drop until July 12, 1974, when the FCC published its definitive ruling on the Fairness Doctrine. In the section devoted to controversial commercials in this document, the Commission sent a message back to the Court of Appeals: since the cigarette-advertising ruling and the automobile-pollution issue were indistinguishable to the court, the FCC simply overruled the former. "We do not believe," said the Commission, "that the underlying purposes of the fairness doctrine would be well served by permitting the cigarette case to stand as a fairness doctrine precedent."[46] The FCC felt that the "kind of logic" represented by the Court of Appeals decision "engages both broadcasters and the Commission in the trivial task of 'balancing' two sets of commercials which contribute nothing to public understanding of the underlying issue of how to deal with the problem of air pollution."[47]

The FCC believed that an interpretation of the Fairness Doctrine such as the one the Court of Appeals had recommended in the Friends of the Earth case would in effect cause the destruction of the American commercial system of broadcasting:

It would be a great mistake to consider standard advertisements such as those involved in the *Banzhaf* and *Friends of the Earth* as though they made a meaningful contribution to public debate. It is a mistake, furthermore, which tends only to divert the attention of broadcasters from their public trustee responsibilities in aiding the development of an informed public opinion. Accordingly, in the future, we will apply the Fairness Doctrine only to those "commercials" which are devoted in an obvious and meaningful way to the discussion of public issues.[48]

The FCC contended that the use of countercommercials was a tortured and distorted application of the Fairness Doctrine, and reminded stations of their obligations to cover consumer problems and of the public-trustee responsibility of the broadcast station "to implement a meaningful discussion of major public issues."[49] Further, the Commission said, such discussion was a method of illuminating issues concerning advertised products which was far superior to a confused debate conducted by commercials and countercommercials.

Thus the FCC sought to write the end to a chapter that had begun with *Banzhaf*. The Fairness Doctrine, the agency said in 1974, was not applicable to the ordinary commercial that simply promoted the sale of a product as contrasted with the Esso commercial that propagandized for the North Slope Oil project.

The final chapter may not yet have been written on *Banzhaf* (the FCC's 1974 policy is again subject to appeal by public-interest groups in the D.C. Circuit), but it is possible to give some overview of what has occurred so far.

The Commission's initial action in the Banzhaf case is fully understandable. As Commissioner Loevinger noted, the FCC believed that the issue was simply a matter of a rectifiable evil. The government had established that cigarette smoking was causing an "epidemic of death," and the public-interest groups therefore cried out for action—whether or not the Fairness Doctrine was involved. Indeed, the Commission and two courts—the D.C. Circuit in *Banzhaf* and also the Fourth Circuit—had pointed out that it was the public interest, not the Fairness Doctrine, that was relevant.

But the Commission did make a technical error; in its decision, as did the Court of Appeals, it also relied on the Fairness Doctrine, to provide "a familiar mold to define the general contours of the obligation imposed."[50] And despite all the Commission's protestations that cigarettes were a unique product, it should have anticipated the intense interest by public-interest committees in expanding the *Banzhaf* ruling. It was a period of political ferment, of the rise of consumer groups inspired by Nader, of opposition by activist groups to Administration military policies. Such groups were vigorously pursuing their aims and recognized that publicity was the key to any success. Broadcasting is the most powerful medium in the country, and the *Banzhaf* decision's mention of the Doctrine seemed to provide an open door.

The FCC adamantly resisted that onslaught; it recognized that the slope was not simply slippery; it was a straight descent. Commercial after commercial—beer, wine, airplanes, products with nonbiodegradable containers, pills, detergents; the list is endless—would provoke countercommercials. The FCC's delayed ruling was intended to stress the first part of the Fairness Doctrine—that the broadcaster must cover such "matters of great public concern" with programing that truly illuminated the issues, rather than with slogans promoting or condemning a product that never dealt with the real controversy.

The FCC's response can be criticized, for the result was that the task of answering, analyzing and otherwise combating commercials raising public or private issues was left mostly in the hands of the broadcast journalist. To equalize the exaggerated claims of the advertiser, the broadcast journalist would require an abundance of air time and a latitude to pursue the issues—neither of which is likely to be forthcoming.

So what is the alternative? Is the government to intervene to make sure that commercial after commercial is answered in some set ratio? How would it take into account other programing on the issue—or commercials for the type of product favored by the complainant (e.g., unleaded gas; small cars)? Whatever the financial effects on the broadcast system, such deep involvement by the government in day-to-day broadcast operations is questionable policy; indeed, it might be contrary to the spirit of the First Amendment.

Perhaps the answer lies not in the Fairness Doctrine but in paid access to broadcast time. Perhaps the answer goes back to 1922 when that real estate developer asked New York City's first station,

WEAF, for time to sell his apartments in Queens. From that instant the commercial die was cast. Free speech was still the American way, but now it was also for sale. "The multitude of tongues" had equal access—except for those who sold such products as soap, gasoline or religion; they were more equal because they could buy their way.

The tricky crosscurrents of this dilemma were illustrated during the energy crisis of 1974. The oil companies, particularly Mobil, protested that their position about the necessity to expand energy reserves was receiving "outrageous treatment"[51] in the nightly newscasts. Although the oil industry was spending $73 million a year in television, the networks refused to permit them to use their minutes to advance their special views. Words such as "offshore drilling," "profits" and "taxes" were off-limits.

All three networks maintained a traditional policy of not selling time for controversial issues other than during political campaigns. With advertising campaigns in many newspapers stating their position on national oil policy, Mobil protested the broadcasters' ban. "We at Mobil think we've been granted reasonable access to express our views in print media," said Herbert Schmertz, vice-president for public affairs. "But the same cannot be said for television, despite the Fairness Doctrine."[52] Concurrently, consumer and conservation groups and some congressmen were criticizing the networks for permitting companies such as Exxon, Gulf, Texaco and Mobil to brainwash the public with a multimillion-dollar "blitz" whose message was that the oil companies were not responsible for the energy crisis and that laws should be changed to benefit them.[53]

In a bold and potentially expensive move, Mobil announced that it was willing to purchase an equal number of commercials for its consumer critics if the networks would sell them time for those advocating its own position. All three networks rejected the idea. ABC claimed that a proposal offering rebuttal commercials would "open a Pandora's box," both for advocacy commercials and counteradvertising, and that the broadcasters would "lose control over their commercial policies."[54]

Both the oil industry and the networks claimed that the First Amendment was being violated, or would be, but eventually NBC agreed to run a low-key message from Mobil asking the public to comment on how it felt about offshore drilling. The oil company ran a large advertisement in the *New York Times* asking: "Why do two networks refuse to run this commercial?" CBS's answer was: ". . . this commercial deals with a controversial issue of public importance and does not fall within our goods and services limitation for commercial acceptance."[55]

The message was, in fact, not controversial. The video portion consisted of a sixty-second view of open sea; a low-key narration recounted the offshore oil-drilling controversy and asked viewers to write letters indicating where they stood. Although NBC agreed to run this because it did not advocate a controversial point of view, in the end Mobil refused the offer. "If we weren't going to get a policy change from all three networks, what was the point?" said Schmertz. "In the face of such censorship, we decided not to accept what we thought was an unfair result by being forced to develop separate commercials based on different networks' standards of acceptability."

The Mobil executive for public affairs brilliantly exploited the access issue to advance his company's image as a tongue-tied giant unable to communicate its constructive ideas on energy because of the networks' intransigence. Schmertz feels that there is a rift between business and the media, and that the networks constantly misuse their own air by broadcasting propaganda helpful to their special interests. He was outraged by CBS's coverage of a Paley speech at Syracuse which asked for an end of FCC controls, as well as a radio broadcast by Mike Wallace in which an imaginary letter to the ghost of John Peter Zenger was used to push the network's opposition to S.1, a Senate bill which Wallace feared could muzzle reporters.[56]

Schmertz believes that air time should be open to all who are willing and able to pay for it. Curiously, many civil-liberties activists share his view. The networks oppose it on the principle that the financially affluent would dominate the air. "Mobil wants to sell its own point of view in the marketplace of its own choosing and on its own terms," said CBS president Arthur R. Taylor. "Mobil has offered to buy so-called 'equal time' for opposing views *if* the request is legitimate." This would, of course, allow the company to retain veto power not only over the choice of opposition "but over the determination of what issues are discussed, as well."[57]

In a strange alliance, Mobil and consumer and conservationist foes are in agreement that the networks' position is grossly unfair and a violation of their First Amendment rights.

Why, the question was asked, should not the party with an editorial message have at least some access to the broadcast system if it was willing and able to pay? This issue was also being fought at the same time, and it came to a head when a Vietnam peace group attempted to buy time on a Washington radio station.

9

THE PAID-TIME CASE:

The President's Use of Television

~~~~~~~~~~~~~~~~~~~~~~~~~~~~~~~~~~~~

> *For better or worse, editing is what editors are for and editing is selection and choice of material.*
>
> CHIEF JUSTICE WARREN BURGER, U.S.
> SUPREME COURT, IN CBS ET AL. V. DNC, 1973

Robert Mitchell's job was to sell time on radio station WTOP, an all-news station in Washington, which reached a "highly sophisticated news-hungry audience," the station's brochure claimed. In June of 1969 Mitchell, who had been a salesman for the station for only one month, received an order for a series of one-minute announcements costing $100 each from the Business Executives' Move for Peace. The BEM organization of some 2,700 executives from forty-nine states had produced a series of anti-Vietnam war messages and was particularly anxious to air its views in the nation's capital, where senators and representatives would be exposed to them. The one-minute spots featured dramatic anti-war messages by Admiral Arnold E. True and Nobel Prize-winner George Wald.

When Mitchell reported to his boss that he had received an order for the BEM spots, the station's sales manager told him to reject it because of WTOP's long-established policy of refusing to sell spot announcements "[dealing with] controversial issues." Not allowed to purchase the air time, the BEM appealed to the station's top management, citing all the commercial messages that WTOP broadcast, and the fact that several other stations in the Washington area had readily accepted their business.

On January 7, 1970, WTOP vice-president Daniel Gold wrote a letter to the BEM stating the station's policy and explaining that newcomer Mitchell had not fully understood it. The station considered the announcements insulting to the President and observed that "subjects of this type deserve more in-depth analysis than can be produced in 10, 20, 30, or 60 second commercials."[1] Two weeks later, the BEM filed a formal complaint with the FCC.

During that same winter of discontent, 1970, the Democratic National Committee tried repeatedly to purchase time on various television stations and on the three major networks to counter the enormously effective use of television by the President of the United States. Richard Nixon was not up for re-election himself, but all of the House, a third of the Senate and many state races were being influenced by a formidable President who commanded access to television and radio almost at will. The networks and most of the major stations refused to sell or grant free time to the Democrats. Convinced that this imbalance was a threat to the two-party system, the Democrats decided to take legal action.

These two separate incidents dramatized the dilemma of regulated mass communications in a democratic system. Involved were issues of public policy, of war, and of the control of political power. In effect, these two cases posed the ultimate question of U.S. broadcasting, the right of commercial speech vs. political speech. The issue was framed when attorney Joseph A. Califano, Jr., who had been President Johnson's assistant for domestic affairs, wrote to the FCC in May 1970 on behalf of the Democratic National Committee: "Are the public airwaves—the most powerful communications media in our democracy—to be used to solicit funds for soap, brassieres, deodorants and mouthwashes, and not to solicit funds to enhance the exchange of ideas?"[2]

Ever since the radio days of the New Deal, when FDR created the fireside chat, the political party on the outs has cried foul against the overwhelming advantage of what is now called "presidential television." Indeed, it is an electronic pulpit of a power that neither Caesar nor Napoleon could ever have imagined. The outs have always accused the White House, the FCC and the networks of collusion. When President Kennedy ruled the airwaves with his tour de force news conferences and his "royal" visits to Berlin, Paris and London, the Republicans saw a plot, as had the Democrats in 1956, when President Eisenhower's electronic red carpet and access during the Lebanon crisis gave him an enormous advantage over Adlai Stevenson.

As the temperature over Vietnam rose, so did President Johnson's insatiable thirst for air time. This led to *The Ev and Charlie Show* (Senator Everett Dirksen and Representative Charles Halleck, later Representative Gerald Ford), using reply time for the slighted GOP.

In President Nixon's first term, the Democratic party and the antiwar movement found his virtually unrestrained management of the airwaves, especially during prime time, so crippling that they began searching for legal remedies. The statistics were staggering; in Nixon's first eighteen months in office he held center stage on all networks during prime hours, more than the combined time of Presidents Eisenhower, Kennedy and Johnson. During one twenty-eight-week period, from November of 1969 to June 1970, the President broke all records; all of the appearances related to the war in Southeast Asia and all were carried live on all commercial networks simultaneously. Moreover, each speech was publicized well in advance and was carried without commercial interruption or reporters' questions. In each instance the networks provided the time without inquiring about content or newsworthiness. Because the presidential appearances blanketed the air, and because in most cities there was no alternative station to turn to, the size of the audience swelled geometrically in comparison to the viewers he might have commanded on any one network. Often Nixon reached audiences of 60 percent of the sets in use.

In 1970 Lawrence O'Brien, perhaps John Kennedy's closest political adviser besides his brother Robert Kennedy, returned to politics as chairman of the Democratic National Committee. The party's prospects and finances were at a low ebb, and the inability to beg, borrow or even buy national air time, except during brief election periods, infuriated the new chairman. In his book, *No Final Victories*, O'Brien reminisces about the time when one network executive turned down, out of hand, the Democrats' request to buy time "to present our case to the American people and solicit funds."[3] Chairman O'Brien talked about this on *Meet the Press* and warned, "I am not going to stand idly by and allow that to happen. They will be hearing further from me."[4]

O'Brien blamed the one-sided television situation on Nixon himself, first for appointing "an able but partisan figure, Dean

Burch, the former Goldwater aide and Republican Chairman,"[5] as head of the FCC. (Burch had complained just as bitterly in 1964 when Johnson used national issues—e.g., the first Chinese nuclear explosion—as an excuse to exploit his party's political interests.) O'Brien also blamed Nixon for assigning Vice-President Spiro Agnew the task of intimidating television reporters and executives by "making thinly veiled threats of FCC action against those [stations and networks] who displeased the Administration."[6]

O'Brien and Califano were admittedly uncomfortable with all three networks, but James Haggerty, a vice-president of ABC, posed a special problem. He had been Eisenhower's press secretary and was a prominent Republican, and Califano believed that he "was keeping the White House fully informed of our conversations." (There is no evidence to support this charge.) But O'Brien didn't think that it was this pressure alone which caused the networks to refuse to sell the Democrats time for fund-raising appeals and for comments on political issues: "I understood the networks' attitude. Why risk the wrath of the President or of some viewers by selling time for 'controversial' political messages when you are doing very well selling your time for non-controversial dog-food and deodorant commercials?"[7] O'Brien's anguished, if simplistic, view of the networks' motives might have seemed more credible if it had evidenced itself during the years when John Kennedy commanded the air at will. But as a frustrated out, he now viewed it differently: ". . . our two-party system can't survive if one party is denied access to the dominant communications medium."[8]

Joseph Califano, who shared O'Brien's dismay, had agreed to serve as the Democratic National Committee counsel in mounting a legal attack on the system. "It was my sense of outrage about television time, and only that, which caused me to take the job."

On April 30, 1970, President Nixon announced the invasion of Cambodia, and utilized his near-monopoly of the national air to defend and promote his decision. O'Brien requested reply time for the Democrats, but of the three commercial networks, only ABC offered thirty minutes of air time. Aggravated and convinced that the networks were discriminating against a major political party on a bitterly partisan issue, Califano filed a request for a declaratory ruling from the FCC:

That under the First Amendment to the Constitution and the Communications Act, a broadcaster may not, as a general policy, refuse to sell time to responsible entities, such as the DNC, for the solicitation of funds and for comment on public issues.[9]

The Democratic National Committee did not single out a particular network or television station for discriminating against them, but claimed that its previous "experiences in this area make it clear that it will encounter considerable difficulty—if not total frustration of its efforts—in carrying out its plan in the event the Commission should decline to issue a ruling as requested."[10] The DNC brief went on to quote CBS's vice-president in Washington, Richard Jenks, who defended the policy against selling time to political parties to promote their positions on public issues because of his company's "belief that [our] news organization can give a fairer presentation"[11] than others. This egocentric policy, Califano charged, "violated the constitutional standards set down by the Court in *Red Lion*."[12]

This claim was similar to BEM's contention that the Commission would be violating the First Amendment rights of the BEM by sanctioning the licensee's policy of refusing to sell time. The BEM argued that refusing to sell announcements which dealt with controversial issues violates the Fairness Doctrine and amounts to "picking and choosing among those topics . . . which it prefers."[13]

The BEM complaint to the FCC had preceded the Democratic National Committee request for a ruling by five months. The Commission considered them separately, but it was only a matter of time before they would be joined, even though the Democratic National Committee suit was directed at the entire industry and the BEM charge was aimed at a single station.

Ironically, WTOP is owned and operated by the Washington Post Company, one of the more responsible managements in journalism, which in its editorials had been an advocate of disengagement in Vietnam. WTOP cited no particular objection to the BEM as an organization but relied on its general policy, which barred the sale of time to all political organizations except during officially designated elections. Such campaigns, the station held, had to be clearly marked on federal or local ballots, and in accordance with the policy, it had previously refused to sell time to the Women's Strike for Peace and to a labor union.

In its original complaint the BEM argued that it was not simply that WTOP had rejected its antiwar commercials, but that the station had failed to cover antiwar views fully. WTOP countered this complaint by submitting a lengthy compilation of news and interview programs which aired the opinions of a broad spectrum of antiwar leaders. Probably no station in Washington covered more protest marches and broadcast more anti-Vietnam opinion than WTOP, and in light of Nixon's open hostility to it and to the other *Post-Newsweek* stations for their coverage of his Administration, the paradox of the BEM's criticism is obvious. The BEM lawyers did not press the Fairness Doctrine issue but relied chiefly on the First Amendment right of access and on the distinction between WTOP's programing time, in which it is free to choose subject and format, and advertising time, in which commercial advertisers may say whatever they desire in their own format.

As the FCC examined the BEM and DNC complaints, the war issue continued to tear the nation apart, and a few responsible leaders of U.S. broadcasting strove desperately to open up the airwaves to serious debate. In June of 1970 O'Brien received a telegram from Frank Stanton, president of CBS, who told him that CBS would voluntarily sell the Democrats sixty-second announcements for the purpose of fund-raising, "without confining these announcements to campaign periods."[14] Stanton also told O'Brien that the network was inaugurating a new series of free-time programs to be called "The Loyal Opposition." There would be four such broadcasts, and Stanton offered the Democratic National Committee twenty-five minutes of time, which would be followed by five minutes of news analysis by CBS News correspondents. The first program was scheduled for 10 P.M. on July 7, and would present the Democratic National Committee's views. If the idea was successful, it would be continued during Democratic as well as Republican administrations.

The first "Loyal Opposition" employed selective sampling of contradictory Nixon statements on tape and film, and was certainly explosive, if not an overwhelming success in presentation or size of audience. It was not specifically oriented to the war; instead it presented O'Brien's own far-ranging indictment of all of Nixon's policies. The broadcast received broad national coverage and O'Brien says Stanton called him the next day to congratulate him, and saying, "Let's have more."

Three days later in a speech in Park City, Utah, Stanton proclaimed the "Loyal Opposition" concept as a permanent but voluntary commitment of CBS and its affiliated stations. He warned that "the mainspring of self-government" was being reshaped by the President's use of television very much on his own terms and with his own timing. Stanton said that such television power "in forging public opinion has been pressed to an unprecedented degree." The CBS president supplied statistics to show that "President Nixon has appeared on network prime television as many times as Presidents Eisenhower, Kennedy and Johnson combined, in his first eighteen months in office." Stanton, still unaware of how disturbed the White House and the affiliated stations were about the O'Brien attack on Nixon, was fittingly proud that his network was attempting to counter the "monolithic force" of presidential television, which was throwing "an enlightened public opinion . . . dangerously off balance."

CBS's enthusiasm for "The Loyal Opposition" did not last long. Stanton was attacked by Republican leaders for permitting O'Brien to "hatchet the President." Even Democratic Senator John Pastore thought O'Brien's remarks had been intemperate: "You know, Larry, you were highly political on that show." O'Brien replied, "Of course I was political; I was *supposed* to be political."[15]

In July, one week after the O'Brien broadcast, the Republican National Committee asked that the FCC order CBS to grant them reply time because O'Brien's was a general attack on the President's policies and was not "issue-oriented."[16] The lawyer's name on the GOP's brief was W. Theodore Pierson, the archfoe of the Fairness Doctrine even before *Red Lion*. "I was still against it, but as long as the Supreme Court says it's the law, I'm going to use it for my clients," said Pierson.

CBS refused the Republicans' demand, asserting that "a conclusion that the ["Loyal Opposition"] broadcast was basically 'party-oriented' can emerge only from a process of judging, on a line-by-line basis . . . the invisible line separating issue-oriented and party-oriented remarks . . ."[17] But the Commission agreed with the Republicans that because time had been given to the Democratic National Committee without any specification of the issues to be covered, the broadcast was party-oriented; accordingly, CBS was directed to grant response time to the Republican National Committee.[18]

At the time, eyebrows were raised at the fact that the liberal members of the Commission, Kenneth Cox and Nicholas Johnson, agreed with the FCC majority. Actually, it was part of a package deal worked out to settle several conflicting complaints. In addition to the Republican demand for time to answer O'Brien, there was also a complaint before the FCC from the Committee for Fair Broadcasting of Controversial Issues against WCBS-TV (New York) and against WTIC-TV (Hartford), contending that five consecutive presidential addresses on Vietnam had gone unanswered. Commissioners Cox and Johnson were sympathetic to this position, while other members, such as Chairman Burch, Robert E. Lee and Robert Wells, were not. These members also supported the Republicans' complaint that O'Brien's "Loyal Opposition" broadcast was "person- or party-oriented rather than issue-oriented."[19]

Evidently a compromise solution was worked out. Burch, Wells and Lee agreed to put a rein on presidential use of prime time for speeches and to require an opportunity for a speech by the opposing side, in a decision called the *Fair Committee Ruling*. In turn, Kenneth Cox and Nicholas Johnson supported the Republicans' demand for time to answer O'Brien on the basis that CBS had failed to specify any issues. Johnson's supporting statement makes clear the nature of the deal: his concurrence on the Republican National Committee complaint was "extremely reluctant,"[20] but he agreed to it because "on balance, the package adopted by five Commissioners of widely differing views was a distinct improvement over the situation as it had existed."[21]

CBS asked the FCC to reconsider, while Califano and the Democrats demanded that Dean Burch, a former campaign chairman of the Republican party, disqualify himself from this sensitive case. With the concurrence of his fellow commissioners, Burch stated that no conflict of interest was involved. Califano compared the situation to "a federal judge who had been chairman of the GOP sitting on a case that involved a fight between two major parties over an issue of such importance." Even though the FCC agreed to review its ruling, which would eventually be decided by the courts, certain senators could not refrain from entering the debate. On August 5 Frank Stanton, testifying before Pastore's Subcommittee on Communications, found himself and his program, "The Loyal Opposition," under blistering attack from Republican Senator Robert P. Griffin of Michigan: "You've given equal time to the hatchet man of the other party. Who's going to answer that?"

At first Stanton insisted that "unless we are forced by the FCC, we won't offer . . . time for an answer such as the Republican National Committee has demanded."

Senator Griffin pushed harder: "You'll . . . allow these hatchet political attacks to continue?"

"I think that if this were to persist," replied Stanton, "if this is the way the 'Loyal Opposition' broadcast series develops, we would have to reconsider." The CBS president was forced to agree that the O'Brien broadcast "would appear to have been person- or party-oriented rather than issue-oriented as CBS stated its intention to be." If the network could not exercise "journalistic supervision to assure fulfillment of its purpose," the "Loyal Opposition" series might have to be curtailed. Stanton also told the committee that there were no present plans for further installments of "The Loyal Opposition"—to which Griffin responded, "This is some improvement."[22]

That same August day, in two separate but related opinions, the FCC handed down its decisions on the BEM and DNC cases. Rejecting the claim that "responsible" individuals and groups have a right to purchase advertising time to comment on public issues without regard as to whether the broadcaster has complied with the Fairness Doctrine, the Commission hailed its own decision as one of major significance, going "to the heart of the system of broadcasting which has developed in this country."[23] The FCC pointed out that a Fairness Doctrine violation could, if documented, entitle a complainant to free time, but it rejected the BEM claim that station WTOP had in fact violated the Doctrine by failing to air views such as those held by members of the BEM. In a 6–1 decision, the commissioners ruled that the general allegation of unfairness in WTOP's coverage had been successfully rebutted by the station's voluminous affidavit citing its widespread coverage of antiwar views.

Commissioner Nicholas Johnson dissented: ". . . a broadcaster cannot accept commercial advertisements, yet reject advertisements which are political in nature."[24] He believed that the BEM had a constitutional right to purchase time on WTOP for its anti-

war messages: ". . . once a licensee opens his forum to the presentation of commercial views, he cannot then close it in a discriminatory fashion—accepting some commercial views, but rejecting all
others."[25]

But the FCC's ruling on the Democratic National Committee's
complaint was not so firm. With Johnson voting with the majority
this time, the Commission held that the Democratic National
Committee had the right to purchase time for the solicitation of
funds to be used in political campaigns. It pointed out that Congress had accorded special status to political parties, in Section
315(a) of the Communications Act, and that solicitation of funds
by them was both feasible and appropriate in the short space of
time allotted to spot advertisements.

O'Brien and Califano dismissed as meaningless this marginal
victory that the Democratic National Committee could buy time
to solicit funds but not to raise issues, and the networks did not
consider it significant enough to appeal. But is it so meaningless?
If the two parties' national committees have the right to solicit
funds in spot announcements, can't the script say: "The Democratic [or Republican] party is the party of the people. It cares
about your pocketbook [statement about health, taxes, etc.]. We
ask your support. Send your contribution to . . ." Since spots are
so useful to political parties, perhaps the Democratic National
Committee won a substantial part of its fight; the only remaining
issue was the right to buy programing time—a lesser matter, since
all too often only the already converted watch such shows.

CBS and the Democrats urged the FCC to reconsider the "Loyal
Opposition" order. On September 24 the FCC, with Chairman Burch voting, praised CBS for its well-intentioned if controversial attempt to inform the electorate by granting the Democratic National Committee twenty-five minutes of television time,
then chided it for permitting O'Brien to present a program that
was "party-oriented" rather than "issue-oriented," and blamed it
for its abstention in this critical area of issues to be covered. Their
holding was "simply that . . . fairness and specifically the 'political
party' corollary required that RNC also be given a similar opportunity to inform the public."[26]

CBS steadfastly refused to accept the ruling and took the decision to the Court of Appeals. In the meanwhile the Republicans
demanded that the reply time be granted, offering to reimburse

the network for the time if the FCC order was eventually over-turned.

Although CBS and the Democratic National Committee were arrayed on the same side on this issue, distrust of the "Loyal Opposition"series grew. O'Brien was under the impression that he had a promise for at least four programs, whereas Stanton had denied to Congress that there was any such long-range commitment. In August 1970 the CBS president invited the Democratic National Committee chairman to lunch and told him that the "Loyal Opposition" program was in trouble with the affiliated stations, "who are raising hell," and that the next and final program would be on November 17. O'Brien called this news a "bombshell," and told Stanton that coming two weeks after the congressional elections, the program would be meaningless. O'Brien gives Stanton credit "for sticking his neck out" but "pressure from the White House and the affiliates was too much."

O'Brien and Califano always suspected that their real sparring partner in these encounters with the networks and the FCC was the White House. What they could not have known—and what most members of the FCC could not have understood—was the depth of that involvement. Charles Colson's credibility, before or after Watergate, is hardly that of an unimpeachable source, but some of his 1970 communiqués (which came to light during the Senate Watergate hearings) provide enlightening reading.

In a memo on White House stationery to H. R. Haldeman on September 25, 1970, just one day after the FCC ruling on "The Loyal Opposition," Colson detailed his attempts to "inhibit . . . the networks," and through the FCC, to "eliminate once and for all loyal opposition type programs":

> The networks are terribly nervous over the uncertain state of the law, i.e., the recent FCC decisions and the pressures to grant Congress access to TV. They are also apprehensive about us . . . The harder I pressed them [CBS and NBC] the more accommodating, cordial, and almost apologetical they became . . .
>
> There was unanimous agreement that the President's right of access to TV should in no way be restrained. Both CBS and ABC agreed with me that on most occasions the President speaks as President and there is no obligation for presenting a contrasting view under the Fairness Doctrine. (This, by the way is not the law. The FCC has always ruled that the Fairness Doctrine al-

ways applies and either they don't know that or they are willing to concede us that point.) [The parentheses are Colson's.] NBC, on the other hand, argues that the Fairness test must be applied to every speech but [Julian] Goodman [president of NBC] is also quick to agree that there are probably instances in which Presidential addresses are not controversial . . .

To my surprise, CBS did not deny that the news had been slanted against us. Paley merely said that every Administration has felt the same way and that we have been slower in coming to them to complain than our predecessors. He, however, ordered Stanton in my presence to review the analysis with me and if the news has been slanted to see that the situation is immediately corrected . . .

CBS does not defend the O'Brien appearance. Paley wanted to make it very clear it would not happen again and that they would not permit partisan attacks on the President. They are doggedly determined to win their FCC case, however, as a matter of principle; even though they recognize they made a mistake, they don't want the FCC in the business of correcting their mistakes.[27]

Colson concluded his memo to Haldeman (and presumably to the President) with the assurance that ABC and NBC would probably issue a policy "generally favorable as to the President's use of TV," and that this declaration would back "CBS into an untenable position." Colson would "pursue with Dean Burch the possibility of an interpretive ruling by the FCC . . . as soon as we have a majority on the FCC." Lastly, Colson cautioned his White House colleagues not to expect much improvement in news coverage, but "I think we can dampen their ardor for putting on 'loyal opposition' type programs."

Even if one discounts Colson's version of the conversations—as Paley and CBS executives do—as well as his gratuitous observations about the furtive and "obsequious" behavior of the executives he attempted to intimidate, the public policies adopted by the broadcast industry provide his account with some credibility. The evidence strongly suggests that Nixon and his chief advisers were determined to prevent Democratic access to television after presidential appearances, and that it was because of congressional and White House pressure that the "Loyal Opposition" program was discontinued. In 1971 CBS won its appeal, with the court holding that the FCC's confused ruling had exceeded its authority.[28] The

series had not been presented for some time, and it was not re-
vived even after the court victory, when there was a clear green
light. CBS obviously had second thoughts; to this day, other than
using the FCC ruling as a pretext, it has not stated its reasons for
discontinuing the series.

During this same period, the Democratic National Committee
also tried to use the Fairness Doctrine to offset the President's use
of television. First Califano instituted what came to be known as
the Free Time case, in which the Democratic National Committee asked the FCC to establish, once and for all, a rule that
provided automatic response time whenever a President used
radio or television to discuss controversial issues of public importance. The FCC declined to do so, and the D.C. Circuit Court
affirmed this decision in February 1972: "DNC asks us to give
birth to a new corollary. We are not the body to pass on such a
request . . . No number of law suits can give this court a legislative
authority . . ."[29]

Next the Democratic National Committee cited four presidential addresses on economic policy, and several television appearances by Administration spokesmen; relying on the FCC's *Fair
Committee Ruling*,[30] it asked for free response time. The networks refused, and again the FCC rejected the request; the networks had reasonably informed the public on the issue of the
economy, and the *Fair Committee Ruling* would not be extended.
To do so, the FCC stated, would convert the desirable discretion
and leeway afforded by the Fairness Doctrine to a more rigid,
mathematical "modified 'equal-opportunities' requirement."[31] In
June 1973, some twenty months later, the D.C. Court of Appeals
affirmed the FCC ruling.[32] Today Califano maintains that even if
the Democrats had won, "the public-dialogue aspects of the issue
were mooted because of the more than two and a half years of
delay."

However, one Democratic National Committee case was not a
loser in the D.C. Court of Appeals, though it had to go all the way
to the Supreme Court: *DNC/BEM*. Technically they were two
separate actions which the FCC had decided in favor of station
WTOP and of the broadcast industry, and which the Business
Executives' Move for Peace and the Democratic National Committee had petitioned the Court of Appeals to overturn.

CBS and ABC decided to intervene in this litigation, thus pitting the networks against the Democratic National Committee. The Court of Appeals for the District of Columbia joined the two cases, and *CBS* v. *DNC* (*BEM* v. *CBS*)* were argued on March 9, 1971. The judgment was handed down fifty-one weeks after the FCC's ruling. In an opinion by Judge Skelly Wright, the Court of Appeals reversed the Commission and held that an absolute and arbitrary ban on the sale of time for discussion of public issues violated First Amendment principles. Judge Wright's opinion against the FCC, the two networks and WTOP was exactly what the Democratic National Committee and the BEM had been praying for:

> For too long advertising has been considered a virtual free fire zone, largely ungoverned by regulatory guidelines. As a result, a cloying blandness and commercialism—sometimes said to be characteristic of radio and television as a whole—have found an especially effective outlet. We are convinced that the time has come for the Commission to cease abdicating responsibility over the uses of advertising time. Indeed, we are convinced that broadcast advertising has a great potential for enlivening and enriching debate on public issues, rather than drugging it with an overdose of non-ideas and non-issues as is now the case.[33]

The Court of Appeals refrained from ordering that the messages by the BEM and the Democratic National Committee must be accepted by broadcast licensees, but specifically stated that "a flat ban on paid public issue announcements is in violation of the First Amendment." The court remanded the cases to the FCC to develop "reasonable procedures' and regulations determining which and how many 'editorial advertisements' will be put on the air."[34]

In his dissent Judge Carl McGowan, while agreeing that the FCC should review the Fairness Doctrine as it applied to paid political advertising, called the reversal of the FCC decision and the ordering of such a review a "constitutional strait jacket which dictates the result in advance."[35]

---

* The various litigants to this multi-party case refer to it by different names. The Washington *Post-Newsweek* stations and the Business Executives' Move for Peace call it *BEM*. Lawrence O'Brien, Joseph Califano, Jr., and the Democrats refer to it as *DNC*. The CBS lawyers remember it as *CBS*. The Supreme Court joined *BEM* and *DNC* and designated it *CBS et al.* v. *DNC*.

There was never a doubt that the paid-time case, or *DNC-BEM,* would be appealed. By the time the Supreme Court handed down its decision in *CBS et al.* v. *DNC,* almost four years had elapsed since the BEM had tried to buy air time on WTOP, and exactly three years since O'Brien and Califano had decided to take their complaint to court. By then—May 29, 1973—American troops were out of Vietnam and Richard Nixon, mired in Watergate, was using less and less of the television time which the suit had accused him of abusing.

The Supreme Court decision in *CBS et al.* v. *DNC* began and ended with *Red Lion*—in the first paragraph with a quotation and in the last with a reference. In between there were thirty-eight other mentions of that case. Yet *Red Lion* was as distinct from *CBS et al.* v. *DNC* as two Fairness Doctrine cases could be. *Red Lion* concerned one individual's right to air time to answer a personal attack, and the right of a station to deny the federal government's order to grant the individual this time. *CBS et al.* v. *DNC* involved the First Amendment rights of a political party and/or organization of partisan activists to purchase time on a radio or television station or network, and the First Amendment right of a broadcaster to reject the purchase of its time for such purposes.

The *Red Lion* decision was an 8–0 majority and required only one opinion, written by Justice Byron White. The Court's rejection of the Court of Appeals decision in *DNC-BEM* raised so many questions that the split Court required five different opinions, four of them alone to explain the majority's reasoning.

Chief Justice Warren Burger, who wrote what is called the "first" majority opinion, struck a mighty blow for journalism, stating that the "unmistakable congressional purpose [is] to maintain—no matter how difficult the task—essentially private broadcasting journalism held only broadly accountable to public interest standards."[36]

In rejecting the Court of Appeals judgment that in this finding for DNC-BEM "it was merely mandating a 'modest reform' "[37] demanding only that broadcasters be required to accept *some* editorial advertisements, Burger scolded the lower court for disregarding the FCC's admirable attempt to stay out of the editing process. He pointed out that granting a constitutional right of access would inevitably push the FCC into reviewing "day-to-day editorial decisions,"[38] such as determining whether a viewpoint or group had been given sufficient broadcast time. "Since it is physically impossible to provide time for all viewpoints . . . the right to exercise editorial judgment was granted to the broadcaster. . . . The broadcaster therefore is allowed significant journalistic discretion in deciding how best to fulfill its Fairness Doctrine obligations . . .''[39]

At times the majority opinion in *CBS et al.* v. *DNC* sounded much like Archibald Cox's losing arguments in *Red Lion:*

> For better or worse, editing is what editors are for and editing is selection and choice of material. That editors—newpaper or broadcast—can and do abuse this power is beyond doubt, but that is not reason to deny the discretion Congress provided . . . The presence of these risks is nothing new; the authors of the Bill of Rights accepted the reality that these risks were evils for which there was no acceptable remedy other than a spirit of moderation and a sense of responsibility—and civility—on the part of those who exercise the guaranteed freedoms of expression.[40]

Although the decisions which prompted the *CBS et al.* v. *DNC* litigation were made in corporate and sales headquarters, without broadcast journalists or even the heads of the news division being consulted, Burger seemed intent on establishing that it was the journalist's decision that should prevail in such crucial matters of access rather than the advocate's pocketbook, no matter how noble the purpose. "It seems clear," he wrote, "that Congress intended to permit private broadcasting to develop with the widest journalistic freedom consistent with its public obligations. Only when the interests of the public are found to outweigh the private journalistic interests of the broadcasters will government power be asserted with the framework of the Act."[41] Although Burger prohibited program-by-program refereeing, he reminded the broadcasters that "license renewal proceedings . . . are a principal means of . . . regulation"[42] of broadcasters' fairness. As an example, he then cited the WLBT decision—written by him—which had stripped Lamar Life of its license.

The Burger decision seemed to discard BEM's First Amendment access arguments in favor of the Fairness Doctrine, and in so doing fashioned the Doctrine into a double-edged sword. It made access more difficult, but as Burger stressed:

> . . . while the licensee has discretion in fulfilling his obligations under the Fairness Doctrine, he is required to "present repre-

sentative community views and voices on controversial issues which are of importance to his listeners," and it is prohibited from "excluding partisan voices and always itself presenting views in a bland, inoffensive manner . . ." A broadcaster neglects that obligation only at the risk of losing his license.[43]

In sum, Burger's opinion was a mixed blessing to the broadcaster, for in this line of reasoning the much-maligned Fairness Doctrine suddenly emerges as the broadcast industry's greatest *protector* rather than its stringent strait jacket. Ironically, CBS, whose president in 1974 would attack the Doctrine as unconstitutional, had relied heavily on its existence in arguing to the Court that BEM's access request was wrong.

To the Chief Justice and the split majority, therefore, the question was "whether the 'public interest' standard of the Communications Act requires broadcasters to accept editorial advertisements, or whether . . . broadcasters are required to do so by reason of the First Amendment."[44] In just so many words, the Supreme Court faulted the Court of Appeals for not "giving due weight"[45] to this sensitive matter, and praised the FCC for upholding the principle that "the marketplace of 'ideas and experiences' would scarcely be served by a system so heavily weighted in favor of the financially affluent or those who have access to wealth."[46] Burger acknowledged the views of the archliberal on the Commission, Nicholas Johnson, who favored purchased access on a first-come, first-served basis, but rejected this approach because "the views of the affluent could well prevail over those of others, since they would have it within their power to purchase time more frequently."[47]

No case that had ever come before the FCC made it more difficult to tell "the good guys from the bad guys" than *CBS et al.* v. *DNC*. Most liberals denounced the Court's decision because it denied foes of the Vietnam war and the Nixon haters the right to purchase time. Yet a year later, when certain energy giants and anti-environmentalists were prepared to spend millions of dollars to propagate their views via editorial commercials, there was some applause for the once despised *CBS et al.* v. *DNC* decision.

This role of government as overseer and ultimate arbiter and guardian of the public interest, as opposed to the role of the monopoly licensee as a journalistic free agent, calls for a sensitive balancing of competing interests. For more than forty years this fragile compact has required "both the regulators and the licensees to walk a tightrope to preserve the First Amendment values written into . . . the Communications Act."⁴⁸

To illustrate those tensions, the Chief Justice turned in his opinion to the inherent differences between privately owned newspapers and publicly regulated broadcast stations:

> . . . The power of a privately owned newspaper to advance its own political, social, and economic views is bounded by only two factors: first, the acceptance of a sufficient number of readers—and hence advertisers—to assure financial success; and, second, the journalistic integrity of its editors and publishers. A broadcast licensee has a large measure of journalistic freedom *but not as large as that exercised by a newspaper* [emphasis added]. A licensee must balance what it might prefer to do as a private entrepreneur with what it is required to do as a "public trustee." To perform its statutory duties, the Commission must oversee without censoring . . .⁴⁹

Seven Justices concurred with Burger's majority opinion; of the four additional majority opinions, the most quoted and the longest came from Justice Douglas. Though he shared the conclusion that reversed the lower court, he reached it by a far different route and denounced the Chief Justice's position that newspapers enjoyed protections not available to the electronic media:

> My conclusion is that the TV and radio stand in the same protected position under the First Amendment as do newspapers and magazines. The philosophy of the First Amendment requires that result, for the fear that Madison and Jefferson had of government intrusion is perhaps even more relevant to TV and radio than it is to newspapers and other like publications. That fear was founded not only on the spectre of a lawless government but of government under the control of a faction that desired to foist its views of the common good on the people.⁵⁰

Justice Douglas harked back to *Red Lion*, which he has never quite forgiven himself for missing: "The Fairness Doctrine has no place in our First Amendment regime. It puts the head of the camel inside the tent and enables administration after administration to toy with TV or radio in order to serve its sordid or its benevolent ends."⁵¹

The gap between Douglas and Burger is a massive one, considering that they were on the same side of a case. Douglas invoked the language of such giants as Madison and Jefferson, and of scholars like Thomas Emerson and Walter Lippmann to inveigh against the Fairness Doctrine; Burger, in contrast, accepted the Doctrine, declaring that it imposed certain journalistic editing requirements on broadcasters and demanding that they "seek out" vital public issues and present them, instead of limiting access merely "to the financially affluent."[52] Thus, the conservative chief of the Court was relying on the Fairness Doctrine as a shield to save broadcasting from the right of access, while the majority's most liberal member was condemning the Doctrine as an affront to the First Amendment.

Justice Potter Stewart, who had always harbored serious doubts about voting with the majority in *Red Lion*, was unwilling, "rightly or wrongly," to identify completely with Burger's majority opinion, and without going so far as to sign Douglas' outright denunciation of the Fairness Doctrine, categorized his views as similar. "It is a frightening specter," wrote Stewart, that the Court of Appeals "requires the government to impose controls upon a private broadcaster in order to preserve First Amendment values."[53]

Although Stewart reluctantly recognized the existene of the Fairness Doctrine, he felt that the FCC's power to regulate fairness had its limits, and that broadcasters must retain important freedoms. Congress never intended that broadcasters should be treated as common carriers: "But surely this [*Red Lion*] does not mean that [broadcasters' First Amendment] rights are non existent, and . . . if those [First Amendment] 'values' mean anything, they should mean this. If we must choose whether editorial decisions are to be made in the free judgment of individual broadcasters, or imposed by bureaucratic fiat, the choice must be for freedom."[54]

Other concurring but differing opinions came from Justices Harry A. Blackmun, Lewis F. Powell, Jr., and Byron White. But even White, the author of the *Red Lion* opinion, argued that radio and television stations should have the "discretion to make up their own programs and to choose their method of compliance with the Fairness Doctrine . . ."[55]

The only dissents came from two Justices who, with Douglas,

form the liberal wing of the Court. William J. Brennan, Jr., joined by Thurgood Marshall, could see no First Amendment reason why licensed broadcasters should be permitted to maintain a policy of "an absolute ban on the sale of air time for the discussion of controversial issues."[56] He believed that it was the action of the federal government in the first place that had enabled the broadcast industry to become "what is potentially the most effective marketplace of ideas ever devised"; this quasi-monopoly use of technology had rendered "the soapbox orator and the leafleteer virtually obsolete . . . Any policy that *absolutely* denies citizens access to the airwaves necessarily renders even the concept of 'full and free discussion' meaningless."[57]

Brennan scoffed at his brethren for raising "the specter of administrative apocalypse" to justify their decision. In reality, however, "the issue in this case is not whether there is an absolute right of access [for BEM and DNC], but rather, whether there may be an *absolute denial* of such access."[58] Brennan, with Marshall concurring, concluded: "The difference is, of course, crucial and the Court's misconception . . . distorts its evaluation of the administrative difficulties that the invalidation of the absolute ban [on all such editorial advertising] might entail."[59]

Brennan and Marshall favored the Court of Appeals invalidation of the flat ban, and of "leaving broad latitude to the Commission and licensees to develop . . . reasonable regulations to govern the availability of advertising."[60]

Brennan did agree with the majority that "truth is best illuminated by a collision of genuine advocates," but feared that with an absolute ban on editorial advertising the public would be compelled to rely exclusively on journalistic discretion of the broadcaster who serves "as surrogate spokesman for all sides of all issues."[61] The Fairness Doctrine was fine as far as it went, but it was desirable to supplement it to promote robust, wide-open debate. Brennan was convinced that "This separation of the advocate from the expression of his views"[62] diminished the effectiveness of that communication. He pointed out that this had been the rationale in *Red Lion*, where it was ordered that Cook himself had the right to reply. WGCB had been willing to *sell* Cook reply time, but the Court had decided that a commercial solution was not sufficient compliance with the Fairness Doctrine. The Brennan-Marshall dissent concluded with an affirmation of the lower court's finding and an endorsement of Judge Skelly Wright's yeasty language:

> It may unsettle some of us to see an anti-war message or a political party message in the accustomed place of a soap or beer commercial . . . We must not equate what is habitual with what is right—or what is constitutional. A society so saturated with commercialism can well afford another outlet of speech on public issues. All that we may lose is some of our apathy.[63]

The many shades of opinion in *CBS et al.* v. *DNC* are confusing, not only because of their conclusions but because of who stated them. Douglas is at least consistent; he will not rest as long as the Fairness Doctrine lives. But White, who wrote the *Red Lion* decision, and Burger, who ordered the removal of a license for WLBT in *Lamar Life,* used the Fairness Doctrine as a shield to protect radio and television from access by political advertisers, while still maintaining it as a sword to prevent broadcasters from engaging in one-sided presentations on public issues. Brennan and Marshall, on the other hand, were unwilling to protect broadcasters from the access of partisan advertisers with the financial resources to buy their way onto the air.

For all the clusters of opinions, three years of litigation had done little to ease the pressure inherent in presidential access, and in the First Amendment rights of those in and out of organized politics who wished time to respond. An equally important result was that though Chief Justice Burger had proclaimed that "editing is for editors," the network which waged the hardest battle stubbed its toe when it tried to create a self-imposed policy, "The Loyal Opposition."

10

PENSIONS:
The Broken Promise and the Splintered Bench

While journalists on the public airwaves are subject to fairness doctrine responsibilities, the risks of government interference are so oppressive as to require a plain showing of journalistic abuse before a government official can issue a direction that the journalist's report must be supplemented with a codicil.

JUDGE HAROLD LEVENTHAL, U.S. COURT OF APPEALS, D.C. CIRCUIT—SEPTEMBER 27, 1974

. . . The majority resolved the problem by standing the teaching of Red Lion *on its head . . . the majority by worshipping at the altar of editorial judgment, attempted to strip the American people of a large part of their ability to ensure access to a full, free and robust discussion . . .*

JUDGE EDWARD A. TAMM, U.S. COURT OF APPEALS, D.C. CIRCUIT—JULY 11, 1975

. . . the court's approach is that it increases rather than decreases the ambiguity of the Fairness Doctrine. The uncertainty of operation . . . both heightens its chilling effect and increases the possibilities of Commission abuse of the Doctrine through "raised eyebrow" harassment as an alternative to overt enforcement and judicial review . . .

CHIEF JUDGE DAVID L. BAZELON, U.S. COURT OF APPEALS, D.C. CIRCUIT—JUNE 2, 1975

For the opening show of a new prime-time documentary series, *NBC Reports*, David Schmerler's assignment in the summer of 1972 was to produce a one-hour investigation of multinational corporations. After three weeks of intense research, Schmerler became convinced that the multinational program was too far-reaching both in complexity and geography to be filmed and edited by its September deadline, so he suggested to NBC News President Reuven Frank that they could meet the September date if they switched to a report on the breakdown of pension plans in U.S. industry. Such a project was already in research at NBC News. By working on a crash basis, "seven days a week, eighty hours a week, we could make it," Schmerler told Frank. Edwin Newman would be the on-camera reporter and narrator.

This was to be the thirty-four-year-old producer's first full-length documentary. Until then his chief credits were for two segments used on the NBC "magazine" *Chronolog*, a forty-five-minute investigation on lead poisoning and a thirty-five-minute treatment of no-fault auto insurance.

Frank, who has produced many documentaries himself and understood what it takes to put such a program together in sixty days, gave the order to proceed on the substitute, and gave it the title, "Pensions: The Broken Promise." He wanted a hard-hitting documentary with clear-cut issues, and that's what he got. Schmerler was aroused and offended by the pension abuses which he had uncovered in his research. "What we were doing was building an emotional program out of people who felt they had been terribly wronged."

CBS had done a critical study of pension programs a year before: producer Paul Lowenwater and reporter Mike Wallace had collaborated on a twenty-minute segment for *60 Minutes*. The CBS program, which was shown on June 8, 1971, had concluded that only one out of seven pension holders would ever receive the benefits which they had anticipated. Though the program was an intense treatment of a controversial subject, differing attitudes were presented, but there was little doubt that the program's viewpoint was highly critical of most pension programs. The *60 Minutes* treatment helped convince Schmerler and Frank that there was ample material for a one-hour program on the topic.

Frank, who is always sensitive to Fairness Doctrine "burdens," kept a tight rein on the program, and would decide on how much "fairness filler," as he called it, would be required.

"Pensions: The Broken Promise" was televised at 10 P.M. on Tuesday, September 12, 1972. The broadcast began with an un-identified man saying that his twenty-three years of seniority had "all fallen away."[1] His bitter plaint and the main thesis of the documentary were then voiced by a woman who defined the problem: "There must be thousands, maybe millions of them that's getting the same song and dance my husband got. When they reached their time for retirement there is no funds left to pay them."

The broadcast centered on interviews with a number of aging workers who described, often in moving, graphic detail, first-hand experiences of pension-plan abuse. Steven Duane, an A&P ware-house supervisor, told Newman what had happened to him when the chain decided to close the warehouse and he was discharged: "So when they finally told us that the men had to be fifty-five and over to collect a pension, I was the big loser. I had a brother the same time as me down there. We were the big losers. Thirty-two years of our life was given up and we had nothing, absolutely nothing to show for it." Duane's plight had originally been brought to public light by the *New York Times Magazine* in 1972. The article was written by Fred J. Cook.

Besides providing first-person accounts of pension-plan injus-tices, the NBC producers included a number of interviews with lawmakers and experts involved with pension-plan reform. New Jersey Senator Harrison A. Williams, Jr., was unequivocal in his condemnation of many private pension plans: "I have all kinds of descriptions of plans here, and all of them just suggest the certainty of an assured benefit upon retirement. Here's a man—this was from a brewery—sitting relaxed with a glass of beer and checks coming out of the air; well, you see, this gives a false sense of security."

NEWMAN: Senator, the way private pension plans are set up now, are the promises real?
WILLIAMS: The answer is, they are not.

One revealing moment in "Pensions" dramatized the impos-sible position that judges and federal regulators face when they attempt to adjudicate fairness. It occurred during a brief inter-view with Senator Williams, chairman of the Labor Committee. The camera was on Newman, and Williams, attempting to illustrate the vague and obfuscating language of pension forms, asked him to read the small type in a pension brochure:

WILLIAMS: We don't want just these golden general descriptions of what can be expected under the plan; we want clear and precise and understandable descriptions of the reality. The worst example that I've seen is *this* description that is wholly unintelligible to anybody but an advanced lawyer.

NEWMAN (reading aloud): "If an employee makes the election provided for in Subparagraph B of the Section Six, his monthly pension as determined under either Section Three or Subparagraph One of Paragraph A of Section Four whichever . . . applies, shall be reduced by the percentage set forth in Paragraph C of this Section Six as if the employee has made the election provided for in Subparagraph One of Paragraph B of this Section Six and shall be further reduced actuarily on the basis of the age of the employee and his spouse at the time such election shall become effective, the sex of the employee and the spouse and the level of benefits payable to the employee's spouse in excess of the level of benefits in the election provided in Subparagraph One of Paragraph B of this Section Six."

Well, maybe I didn't read it very well?

WILLIAMS: Well, of course you understood it, though.

NEWMAN: Perfectly!

Edwin Newman is not an actor, but he does have the rubbery, expressive face of a Walter Matthau. When he answered Williams' question, it was clear to the viewer, though not to one who read the script, that "Perfectly" meant something quite different. In fact, the printed version of the script in the court's exhibits does not contain the answer. A regulatory examiner or an appellate judge trying to apply positive or negative measurements to such a sequence could interpret the response in such a way as to make a mockery of the concept of fairness. Neither Newman nor Schmerler had planned to include this exchange, yet it was one of the most illuminating moments of the broadcast.

At the end of the broadcast Newman summed up the program, beginning with a disclaimer that was to become subject of much legal discussion: "This is a depressing program to work on, but we don't want to give the impression that there are no good private pension plans. There are many good ones, and there are many people for whom the promise has become a reality. That should be said."

Then Newman went on to discuss the pension abuses that had prompted the broadcast in the first place. He noted that the program had taken only a quick look at certain technical issues, such as the vesting and funding of plans; these issues, he told his audience, were matters for Congress to consider. He also alerted individual pension-plan participants to take a close look at their own situation, and then ended by saying, "Our own conclusion about all of this is that it is almost inconceivable that this enormous thing has been allowed to grow up with so little understanding of it and with so little protection and such uneven results for those involved. The situation, as we've seen it, is deplorable. Edwin Newman, NBC News."

Between the opening of the program and that sign-off there was approximately fifty minutes of reporting, plus two and a half minutes of commercial copy and three and a half minutes of public-service messages to take the place of the unsold sponsor holes. The interviews with pension holders and employers from various sections of American industry and with experts were, like Newman's probing narration, critical and presented with no intent to balance every negative fact with a favorable one. Still, some interviews were held with defenders of pension plans. An executive of the National Association of Manufacturers commented, "You must remember that the corporation has set up this plan voluntarily. They have not been required by law to set it up." Also, "Over a good number of years the track record is excellent. It's unfortunate that every now and then some of the tragic cases make the newspapers and the headlines . . . That's not to say there aren't a few remaining loopholes that need closing, but we ought to make sure that we don't throw out the baby with the wash water." Schmerler says that he urged the NAM spokesman to say more in defense of pension plans, but that he declined to be more specific. An executive of the Bank of California expressed the view that pension holders had no reason to complain: "After all, the pension is a gift from the employer."

There was no attempt by NBC to create a stopwatch balance, and some observers believe that the producers and their reporting staff could be faulted for not pursuing some of the worst pension-plan offenders. Producer Schmerler says that he wrote each of the companies criticized in the broadcast, inviting them to appear, but that none accepted. Experienced journalists know that such written offers are often not enough; pursuit by phone, personal contact and even seeking out a mutual friend is sometimes required to convince reluctant subjects to participate in a documentary. Schmerler admits that the broadcast would have been more balanced if there had been a more persuasive defender of pension systems, "but every time we thought we had found someone to speak for the other side, either we couldn't get them, or when we set up the cameras they would refuse to say that pension plans are good. Instead, they would fudge the issue and say, 'There are a lot of problems.' "

Unlike Reverend Billy James Hargis and the Red Lion station, NBC in "Pensions" made "a reasonable effort" to obtain interviews with articulate defenders of the pensions systems. The Red Lion and the "Pensions" broadcasts were separated by eight years, and the facts of each are as varied as their economics. The Hargis attack involved a single daytime radio station and took up two minutes out of fifteen minutes of air time costing $7.50. "Pensions" involved a major network of 175 stations and an hour of prime-time television, which if used for its normal entertainment fare might have stimulated revenues in excess of $300,000. Moreover, "Pensions" cost its broadcasters $170,000 to produce. The Red Lion program was the product of a nonjournalist, Reverend Hargis, whose goal was to attack Fred Cook, while the creators of "Pensions" were career journalists whose objective was to present a compelling examination of employee pension programs in the United States. No one at NBC has ever claimed that "Pensions" was a perfect or "objective" broadcast—only that producer David Schmerler and correspondent Edwin Newman intended to focus their searchlight accurately on the dark side of an otherwise healthy business situation. Dr. Hargis and Red Lion Broadcasting professed no fairness to Cook; the "Pensions" broadcast contained no personal attacks, but its premise was a bias against pension plans that did not deliver what they promised.

Following the Red Lion broadcast, the request for reply time came from the target of the personal attack, Fred Cook. However, the formal complaint in the "Pensions" case was filed by a group of citizens organized into a media-watchdog committee, Accuracy in Media, Inc. AIM's interest in the broadcast was prompted by a Los Angeles actuary, Richard H. Solomon, who felt that the program had unfairly represented his profession. Calling the NBC documentary "a distorted picture," Solomon demanded that the network give him and other pension-plan consultants reply time.

Solomon had recorded the broadcast on a cassette audio re-corder—even before he knew he would disapprove of it. Fearful that NBC would brush off his criticism, he sent copies of his first protest to his local congressman, to Vice-President Spiro Agnew and to AIM. Whether or not Solomon had prior contact with AIM is uncertain; what is clear is that he was correct in assuming that AIM would be interested in seeing a carbon of his protest letter to NBC.

AIM's purpose is the vigilant surveillance of news production, print and broadcast. Its membership contains many names gen-erally associated with the right-wing, even Agnewian view of the press: Abraham H. Kalish; Marine Corps General Lewis W. Walt; Eugene Lyons. AIM's founders and original directors in-cluded some moderates: Dr. Harry Gideonese of Freedom House; Dean Acheson, Secretary of State under President Truman; the journalist Edgar Ansel Mowrer. While the source of AIM's fund-ing is not clear, its current head, Reed Irvine, an economist in the Federal Reserve System, does little to dispel the charge that some of the same wealthy people who help support conservative politi-cal causes are the funders of AIM. The identities of all of AIM's financial backers are not revealed, although knowledgeable sources will confirm that one wealthy individual who made a major contribution to the group was Shelby Cullom Davis, a major contributor to Nixon's campaigns who eventually was appointed ambassador to Switzerland by the former President. AIM's largest contributor, a wealthy Connecticut industrialist, refuses to be identified.

AIM's stated goal is to promote greater accuracy in media, but it admits that few of its claims have ever been directed against William Buckley, Paul Harvey or any other right-wing broad-casters or newspapers. Rather, it has focused on Public Broadcast-ing System programs* on sex education, on justice and on Chile;

* AIM did not limit its criticism to the commercial broadcasters. In 1973 it asked the FCC to determine whether broadcasts funded by the Corpora-tion for Public Broadcasting were subject to more severe limitations because of some ambiguous language in the Public Broadcasting Act of 1967. Con-gressman William Springer, a long-time critic of broadcast journalism, had insisted that Section 396(g)(1)(A) of the Communications Act be amended to provide that CPB be authorized to

facilitate the full development of educational broadcasting in which pro-grams of high quality, obtained from diverse sources will be made available

on NBC for its report on drugs and Communist China; on CBS
for the revival of a documentary of gun control; and on the *New
York Times* for its updating of the Alger Hiss case. When asked
why AIM's complaints and monthly newsletters generally ignore
conservative media, Irvine replies with a wry smile, "I guess you
could say that conservatives are always getting screwed by the
media." Abraham Kalish, who was AIM's first executive secretary,
puts it another way: "The right wing corrects its errors; the left
doesn't."

No one in AIM, including Irvine, saw "Pensions" on the air
or on video tape later.

After "Pensions" was broadcast, almost all of the companies
which had refused to appear condemned the documentary and
wrote NBC that it had either missed the point or oversimplified
the issue. (It is no secret at NBC that the first recorded complaint

---

to non-commercial educational television or radio stations, *with strict adherence to objectivity and balance in all programs or series of programs of
a controversial nature.* (Italics added.)

This language, which Chairman Harley O. Staggers of the House Interstate
and Foreign Commerce Committee explicitly said "did not impair or affect
the existing statutory duty and responsibility of the [public] station licensees," was tested when AIM filed a complaint against the Public Broadcasting System charging that two programs, "The Three Rs . . . Sex Education" and "Justice," had violated not just the Fairness Doctrine but also the
special "objectivity and balance" requirement of Section 396(g)(1)(A) . . .
The FCC turned down AIM's fairness complaint against PBS on the
sex-education and justice programs, but also refused to consider Section
396(g)(1)(A).
Thus the FCC established that it would regard public-broadcasting stations
as having Fairness Doctrine obligations no more or less than those of commercial licensees. This decision was appealed by the parties, and once again
the Court of Appeals with its traditional involvement in fairness litigation
was asked to decide whether public broadcasting would have a double layer
of fairness.
Finally, on October 16, 1975, the Court of Appeals for the District of
Columbia ruled that public broadcasting programs were not bound by any
FCC standards of objectivity and balance other than the Fairness Doctrine.
The court said that the Congress merely established a set of goals to which
the directors should aspire. "We leave the interpretation of this hortatory
language to the Directors of the Corporation and to Congress in its supervisory capacity. We hold today only that the FCC has no function in this
scheme of accountability established by 396(g)(1)(A) and the 1967 Act in
general other than that assigned to it by the Fairness Doctrine."[2]

came at nine-thirty the morning after the broadcast by an executive in the network's own personnel office whose area of responsibility included pensions.) Nevertheless, of the nearly thousand
letters received after the program, almost all were laudatory, and
press comments were overwhelmingly favorable. AIM called the
program "a useful lie."

Although "Pensions" received both an American Bar Association and a Peabody award, the strong remedial action that Congress applied to the problem in the pensions-reform law of 1974
could be considered NBC's most enduring prize. It was an
example of tough investigative reporting, and its coverage did not
pretend to be fastidiously fair to all concerned. Its makers were
muckrakers with their eyes and hearts open, not blind disciples of
the goddess of justice. One nationally recognized expert in pension plans and abuses observed, "For years there had been attempts
to get pension reform through Congress, and this one program
probably did more good than all the other efforts."

The most serious critique came from actuary Richard Solomon,
who charged at the time of the broadcast that the program was
overemotional and flawed with "significant misstatement of facts."
Specifically, he argued that the statement "Most plans require you
to work in the same place for twenty-five years or more" was false,
that "The average period required for at least partial vesting was
probably between eight and twelve years . . . for full vesting . . .
between ten and fifteen years."[3] The broadcast had also stated:
"A lot of people lose their pensions because the plan runs out
of money." According to Solomon, "If you consider a lot of people
any number between ten and five hundred thousand, . . . this statement is correct," but he recited a recent government survey indicating that "the percentage of plans that fail is infinitesimal."[4]
Solomon admitted that this information was not available at the
time of the broadcast, but neither, he said, was there information
that would support NBC's conclusions.

Solomon further claimed that the program's statement that
"Workers get smaller pensions than they expect partly because
many plans treat highly paid executives much better than lower-
and middle-level executives" was absolutely false. The actuary
retorted that it was "a cardinal principle of the IRS that plans
may not discriminate in favor of the highly paid employees."[5]
Other experts in this field believe that Solomon oversimplified

the issue and that he was guilty of the same kind of overgeneralization that he attributed to the broadcast. The difficulty is that there ·e few reliable statistics for either side to depend upon.

Solomon went on to criticize the broadcast for reporting that some people of sixty-two to sixty-five find that their retirement income is cut by as much as 70 percent. He admitted that this can be true, but pointed out that it is "misleading without further clarification."[6]

Many of Solomon's comments are marginal or subject to various interpretations, but some are not so easily dismissed. NBC News did not claim they should be, whether major or minor, but it contended that "Pensions" had been a fair and honest program, and that the tangential errors did not cast doubt on the documentary's inherent integrity or on its conclusion that conditions in too many pension plans were "deplorable."

As journalists, the NBC newsmen admit that they made a number of judgments during the filming and editing of "Pensions." Until this program, such judgments had been viewed by the FCC through the weakly tinted glasses of a Fairness Doctrine interpretation which avoided Commission interference with content. FCC Chairman Dean Burch had pointed out that the Commission was staying out of the editing rooms and avoiding the posture of "a super-broadcast journalist." In a concurring opinion to a Commission ruling in 1971, Burch raised the basic issue: "I question whether a process of categorizing and quantifying presentations, times and formats, in order to rule on the reasonableness of the licensee's judgment, does not involve the Commission too deeply in day-to-day journalistic practices."[7]

But this concern, however eloquently voiced, was not strong enough to keep the FCC from taking just such a look at "Pensions." What brought Burch and the other commissioners into the case was a letter from AIM written two and a half months after the September 12 broadcast. The nonprofit organization first wrote to NBC on November 6, but claimed that it had received no reply. Then, in a series of letters to the FCC, AIM charged that "Pensions" presented a "grotesquely distorted picture of the private pension system of the United States . . . giving the impression that failure and fraud are the rule."[8] It accused NBC News of brainwashing[9] and of "a one-sided, uninformative, emotion-evoking propaganda pitch"[10] on an issue of public importance—

the performance of pension plans. It also charged that although Newman had stated that there were some good private pensions, the program "did not discuss any good plans or show any satisfied pensioners."[11] AIM's action was designed to convince the FCC to order the network to schedule additional coverage of pensions in order to correct the deliberately distorted presentation that NBC had employed in order to foist its ideological views of events.[12]

NBC denied AIM's allegation of distortion, maintaining that the broadcast had not concerned a controversial issue of public importance. It was neither a discussion of *all* private pensions nor a recommendation for specific legislative remedies. "Rather, it was designed," said NBC, "to inform the public about some problems . . . which deserve a closer look."[13] NBC and its president, Julian Goodman, refused to provide additional time because they felt "Pensions" had been a fair show. (Reuven Frank was so convinced of its fairness that when he first saw a rough cut of the program, he complained, "Where is the controversy?")

The Broadcast Bureau of the FCC also rejected AIM's allegation of distortion but upheld the charge that NBC had violated the Fairness Doctrine. The staff report, written by a former editor of NBC News, Bill Ray, denied the network's claim that the program had not presented one side of a controversial issue, and concluded: "Its overall thrust was general criticism of the entire pension system, accompanied by proposals for its regulation."[14] Official notification that "Pensions" had violated the Fairness Doctrine was received on May 2, 1973, the same day that executive producer Elliot Frankel stood before a luncheon audience at the Pierre Hotel to receive the Peabody Award.

Not content with its progress, AIM further exacerbated the issue and infuriated NBC by sending letters to NBC affiliates shortly after the FCC staff decision was rendered but before the full Commission had acted, asking if they had carried "Pensions" and threatening each station with Fairness Doctrine complaints at license-renewal time if they did not correct "the lack of balance in 'Pensions: The Broken Promise.' "[15] NBC considered this a brazen attempt at intimidation of its stations, many of which were nervous about presenting hard-hitting network documentaries.

Smarting under AIM's utilization of the staff's preliminary ruling and aware of Burch's and other commissioners' proclaimed determination not to enter the thicket of content, NBC appealed the Broadcast Bureau's staff ruling to the full Commission. On December 3, 1973, Burch and four of his colleagues upheld the decision of its staff. While commending NBC for a laudable journalistic effort, the Commission found that the network had not satisfied its fairness obligations and ordered it to do so immediately. The commissioners agreed with AIM and its own staff that the "overwhelming weight" of the "anti-pension" statements required further presentation of opposing views. Thus, for the first time in its history, the FCC applied the Fairness Doctrine sword to a network television documentary, and ordered NBC "to submit a statement within 20 days of the date of this decision, indicating how it intends to fulfill its fairness obligations in accordance with this opinion."[16]

NBC, which might have fulfilled the Commission's order by scheduling a follow-up report on the *Today* show or on the NBC Nightly News with John Chancellor, flatly refused. David Brinkley, who had played no role in the documentary, wrote an affidavit in support of the network's refusal to comply with the FCC order, observing: "To be found guilty of 'unfairness' for not expressing to the government's satisfaction the view that most people are not corrupt or that pensioners are not unhappy is to be judged by standards which simply have nothing to do with journalism."[17]

The FCC's position was that the Brinkley position was wrong; it was not a matter of journalism but rather a matter of law which Congress had passed and the FCC had interpreted. An appeal to the D.C. Circuit Court was entered by NBC, with amicus curiae briefs by CBS, the Radio-Television News Directors Association, the National Association of Broadcasters and the *New York Times*. To the amazement of broadcast insiders, a brief was also filed by Henry Geller. When he was the FCC's general counsel, Geller had advocated the use of the Fairness Doctrine in *Red Lion*; now, as a private citizen, he was intervening against it. Arrayed against NBC *et al.* were the FCC, AIM, the Office of Communication of the United Church of Christ and several liberal public-interest law firms, including the Center for the Public Interest and the National Citizens Committee for Broadcasting.

While NBC pushed its appeal, the FCC demanded that it fulfill immediately the terms of its order and correct the "imbal-

ance" of "Pensions." Again the network refused to comply, until
the Court of Appeals had a chance to hear the case. Floyd Abrams,
NBC's thirty-seven-year-old attorney who with Alexander Bickel
had represented the *New York Times* in the Pentagon Papers
suit, believed this to be a significant case. He argued that com-
pulsive government programing "against the will of the licensee
prior to judicial review cannot be undone by an after-the-fact
reversal of the Commission's decision in this case."[18] The FCC
countered with the claim that "Pensions" was a "textbook" fairness case, and that with pension reform before the Congress at
that moment, fairness delayed was fairness denied. Abrams told
the Court of Appeals for the District of Columbia that "Pensions"
had not dealt with the specific legislation before Congress, and
that if NBC was forced to comply with the FCC order now, even-
tual reversal of such "coercion" would have no meaning. The
result, said Abrams, was that with an FCC "uninhibited by the statutory right of review, broadcast journalists may all-too-early err
on the side of caution."[19]

Judge Harold Leventhal of the Court of Appeals understood
that a swift hearing of NBC's appeal was essential because of the
currency of the pensions issue. Proposing an extraordinary procedure, he therefore asked Abrams if he and his client would be
willing to eliminate the preparation of lengthy briefs and to argue
the case in court as soon as possible.

On argument day, February 21, 1974, Abrams based NBC's
case on the fact that "the cornerstone of the fairness doctrine is
good faith and licensee discretion." He added that in the NBC
case, the licensee's discretion had been "overruled by the Commission in a way which neither the Fairness Doctrine nor the
First Amendment would allow."[20]

One of the points that interested Judge Leventhal was Abrams'
claim that the FCC staff and members who had decided the case
were basing their criticism only on a reading of the script. "Are
you implying that the FCC did not see the program?" asked the
judge.

"That is my understanding, your honor," Abrams answered.
"They certainly did not see an NBC copy of the program. They
did not ask us for a copy of the program. And I understand that's
their usual practice." Millions of Americans had watched the original telecast, but the inference was that even if the commissioners

had been members of that audience, they had not examined the broadcast in light of AIM's charges.

Leventhal wanted to know whether it was significant that the commissioners had only read the script and not seen the program. Abrams responded that "television is a visual medium . . . And with respect to the legislation . . . when Ed Newman said, 'These are issues for Congress to decide,' . . . his tone of voice was such as to suggest to me, as a listener of the program, that he was saying Congress and not NBC, or Congress and not me . . ."

Leventhal was exploring a sensitive issue never before touched in broadcast cases: the difficulty of judging a news report or documentary in script form long after the climate of the original impact in a medium which cannot express qualities of sound, pictures of people, tones and accents of delivery. Anyone who has ever produced a documentary understands the disparity between printed text and live action. Three pages of hortative pleading may be outweighed by a one-sentence oath delivered by a person with a fire in his belly, or by the kind of exchange that occurred between Senator Williams and Newman.

Leventhal said he wondered whether a Commission regulating television and broadcasting could make decisions without viewing the programs, especially in a case-by-case framework of review.

Abrams suggested that while the action taken by the FCC in connection with the "Pensions" program was illustrative of the dangers of the Fairness Doctrine, the case-by-case method of review could be made to work properly. He argued that the Commission could exercise discretion, actually watching programing only in situations when its prior reading of a written script indicated the likelihood of a fairness problem.

Abrams contended "that the need for reform in this field [pension plans] is not a controversial issue of public importance." To support this claim, he cited a recent unanimous Senate vote for pension reform. He also pointed out that all groups testifying before Congress had supported the idea of some kind of legislative reform.

Concluding his argument, Abrams quoted Chief Justice Burger from the *CBS et al.* v. *DNC* case: "For better or worse, editing is what editors are for and editing is the selection and choice of material."

Arguing for the FCC, its new general counsel John Pettit agreed that while editing was for editors, the Fairness Doctrine must be applied to such unbalanced editing as NBC's. Pettit maintained that "the Congress, the Commission and the Courts have made it clear that it is the right of the viewers and the listeners, not the broadcasters, which is paramount." He noted that in *Red Lion,* the Supreme Court had upheld the personal-attack rule "which far more than the Fairness Doctrine limits the discretion of the licensee . . ."

Pettit contended that the program was clearly controversial, and that NBC's claim that the subject of the program was not "unreasonable" was not valid. He scoffed at the network's fears of an FCC reign of terror, citing that in fiscal 1973 the Commission had "received some two thousand four hundred and six complaints" on which it had "issued one hundred and eight rulings . . . five of these rulings . . . adverse to the licensee . . . and only two of these . . . were general fairness doctrine cases . . . one of which you find before you today."

He went on to say that the FCC felt that the thrust of the NBC presentation had been to suggest that "the overall performance of the private pensions system . . . was deplorable."

When Judge Charles Fahy asked about the statement at the end of the program which said that there were many good plans, Pettit proceeded to read aloud Newman's closing remarks about the "deplorable situation." Judge Leventhal responded by quoting Newman's conclusion: "We don't want to give the impression that there are no good private pension plans. There are many good ones . . . and that should be said."

Speaking for the FCC, Pettit insisted that Newman's ending did not correct the basically negative attitude of "Pensions" and argued that NBC's unwillingness to schedule any remedial remarks was a dereliction of their fairness responsibilities. Pettit added, "It is not a question of making NBC go to any expense . . . They have the vehicle in the *Today* show."

During the two hours of argument, other provocative statements came from the United Church of Christ, whose attorney, Ellen Shaw Agress, ridiculed the timorous licensees "who are crying wolf again." She noted, "It would rip the guts out of the Fairness Doctrine to lower the standards any more."

Although argument day had been expedited in order to reach a prompt decision, it was months after the oral arguments and almost two years after the broadcast that the Court of Appeals delivered its verdict. In the interim, "Pensions" continued to win awards and be acclaimed and denounced by experts who had never seen it. More significantly, during the summer of 1974 Congress unanimously passed its comprehensive pension-reform bill prescribing far-reaching changes.

Because there had been no formal briefs, the oral arguments were far more decisive than usual. In his quiet way Floyd Abrams had hit hard at the FCC's misuse of the Fairness Doctrine and had wasted little time on the customary First Amendment rhetoric. When the court handed down its decision, two of the three judges identified themselves with his argument about the misapplication of the Fairness Doctrine. "Petitioners urge that the Commission's decision be set aside as a misapplication of the fairness doctrine and a violation of the First Amendment. Since we reverse on the former ground, we have no occasion to consider the latter,"[21] said the majority.

Writing for the majority, Judge Leventhal was blunt in stating that the FCC had been unable to prove "that the licensee had failed to provide a reasonable opportunity for the presentation of contrasting approaches,"[22] while carefully restating the Supreme Court's upholding of the Fairness Doctrine as a principle. "The broadcaster cannot assert a right of freedom of the press that transcends the public's right to know."[23] But in this particular case, said Leventhal, ". . . when a court is called on to take a 'hard look' whether the Commission has gone too far and encroached on journalistic discretion, it must take a hard look to avoid enforcing judicial predilections."[24] (In other words, the penchant of judges to play the role of conciliator must be resisted.) "And . . . recognition of the other's viewpoint in the broad interest of fairness, must yield to a vigilant concern that a government agency is not to . . . second-guess the journalist."[25] Leventhal's point was that the Communications Act gives discretionary responsibility to the journalist, unless there is persuasive proof *that the broadcaster has acted unreasonably or in bad faith.*

Conceding that the FCC had acted in good faith, the court nevertheless held that it had exceeded proper regulatory restraints on this occasion. "But we are here concerned with the area of investigative journalism," wrote Judge Leventhal, "[and] there is the greatest need for self-restraint on the part of the Commission. . . . Investigative journalism is a portrayal of evils."[26] He agreed that the "Pensions" audience might have gained the impression that the evils reported were "the rule rather than exception. But the question is not the Commission's view of what . . . would be reasonable . . . but whether the licensee, who had this rule, had been demonstrated to have maintained an approach that was an abuse rather than an exercise of discretion."[27]

Then Leventhal's opinion plowed new ground on the issue of whether the statement that there was "a need for reform" was necessarily a controversial issue, as AIM and the FCC had contended. The court maintained that some specific proposals for reform might be controversial, "but they were not the subject of the Pensions broadcast."[28] In short, the opinion affirmed what journalists had been trying to explain to nervous management lawyers for a long time—that in a documentary about society's ills, whether pension-plan failure, the living conditions of migrant workers, or documented proof of police corruption, the issues may not have two equal sides. Moreover, remedies may very well be controversial and require special fairness balancing. "Pensions," said the Court of Appeals, was not such a case because no specific legislative action had been advocated by the broadcasters.

The court took note of AIM's exhibit of a Washington *Post* study of the pension situation as being more balanced and containing pro and con arguments, but dismissed its relevance because of the difference in technique between newspapers and broadcasting. To force television, with its ability to portray intense interviews, to "adopt techniques congenial to newspaper journalism" would be "an impermissible intrusion"[29] by government, wrote the court.

Acknowledging that *Pensions* had "not been an easy case to decide,"[30] the court rejected the Commission's contention that even though no special solutions had been recommended, the "overall impact" of the "Pensions" program had been one-sided and unfair. Like AIM members, the FCC commissioners and staff, the judges had never viewed the film itself.

> We have analyzed the various segments of the "Pensions" broadcast and have not found them to justify the Commission's invocation of the fairness doctrine. We also take account of the Commission's statement that its decision was based upon the

"overall impact" of the program. In some fields the whole may be greater than the sum of its parts—according to the principles of Gestalt Psychology. In general, however, the evils of communications controlled by a nerve center of Government loom larger than the evils of editorial abuse by multiple licensees who are not governed by the standards of their profession but [are] aware that their interest lies in long-term confidence. The fairness doctrine requires a demonstrated analysis of imbalance of controversial issues. This cannot be avoided by recourse to a subjective and impressionistic recording of overall impact.[31]

There was one unexpected note in Judge Leventhal's majority opinion: in an attempt to nudge the FCC, he devoted five pages to the amicus curiae brief of Henry Geller. Though Geller had filed his remarks as a private citizen, the court made a point of identifying the former FCC chief counsel as "a serious student of the fairness doctrine."[32]

According to Leventhal, the Geller view was "that under the law the FCC could not properly issue the ad hoc fairness ruling on this program but was limited to consideration of the matter only in connection with NBC's application for renewal of license, and then only to determine if some flagrant pattern of violation of the fairness doctrine is indicated by NBC's overall operation . . ."[33] The drift in Fairness Doctrine procedures toward the role of a program-by-program umpire had led the Commission "ever deeper into the journalistic process."[34] The net result, particularly among small stations, "has been to inhibit the promotion of robust, wide open debate,"[35] for even when a small station could win a fairness complaint, substantial time and funds had to be expended before the process was completed.

Geller's theory would not be considered in *Pensions*, declared Leventhal, but looking to the future, he advised the FCC that the point made by the former chief counsel was "a serious one, and it deserves serious consideration."[36]

Although Judge Fahy concurred with Leventhal's opinion and language, he could not resist the opportunity to warn the television industry: "One may hope that this latitude will not encourage in a different context abuses which, even though protected by the First Amendment, should be discouraged, or lead to claims of such protection which could not be sustained."[37] Fahy's concern seemed to be slightly off target, especially in view of the

majority opinion, which had purposely avoided the First Amendment arguments of both sides. However, Fahy clearly wished to
register that the freedom he was defending from government intrusion was not a license to unleash violence in programing. It
was time, he noted, for broadcasters "to stop asserting 'not proved'
to charges of adverse effects from pervasive violence in television
programing."³⁸ During the dancing in the streets which followed
the *Pensions* decision, few broadcasters remembered that one
judge on their side was warning them that they would have to
take some self-imposed steps to soften the impact of television on
"anti-social styles of life."³⁹

The dissent in the *Pensions* opinion came from Judge Edward
Tamm, who had helped forge the Fairness Doctrine in *Red Lion*
and was clearly perturbed that it was being weakened by Leventhal and Fahy. Tamm charged that the majority's finding had
concluded "that fairness, meaning a presentation of both sides of
a question of public interest, is not a practically enforceable obligation of a licensee of the public airwaves."⁴⁰ Tamm pointed out
that "digesting . . . eighty thousand feet of film into a two thousand
foot final product,"⁴¹ distinguishes the rights and obligations of
telecasters from those of the press. He scoffed at NBC's position
that "under the label of investigative reporting . . . a few factual
bones covered with the corpulent flesh of opinion and comment
fulfills the obligation of a network to give a fair picture to the
public."⁴²

Tamm was also disturbed by the tremendous power of the
broadcast industry and the tendency of the documentary maker
to produce "a manipulated and selective presentation which ignores all viewpoints and positions other than his own."⁴³ He did
not equate the public's right to know with the "absolute right"
of broadcasters "to exercise their constitutional infallibility" in
deciding what the public should see and hear. Vigorous in his
defense of the Fairness Doctrine, he wrote:

> The fairness doctrine . . . is not a censorship, it is not a prior
> (or subsequent) restraint, is not a usurpation of what the major-
> ity describes as "Journalistic Discretion" but is merely a policy
> that requires in the public interest all viewpoints be presented
> in factual matters . . . The doctrine, as it has been utilized here,
> is the yeast of fairness in the dough of the telecaster's right to
> exercise his journalistic freedom. The resulting problem of the

Commission is then the securing of responsibility in the exercise of the freedom which the broadcasting industry enjoys.[44]

Judge Leventhal not only disagreed with Tamm but seemed to rebut him in a supplemental concurring statement to his majority opinion: "A judge confronted with a problem like this one has a natural tendency . . . to try to strike a middle ground between the antagonists—here, between NBC and AIM."[45] Leventhal agreed that small independent stations might not have the legal staffs or budgets and might compromise on content to avoid trouble, and took the legal profession to task for overlooking the "stultifying burden on journalism"[46] that the bureaucrat may cause by peeking over his shoulder.

Disappointed by the Court of Appeals decision and stunned by the language of the majority opinion, the FCC considered appealing to the Supreme Court for final review, and was urged to do so by AIM. "We thought we had such a commitment from our partners," said AIM director Reed Irvine, who clearly wanted an appeal. However, the new FCC chairman, Richard E. Wiley, who as a commissioner had committed the FCC to the original litigation with "no real enthusiasm . . . it just wasn't the right case," decided against carrying the matter further.

NBC and Floyd Abrams had won a decisive round. Members of the Washington communications bar could not recall an occasion when a single advocate, without benefit of a formal brief, had made such an impact on the outcome of a landmark case. But it turned out not to be the final round. Soon after the decision by the three-man Court of Appeals, word circulated in Washington communications circles that some of Judge Leventhal's colleagues were troubled by his "big wind" decision which seemed to have the effect of softening the Fairness Doctrine without quite voiding it. The implication was that if the FCC or AIM asked for an en banc review by the entire ten-judge court, it would be favorably received.

The FCC heard and ignored this signal, but AIM, as it always said it would, petitioned for a rehearing because of "the narrow margin by which the case was decided," and "inasmuch as the majority opinion serves to erode and substantially weaken the Fairness Doctrine."[47] The petition filed restated AIM's indictment of "Pensions" as "a useful lie," and told the court that its prior decision "will have an impact on the fairness doctrine . . . similar to a finding that the Fairness Doctrine was unconstitutional."[48]*

It came as a shock to NBC when on December 13, 1974, AIM's request for the en banc hearing was granted and the Leventhal opinion was accordingly vacated, though the stay of the FCC fairness order that Leventhal had granted NBC was extended until the en banc judgment was rendered. This meant that NBC did not have to comply with the FCC command to provide more coverage on the pensions issue until the matter had been completely adjudicated by the full court.

The court ordered that written briefs be delivered to its clerk within forty days; oral arguments were to be heard on April 2, 1975, six years to the day after the *Red Lion* debate in the Supreme Court.

But the en banc arguments never took place. Two weeks before Chief Judge David Bazelon was scheduled to gavel the ten-man court to order (retired Judge Fahy was the extra member), a majority of the judges decided that they did not wish to hear the case. Bazelon had wanted the en banc hearing, hoping that at least five of his colleagues would agree with him that it was time to consider the constitutionality of the Fairness Doctrine. Moreover, even before this decision by the court, the FCC, which had never liked the merits of *Pensions* and apparently did not look forward to its Fairness Doctrine being challenged on the basis of AIM's

---

* It is unusual for a full (en banc) Court of Appeals to decide to examine a case already adjudicated by three of its members; in effect, a rehearing en banc is a procedural way for an appellate court to take a second look at its own decision. Section 35 of the Rules of the Appellate Procedure provides:

A majority of the circuit judges who are in regular service may order that an appeal or other proceeding be heard or reheard by the Court of Appeals *en banc*. Such a hearing or rehearing is not favored and ordinarily will not be ordered except (1) when consideration by the full court is necessary to secure or maintain uniformity of its decisions, or (2) when the proceeding involves a question of exceptional importance.[49]

In plain language this means that the full court has a procedural method of overturning any three-judge decision it is concerned about, or before such an opinion goes up for review to the Supreme Court. The vote is secret, but in this case it was no secret that most of the Court of Appeals judges considered themselves authorities on the Fairness Doctrine.

position, had suggested that the case was moot. Since the Employment Retirement Income Security Act of 1974 was now law, the Commission questioned the value of continuing the debate on an issue which Congress had already decided. AIM and Reed Irvine were furious about the FCC's "cowardly" stance, but still no one expected that the court would make such a decision on the eve of an en banc hearing which had attracted large national attention.

Chief Judge Bazelon, who was away on vacation at the time, saw no reason for his court's vacating the order for a rehearing and rejected the suggestion that the case was moot. "If this is the cause [mootness], I am at a loss to understand the court's action,"[50] he later wrote.

With the vacating of an en banc hearing, *Pensions* was remanded back to Judge Leventhal's three-man panel so that they could rule on the mootness issue or reaffirm their original opinion in favor of NBC. But Bazelon was not content to wait until the Leventhal panel issued its final opinion; in June of 1975 he issued a blistering attack against the eight judges who had vacated the en banc hearing, against the arguments of the NBC lawyers, and against the Leventhal decision which had declared that the "Pensions" broadcast had not violated the Fairness Doctrine.

In essence he argued that the courts had only increased the ambiguity and uncertainty of the Fairness Doctrine, whose chilling effect and abuse by the Commission he still believed to clash with the First Amendment. As for NBC, he contended that just as AIM had argued, the network had broadcast a controversial subject and been on the side of the need for reform. He disagreed strongly on the question of mootness: "I certainly hope we have not yet reached the stage where a majority of Congressmen can by their votes determine that an issue is no longer 'controversial.' "[51]

Bazelon was particularly scornful of Floyd Abrams' arguments for NBC that had been accepted by the Leventhal panel. He felt that his colleagues on the court had, by a semantic trick, and by divide-and-conquer tactics, "provided licensees with a litigation strategy for avoiding adverse Fairness Doctrine rulings."[52]

Bazelon also felt that "a very serious constitutional question" had been "obscured by the court's decision"[53] and that broadcasters "will find the First Amendment less strong than before and may one day reap the harvest of that ambiguity being used in an unauthorized manner to control their expression."[54]

Finally, Bazelon feared that the *Pensions* brief and opinion would "only serve to denigrate and compromise a genuine journalistic achievement."[55] In language that stunned NBC lawyers and bewildered newsmen, he warned:

> I wonder what the professional journalists who prepared the "Pensions" program think about NBC's litigation position in this case that their program was not really controversial. My own thought is that NBC has by its litigation position done more to attack and undercut the "Pensions" program than anything AIM could have done through the FCC. This is the saddest commentary of all.[56]

Six weeks after Bazelon's scolding and thirty-four months after the original "Pensions" broadcast, the Leventhal panel issued a quarrelsome, confusing opinion in this star-crossed litigation. Even the printer appeared to be affected; the first printing of the case summary began: "The Federal Trade Commission issued an order under the Fairness Doctrine . . ."

As the court pointed out, the FCC had for a long time wanted this case "to be ended without a definitive decision on the merits,"[57] claiming that the President's signing of pension-reform legislation in 1974 had rendered moot its original ruling that NBC provide contrasting views to its "Pensions" broadcast. Neither AIM nor NBC wanted the case to end without a decision on the merits, but the FCC got what it wanted, having the court return *Pensions* to its own jurisdiction, where it would be allowed to die. Technically, the court did not vacate the majority ruling on the ground of mootness, but the final opinions made it clear that the issue had been ducked. Judge Fahy wanted the mootness issue to be understood as an exercise of the court's equity powers:

> The Commission seeks the remand on the theory of mootness. It is clear, however, that this theory is simply the medium advanced by the Commission to enable the case to be ended without a definitive decision on the merits. The essence of the matter is that the Commission seeks permission to vacate its order.[58]

Concurring in part, dissenting in part and denying legal mootness, Judge Leventhal reluctantly agreed to return the case to the

Commission on that basis, thus allowing his original Appeals Court decision to be set aside:

> This has been a Big Case with issues large in law and judicial approach. This is the way it ends: All the judges on the panel . . . agree on the dissolution of the order of the Federal Communications Commission that the National Broadcasting Company's Pensions telecast violated the Fairness Doctrine. But the reason differs from judge to judge.[59]

The mootness argument was not the only one that separated the three-judge panel. Judge Leventhal obviously wished his original ruling that NBC had not violated the Fairness Doctrine to remain as precedent: "Fairness rulings raise the problems of a chilling effect on broadcasting journalism. And specifically NBC, with its owned and operated stations, faces the possibility that the Pensions broadcast will haunt their renewal applications."[60] Although Judge Tamm concurred in the decision because he believed the case to be moot, he remained steadfast in his stance calling the original judgment a "tortured interpretation of the fairness doctrine"[61] and attacking his colleagues who had improperly "worship[ped] at the altar of editorial judgment."[62] Judge Fahy, who originally constituted one half of the majority, still hoped that the original opinion would remain for its "influence in the development of the law,"[63] but was not prepared to let the ruling stand as the definitive Fairness Doctrine holding.

Obviously this strange ending of this "big case" was a tactical compromise. When the three judges exchanged memoranda among themselves, it was clear that Leventhal wished to let the original order against the FCC stand. Tamm still bristled under this assault on the Fairness Doctrine and produced "an extended critique." Fahy's was the key vote, because while he still believed that the Commission's decision against NBC should never have been entered, he did not feel that *Pensions* was the case on which the future of the Fairness Doctrine should stand or fall. Sending the case back to the FCC, which no longer sought enforcement, reduced the chances that the Supreme Court would agree to take on an issue that had become "abstract" and "meaningless," to use Fahy's words. Nonetheless, AIM still intends to ask the Supreme Court for a writ of certiorari.

As a result, "The Commission's hope and purpose of vindicating the Fairness Doctrine cannot be achieved,"[64] said Leventhal's panel. NBC had achieved a moral victory, but not the clear-cut legal triumph it had sought. In future fairness cases, broadcasters can point to the fact that in the original decision, two judges of the Court of Appeals had warned the FCC that "to overrule and discard the journalistic judgment of the broadcast licensees" is to undermine "the very premise of the legislative structure."[65] This opinion would have no precedental force, but as Judge Fahy wrote, "The views advanced in the opinions . . . would remain for their influence in the development of the law."[66] And the case itself might establish a mood: If the FCC could not win this case, on which it had staked all, what fairness case involving a TV documentary could it win? The grand en banc hearing that Chief Judge Bazelon had planned came to naught, and Judge Tamm was now willing to call the case moot, and his colleagues' work "evanescent."[67] The Court of Appeals of the District of Columbia, which is regarded as the upper house of the FCC, had again demonstrated how splintered and contentious its members are when faced with the vagaries of the Fairness Doctrine.

The final sorry note is that as far as can be ascertained, not one of the ten judges or seven commissioners, or the head of the Complaints and Compliance Bureau, or any of the executives of AIM, ever saw "Pensions: The Broken Promise," either when it first appeared or a tape of it later. Today the FCC wants to forget the whole case; NBC cannot afford to.

11

DISTORTION IN THE NEWS ... OR ABOUT THE NEWS?:

The Case against the Cronkite Show

~~~~~~~~~~~~~~~~~~~~~~~~~~~~~~~

CBS News, Weighed and Found Weighted

EUGENE H. METHUIN, WASHINGTON STAR
NOVEMBER 2, 1974

CBS News Reports National Defense News Unfairly

OMAHA WORLD HERALD
NOVEMBER 10, 1974

How Could Anyone Form a Responsible Opinion on National Defense Needs on the Basis [of CBS reporting] Like This?

INDIANAPOLIS STAR
DECEMBER 7, 1974

FCC-CBS Confrontation in Offing ... CBS Television News May Face Court Action

LONGVIEW (TEXAS) JOURNAL
OCTOBER 23, 1974

The seventh news item on the Cronkite broadcast of June 27, 1972, was about the meeting of the Platform Committee of the Democratic Party in Washington, with Dan Schorr reporting on the various planks. The story lasted four minutes and dealt with the Democrats' campaign promises on economy, defense, wages and prices, busing, drugs, tax reform, welfare, crime and abortion.

Nineteen words by Schorr summarized the Democrats' plank for Vietnam draft dodgers: "For those who have evaded service, 'amnesty on an appropriate basis after the war when the prisoners are returned.'" These words spoken by correspondent Schorr were coded, broken down and analyzed as part of *TV and National Defense,* a 200-page study which determined that "The CBS Evening News with Walter Cronkite" had in 1972 and 1973 violated the Fairness Doctrine by underplaying the Soviet and Communist Chinese threat to U.S. national security.

The study was prepared and funded by the Institute for American Strategy, "a 'Cold War college' to train leaders for the battle against Communism," as the *Wall Street Journal* described it.[1] *TV and National Defense* was published on October 23, 1974, and was written by Dr. Ernest Lefever, a former minister and currently a senior fellow of the Brookings Institution, who claims he seldom watches television and only watched the Cronkite program once in his life before he worked on the study, and very seldom thereafter. Lefever and the institute view the Cold War as the "one" cause more vital than all others, and consider it their mission to make certain that the news media, and particularly television, inform the American people that "threat to U.S. security is more serious than perceived by the government, or that the United States ought to *increase* its national security efforts."[2]

The IAS analysis received national attention, most of it favorable, when it was published. It is not the first time that a major news organization has been subjected to such intense analytical scrutiny, but the study is significant because it may become the basis of a complaint to the FCC under the Fairness Doctrine. The IAS demand for compensatory programing is based on an investigation by a team of social scientists claiming that CBS News had by omission and commission systematically ignored and distorted a widely held position on a controversial issue of public importance. In that failure, Lefever claimed, "CBS News shortchanged the American people and thus compromised its public trust."[3]

For the first time, tapes provided by the Television News Archive of Vanderbilt University* were utilized for such Fairness

* The Vanderbilt Television News Archive is supported by a variety of foundations, corporations and individuals. The Ford Foundation has contributed approximately 17 percent of the archive's total budget. In my capacity as a consultant to the Ford Foundation, I recommended its 1973 grant of $200,000.

Doctrine review. Since 1968 Vanderbilt has been recording, preserving and indexing the nightly news broadcasts of all networks, and long before this instance, CBS had protested the operation as a violation of its copyright. The network has brought suit in Federal court to halt Vanderbilt's use and distribution of its news broadcasts to scholars and others.

The confrontation between the Institute for American Strategy and CBS is not only an examination of how Cronkite and his team cover the subject of national defense; it is also a test of the methods by which Lefever and his team made such a determination. At stake is the larger issue of whether statistical content analysis can be applied to the fast-breaking decision process of news gathering, which has been termed "the first draft of history" and which may defy scholarly analysis done months or years later, when the political climate, viewer appetites and restrictions of time cannot be accurately calibrated. This case also raises some disconcerting questions about how much primary source material was actually studied, and how much the study depended upon secondhand unauthenticated summaries catalogued for ordering and retrieval purposes only.

It is perfectly understandable and proper for those who make policy, as well as those who attempt to influence it, to be critical of the media—the military establishment no less so than civil rights militants. What is open to question is the use of such an indictment by a special-interest group as the principal evidence in a Fairness Doctrine case.

James J. Kilpatrick, a firm believer in military power, thought the study a valuable contribution and felt that CBS News, for whom he does a brief weekly TV commentary, had some explaining to do. But while the columnist felt that dividing public opinion into "hawk, sparrow and dove" was "fairly within the range of statistical analysis," he had some reservations about applying this analysis to Fairness Doctrine violations.[4]

The potential impact of the Lefever-IAS study on future Fairness Doctrine complaints by other pressure groups concerns those who care about the independence and vigor of broadcast news. To understand the implications of potential FCC action based on the IAS analysis and complaint, one must look back to the institute's founding, purpose and earlier encounter with the Fairness Doctrine.

TV and National Defense was not conceived by Lefever but by

John M. Fisher, a World War II bomber pilot and former FBI agent, who was recruited by General Robert E. Wood, chairman of Sears, Roebuck, to establish a research library and data bank on Communist subversives. General Wood was a founder of "America First" in the late thirties, and a staunch supporter and backer of Senator Joseph McCarthy in the early fifties. Fisher, a protégé of Wood's, left the FBI in 1953 to become Sears' executive assistant in personnel, specializing in security-clearance matters. As McCarthyism and security clearances for private industry became less acceptable, Wood and Fisher decided to convert the Anti-Communist Research Library into the American Security Council, in order to concentrate on Cold War strategies "against the Soviet threat of world domination." After General Wood's death in 1964, Fisher moved the organization to Culpepper, in the Blue Ridge Mountains of Virginia, where the data bank on subversives became a more general library on world Communism.

More than 1,700 companies pay dues to IAS based on the number of employees, but in 1970 the *Times* reported that few of these "manufacture guns or bombs or warships; instead they sell mattresses, newspapers, television sets, razors and insurance."[5] With an impressive board of former generals, admirals and captains of industry committed to the development of enlarged weapons systems, the council campaigns against senators and congressmen dedicated to trimming the Pentagon's budget. It has lobbied vigorously for the ABM, the Trident, the B-1, and for a strike force capable of destroying the Soviet Union. In the early seventies, the American Security Council created a tax-free arm, the Institute for American Strategy. Today the combined organizations, with a membership of 190,000, and a budget of $2 million, occupy a five-building complex on 850 acres in Boston, Virginia, near Culpepper. The institute conducts eight to ten seminars a year in which congressional assistants, governors' aides, corporation executives and educators attend two-day conferences on national security and the Cold War.

Both the institute and the council continue to be the lengthened shadow of one man, John Fisher, who is president and chief executive of the board of both organizations. The largest and by far the busiest building at Boston is the direct-mail center. The direct-mail business that Fisher learned at Sears still serves him well; he is considered to have few peers in the highly specialized skill of composing fund-raising letters. A battery of semi-robot typewriters send out anywhere from three to ten million letters a year soliciting funds from citizens apprehensive about the Soviet threat. Fisher avoids Birch Society rhetoric or assaults on the motives of doves or liberals. His enemies are Russia and Red China, and his council and institute are committed to keeping America powerful enough to defeat all the "announced plots" of the Marxists to control the world. His letters appeal to the fears of those who believe that détente is a myth designed by Kissinger and the Soviets in order to lull the United States to sleep.

In the early seventies, long before the study on CBS News, Fisher and the Institute for American Strategy had their first experience with television and the Fairness Doctrine. Frustrated by the news media's lack of attention to their hard-line view on military strategy and spending, the institute decided that the networks' news treatment of those leaders concerned with U.S. military superiority was "to ignore them or to criticize them." Fisher's fund-raising letters warned that the "basic view offered the viewer by the networks is between the status quo and doing less."[6] With this in mind, the institute methodically divided the public-opinion spectrum on national defense into three carefully selected categories:

"A" view: The Administration is not doing enough to build up and protect America's defense interests. The USSR is militarily ahead of the U.S., and the U.S. needs to spend more to achieve superiority.

"B" view: The USSR and the U.S. are and should be at parity. The Soviets are mellowing and may be willing to give up their goal of world domination.

"C" view: The Soviets pose no threat to the free world, and the U.S. should reduce its defenses.

Convinced that the "B" and "C" views received the lion's share of coverage on television, the institute asked potential funders: "Can *you* think of *any* favorable network mention of the 'A' views during 1971 or 1972?"[7] To balance this situation, the IAS decided to fund a television film of its own, a short documentary which cost $80,000 and was called "Only the Strong." Moreover, the institute was prepared to spend a further $250,000 for distribution and sponsorship of its twenty-six-minute polemic on military preparedness.

"Only the Strong" was made primarily with stock film from Soviet and American libraries, most of which had been previously shown. The narration stated: "The Soviets moved ahead of us in 1969, and now in some respects have the same advantage over us as we had over them at the time of the Cuban missile crisis." The film also warned that the Russians "have about five times as much missile megatonnage, and thus could divide theirs into five times as many warheads as we have,"[8] and further that the proposed SALT agreements favored the Russians. A series of interviews with beribboned generals offered statements by those who shared the A view. Much of the film was based on a minority statement by a six-man ad hoc committee that had differed with the 1970 Blue Ribbon Defense Panel appointed by President Nixon.

None of the networks were willing to run or permit sponsorship of such a film, and Fisher says he was told that it was the Fairness Doctrine that prevented them. In fact, CBS and NBC have a policy against running film produced outside their organizations, regardless of their source, and ABC rarely accepts such productions. Fisher adds that the Metromedia station in New York gave him a price of twice the standard rate card "so that they could afford to grant time to someone on the other side to answer." Resenting the implication, Fisher turned down the offer.

Some eighty independent stations did agree to sell Fisher time, but even before the film was shown, a Fairness Doctrine complaint was sent to the stations. In a joint letter the president of the Arms Control Association, William C. Foster, and the director of the Center for Defense Information, retired Rear Admiral Gene R. LaRocque, claimed that " 'Only the Strong' provided a biased, one-sided view" and contained serious errors and omissions.[9] They warned stations against scheduling the film, and that if they did, Fairness Doctrine rules demanded balanced programing—which they were prepared to supply.

Fisher countered with the claim that he, too, believed in the true principles of the Fairness Doctrine, and that since "B" and "C" positions already dominated the airwaves, "Only the Strong" would correct the imbalance. Fisher estimates that eventually there were eight hundred different showings, but he could not understand the decision of the networks and some large independent stations not to run it. This "misapplication of the Fairness Doctrine," as Fisher put it, coupled with such aggravations as the evening news and the CBS News production in 1971 of "The Selling of the Pentagon," convinced him and his board to investigate the bias of television in its coverage of national defense.

In essence, the analysis was designed to document their conviction that the hawk position was not being represented fairly on television—indeed, was virtually ignored. IAS drafted Dr. Ernest Lefever of the Brookings Institution "to pull it all together and write it up, when we found ourselves in kind of a mess with the transcripts. Ernie kept us from making a lot of mistakes," Fisher says candidly. According to Lefever, for a long time he had wanted to do an analysis on the media and foreign affairs; he says somewhat bitterly, "Brookings would never approve such a study. I heard that IAS had tapes of the nightly news broadcasts, and I thought I might make an arrangement to use them . . . I signed on in 1973 as an anonymous consultant, but I soon discovered that Fisher wanted my name and the prestige of the Brookings Institution."

With some amusement, Lefever tells of joining Fisher's project and looking up his own card in the five-million-card data bank. "There wasn't much there . . . minister and pacifist . . . I wouldn't have been cleared in 1953." This was an allusion to his record in World War II as a conscientious objector; as a young minister, Lefever had a draft deferment on religious grounds and served in Europe as a volunteer in prisoner-of-war camps. "That's where in 1946 I first saw the evils of Communism," he explains.

TV and National Defense began as an analysis of one year of news of all three networks, but became a study of only one network for a two-year period. "We set out to examine the news programs of ABC, CBS and NBC," Fisher says, "but in the interests of depth and thoroughness we decided to confine our analysis to just one network. We chose CBS because it has the greatest evening news audience and the largest number of affiliated stations." On the basis of its study the Institute for American Strategy determined that CBS "bred a distrust of governmental authority and military responsibility" and "tended to discredit in advance anything a military spokesman had to say."[10] In addition, IAS charged that "the unfair and lopsided reporting of Vietnam had a damaging effect on the fidelity and balance of CBS coverage in other national security areas."[11] Further, CBS "frequently excluded views on key issues that ran counter to the broadcast opinion of its own newsmen[12] [and] . . . presented the U.S. military establishment in an unfavorable light most of the time . . . CBS-TV Evening News failed to provide a 'reasonable opportunity' for broadcasting the views of millions of Americans who were skeptical about the politics of détente, the SALT arms control agreements, or increased U.S. trade with Moscow and Peking."[13]

There was little doubt that the study would support the institute's worst expectations. Many surveys commissioned and conducted by special-interest groups tend to confirm the funders' beliefs, and the IAS study was no different in this regard. It had designed the ground rules in such a way that the general findings would necessarily show that the CBS Evening News devoted little time to view "A"—which Fisher and Lefever describe as more defense-minded than that of the Nixon Administration and the military establishment. In their coding, the "B" view represented that of the President and the Secretary of Defense, who at the time of the study were bombing North Vietnam and invading Cambodia in an effort to exert pressure on the enemy and force a negotiated settlement. Consequently, in the spectrum of opinion that IAS carefully constructed for its study, the Pentagon—a part of the executive branch which most analysts would place in the extreme "A" category—was accorded a "B" position. All others—whether Senators Hubert Humphrey, Edward Brooke, Jacob Javits, Edmund Muskie, or Clark Clifford, or such "peace mongers" as Jane Fonda, Abby Hoffman, and Benjamin Spock— were lumped together as "C." In short, the IAS analysis used the two categories, "A" and "B," for what most reasonable observers would categorize as the hawkish position, and only one category for the doves of every persuasion and gradation. Independent content analysts who have examined the study suggest that at least five categories were required for proper coding; in such complex issues as war and peace, overkill and sufficiency, views simply cannot be easily divided into three broad categories.

"In the final viewpoint analysis [for 1972], 274 different news items were examined and coded. This included 725 separately coded passages within news items,"[14] the IAS study stated. Lefever and the staff examined extracts of 2,235 sentences consisting of 44,789 words. A chart broke these down as follows:

[Table 4-1]
Viewpoint Distribution: Summary

	SENTENCES		WORDS	
	Number	*Percent*	*Number*	*Percent*
Viewpoint A	79	3.54	1,672	3.73
Viewpoint B	774	34.63	15,690	35.03
Viewpoint C	1,382	61.83	27,427	61.24
Totals	2,235	100.00	44,789	100.00

The above table shows that CBS Evening News gave preponderant (over 61 percent) attention to Viewpoint C and scant (under 4 percent) to Viewpoint A. Most of this disparity between C and A is attributable to the high proportion of Vietnam sentences (1,719 out of 2,235) and the high proportion (69.87 percent) of C material in these Vietnam sentences.[15]

Statisticians, including some of Dr. Lefever's colleagues at Brookings, who have examined the survey believe that the method of viewpoint coding was misleading. They question the technique of discarding 80 percent of the original news items extracted for examination and analyzing only the remaining 20 percent as if it were a broad sample of the national-defense and -security stories of the period. According to the Institute for American Strategy, the original plan included a "D" category. "If the national security item presented no viewpoint, it was designated as 'D,' " Lefever wrote.[16] At first a grand total of 1,396 CBS News news items were considered national-security news stories by IAS. Of these, 1,122 were dropped from the study because they were "D" items—meaning that no viewpoint was expressed. By dealing with only 274 of the original 1,396 items, the study deliberately excluded 80 percent of the news reports that by its own definition had no viewpoint. But a casual reader of the charts is led to believe that the carefully screened remaining 20 percent represents the total. By IAS's distorted yardstick, the "C" position received more time than the "A" and "B" positions combined. However, the "D," or neutral, viewpoints total more than four times as many as "A," "B" and "C" together.

The study also failed to take into account the obligation of a national news organization to report what the major candidates were saying. With Richard Nixon and George McGovern being the nominees whose views IAS labeled "B" and "C," and with no "A" candidate in the race, the hawk point of view was bound to be accorded less coverage. Also excluded from consideration was the complexion of the 1972 presidential campaign. If Senator Henry Jackson had won the Democratic nomination, there would have been more "B" and "A" views reflecting his hawkish stance on defense. Similarly, if George Wallace had not been shot and had continued his third-party candidacy, there would have been still further "A" views. Such a survey conducted in 1964, when Goldwater was running for President on a hawk platform, would almost automatically have shown CBS televising more "A" than "C" views. In addition, the study evaluated sentences spoken by CBS reporters such as Dan Rather and Marvin Kalb with the same weight as those of the public figures they were reporting. For example, Dan Schorr's account of the Democratic plank on amnesty was treated no differently than if he had personally advocated this "C" position. Even more serious is the selection of items and sentences scrutinized during June 1972 suggesting that the inclusion of Schorr's verbatim mention of "amnesty on an appropriate basis" was arbitrary when examined next to sentences that the study omitted. Immediately after Schorr's report, Cronkite quoted an official spokesman for Governor Wallace who charged that the platform "was a suicide note for the Democratic party."[17] Apparently this rebuttal was not included in the data. An even more curious omission is a thirty-second report on a revolutionary U.S. Air Force helicopter which fires missiles and destroys enemy weapons on the ground.[18] The film was supplied by the Defense Department, and was so identified by CBS; the Cronkite narration was positive, and yet it seemed to be ignored in the content analysis that presumed to examine CBS News coverage of national-security issues.

Equally baffling is the categorizing of a conversation on the consequences of defense budgeting between Defense Secretary Melvin Laird and Senator William Proxmire. Though he dissented from the drastic budget cuts that George McGovern proposed, Proxmire was placed in the same "C" category as the Democratic presidential candidate, whereas Laird's performance was given a "B" rating in spite of his dramatic allusion to surrender: "I would say that the thing to do if you go the $30 billion route is to direct the Department of Defense to spend at least a billion dollars in white flags so that it can run them up all over, because it means surrender."[19] In this emotional exchange with Senator Proxmire, Laird was telling the nation that McGovern's recommendations were a form of surrender. It appears that only IAS's pre-set programming that *all* Administration views were "B" prevented Laird's remarks from being tallied under the "A" column.

The study's analysis of Vietnam coverage offers another example of skewed coding. Senator Barry Goldwater's statements on Vietnam were labeled as "B" views in spite of such strong comments as this one, made on December 21, 1972: "I'm for bombing them and bombing them and bombing them, and keeping it up until they come to the table and say, 'I want to quit.' "[20]

The Institute for American Strategy defends placing such a statement in the "B" category because of its context: "Senator Goldwater's statement was made in support of President Nixon's renewal of the bombing in North Vietnam. Since government policies were classified as 'B,' this was so classified."[21] Similarly, South Vietnamese Foreign Minister Tran Van Lam's and Senator Strom Thurmond's statements were also classified as "B" because they, like the Nixon Administration, supported bomb strikes against the North. This technique of coding is based on what social scientists term a "floating center." In layman's language, this means that no matter how hawkish the Nixon Administration's position became, it remained by definition "B," thus shrinking the potential number of "A" statements that CBS could possibly broadcast, while simultaneously expanding the range of opinion that would be tabulated in the "C" category.

The consequences of a "floating center" meant that after December 18, 1972, when the Nixon Administration began the policy of bombing North Vietnamese harbors, only an advocate of total destruction of North Vietnam could be classified as making "A" statements. Under the same logic, all those who supported our Vietnam war effort but stopped short of endorsing massive bombing in the North would be transferred from the "B" to the "C" category.

On U.S. policy in Vietnam, the *TV and National Defense* study shows CBS News favoring "C" over "A" views in "Theme Analysis" by a ration of 5 to 1; in "Viewpoint Analysis," by 48 to

1; and in what it calls "Proper Name Analysis," by 36 to 1.[22] But in defining "A" as an extremely narrow category and "C" as an extremely broad one, it was virtually predetermined that such a bias would emerge. Some of this methodology is as worthy of scrutiny as what IAS was studying.

Ostensibly to demonstrate its coding technique, IAS published forty sentences from its "Viewpoint Analysis" purporting to represent the month of June 1972. Employing phrases such as "exactly as they were broadcast during June, 1972,"[23] the study induces the casual reader to believe that he is examining the total defense news output of the CBS Evening News for the thirty-day period. Dr. Lefever is careful to mention that "simply to shorten the example, we eliminated the 19 sentences that happened to fall on June 15."[24] Though they were used elsewhere in the study, there is no way for the reader to know which nineteen sentences were excised from the June 15 broadcast, or how they were categorized. Significantly, the reader is left unaware of the character of the particular news day—one marked by nervous skepticism and cautious approval because of a U.S.-Soviet arms-negotiations report. A viewing of the tape supplied by the Vanderbilt Television News Archive indicates that almost one third of the Cronkite program that evening was devoted to defense and Vietnam information—a particularly useful broadcast to study, it would seem.

To be specific, the June 15 program began with a two-minute, ten-second report by Dan Rather quoting President Nixon as saying that the SALT agreements were as significant as Woodrow Wilson's attempt to bring America into the League of Nations, and that it would be as much a tragedy if the Congress failed to ratify them. "Our clients," said the President, "are the children of future generations." Three senators and one congressman expressed approval or doubts about the SALT treaty, including Senator Jackson, who feared it would give the United States "sub-parity; they have fifty percent more in number of missiles. It's that simple." Rather predicted that the Moscow agreements would pass by a large majority, but added that President Nixon and his staff were "confident they will get through the programs they want for additional submarines and B-1 bombers."

Next was an extended Vietnam report highlighting the South Vietnamese victory at the battle of An Loc. "It will go down in history as the greatest victory in the history of warfare," said one American general. Also included was a brief report in which Senator Proxmire regretted that General John Lavelle, who had been forced to retire "because of twenty unauthorized air strikes in North Vietnam, had not been court-martialed." Another report dealt with Soviet President Nikolai Podgorny's visit to Hanoi, and the importance of the cancellation of American bombing of Hanoi for that period. In all, there was a wide variety of military and Vietnam stories, and it is difficult to understand why it was not an ideal night for the institute to include in its illustration.

Even granting the IAS admission that the June examples were merely to serve as illustrations, the casual reader of the study is left with the impression that this slender sample reflected most of CBS's coverage of defense issues for this thirty-day period. When one realizes that a very large percentage—approximately four fifths of the items—were eliminated because they had no point of view (the "D" category), it seems odd that in a 200-page book, a news day crowded with defense and Vietnam-related activities was excluded, especially when the nineteen sentences from June 15 represent one third of the true total June sample.

Dr. Lefever makes the point to interviewers that as a scholar he forbore watching Cronkite, instead studying the transcripts and abstracts from selected tapes provided by the Vanderbilt Television News Archive. But he and the IAS staff erred in depending on abstracts which are intended as a user's guide, rather than looking at the complete video tapes available from the same archive. An example in point is a Cronkite story on détente. In the chapter "News CBS Did Not Report," the study noted that "On December 12, 1972, CBS reported that the USSR announced a reduction of its military budget because of détente with the West."[25] This is what the abstract from the Vanderbilt archive says, but the videotape from the same source has an additional eleven words which change the meaning and would have changed the study's categorization. What Cronkite went on to say was, "But the official [Soviet] military figures aren't considered to be very reliable."[26] How many other views were incorrectly coded because the abstracts were, by definition, incomplete?

For a scientific study which pretends to analyze the omissions and distortions of a major news organization over a two-year period, there are omissions and distortions by the Institute for

American Strategy and by Lefever which far exceed any charges that they make. The IAS research team disregarded a clear-cut warning by the Vanderbilt archive that only its video tapes and not its abstracts should be used as the basis of research. Each of the monthly indexes and abstracts state on page one:

> The abstracts are primarily designed for identification of the news items for subsequent retrieval on the video tapes of the programs. The abstracts are condensations, not verbatim transcripts, and the words never should be attributed to the speakers as direct quotes, nor should they be cited as evidence of precisely what was or was not said on the news programs. The tapes themselves must be used for authoritative study, quotation, and reference.

Although *TV and National Defense* claims to have examined two years of news programing in depth and has as its subtitle "An Analysis of CBS News—1972–1973 Conducted by a Team of Scholars," the institute chose to ignore that Vanderbilt warning. Only on rare occasions did the team view the video tapes of the CBS Evening News for its 261 broadcasts of 1973. Clearly, the implication by the publisher and author is that a scrupulously scientific examination of all the video tapes from the Cronkite news had been made, and most of those reviewers who praised the study inferred this. But the fact is that IAS relied almost solely on the index and abstracts, or on Vanderbilt's categorization of CBS news items for 1973. Except for a handful of broadcasts, IAS ordered or leased no video tapes of the news programs, and because the Vanderbilt archive makes no transcripts of these broadcasts, the IAS analysts did not have access to those 1973 programs which they claimed to have scrutinized in detail.

When asked about this ambiguity nine months after publication of the study, Dr. Lefever made no pretense about it. "We depended almost completely on the Vanderbilt abstracts and indexes for 1973, except for a relatively few where we thought we detected minor contradictions. . . . We found the Vanderbilt abstracts extremely accurate and dependable. Except in rare instances, we did not order the video tapes from Vanderbilt." What this means to the reader of the IAS study—which includes the Federal Communications Commission—is that the critique of one of the two years under study is based on a reader's guide or index intended for identification and retrieval. It is as if scholars had attempted to evaluate the content of the *New York*

Times from its daily news index of what stories appeared in each edition.

Aside from the misuse of the Vanderbilt indexes and abstracts, there are subtle and obfuscating half-truths that prevent the reader from realizing that judgments and evaluations for 1973 were not based on video tapes or even transcripts. There are fleeting small-type mentions of the use of the abstracts and index: "We are informed by the Vanderbilt Television Archive that due to unavoidable mechanical imprecision an error of one minute is possible though not probable. . . ."[27] But in a report that intermingles an analysis of 1972 and 1973, and which is dominated by phrases that refer to the Vanderbilt video tapes ("All CBS Evening News broadcasts for 1972 and 1973 were examined by subject and theme analysis"[28] and "grappling with the transcripts for several months"[29]), it requires a linguistic detective to discover that in a study of a visual medium, tapes had been virtually ignored for one of the two years. With the built-in skew of a "floating center," the use of video tapes rather than abstracts may not have altered the results, but dependence upon secondary sources is shoddy practice for a study presuming to examine another organization's standards. What the reader, the FCC and CBS News deserved was a forthright disclaimer that only in rare instances were tapes studied of the 261 broadcasts for 1973. It is interesting to speculate about what IAS would have charged if it had discovered such an omission by CBS News.

By not screening many of the tapes, Lefever and the Institute for American Strategy may have lost much of the context and intensity of a given news day. To give a specific example, on August 24, 1972, *TV and National Defense* cites the CBS Evening News for missing a significant antidisarmament statement by Russia's M. A. Suslov and General V. G. Kulikov:

> *August 24, 1972:* The *New York Times* reported that M. A. Suslov, the top Soviet ideologue and a member of the Politburo, warned against U.S. Congressional attempts to put restrictive interpretations on the SALT I agreement and that General V. G. Kulikov made it clear there was no change in American "imperialism" or "aggressive plans."[30]

Lefever contrasts the above account in the *Times* with what he implies were the main events covered by the Cronkite program:

That evening, CBS News reported on the Bobby Fischer-Boris Spassky chess match in Iceland, a North Vietnamese assault in the Que Son Valley, and an attack against U.S. policy in Vietnam from Viet Cong spokesman, Madame Nguyen Thi Binh.[31]

The study clearly ignored the kind of news day August 24th was. (Lefever now concedes that he did not think it important enough to investigate.) On the previous night Richard Nixon had been renominated for a second term, and the Vanderbilt tape indicates that almost two thirds of the program's 22½ minutes was devoted to the first day of his campaign. But the opening and longest segment was an appearance by the Commander in Chief before the American Legion in Chicago. A strong national defense was the impassioned keynote of the President's address: "There are naturally some small anti-military activists who totally disagree . . . But I have never gambled, and I never will gamble with the safety of the American people under the false banner of economy. Instead of making moral heroes of a few hundred who deserted their country, let's honor the real heroes who have served their country."[32] The Legionnaires responded with a standing ovation. Later in the broadcast they were shown sitting on their hands when the Democratic candidate from South Dakota addressed them.

When the history of détente—a word that in 1975 Kissinger and his staff no longer liked—is finally written, it may well be concluded that most of the news media failed to provide sufficient coverage and analysis of the Soviet rhetoric and the Soviet terms. Preoccupied with the end of the Vietnam war and with President Nixon's summitry in Moscow and Peking, broadcast news organizations, like the majority of newspapers and magazines, may have accepted the spirit of détente as they did the spirit of Geneva during Eisenhower's era or the spirit of Glassboro when Johnson was exchanging bear hugs with Kosygin.

The IAS study may be right when it claims that too little of the "news hole" of the CBS Evening News in 1972 was filled with significant reports on national-security and foreign policy, other than Vietnam. (In newspapers and other forms of journalism, the "news hole" is a term for the amount of space left for news material after the advertising lineage is established; in television, it is the time between commercials.) The news hole in each of the three networks' evening news is 22½ minutes an evening, or approximately 97 hours a year. Cronkite and the producers of the CBS Evening News might well have preferred something more than the 1,537 minutes that the study indicates was devoted to defense and international affairs, particularly when 71 percent—1,092 minutes—of it was about Vietnam. This left only 445 minutes for the Middle East, USSR-U.S. relations, the SALT negotiations, China, international economics, and 3 minutes and 20 seconds on USSR military developments, according to the IAS figures.[33] But with a news hole of less than 100 hours per year, who is to say what stories—presidential elections, Watergate, space, crime, the economy, busing and civil rights, among others—should be minimized to make room for what IAS and Lefever believe to be the most crucial story of our times? Yet, says Lefever in disbelief, "CBS Evening News in 1972 gave more time to Vietnam each evening than to all reports of Soviet military developments for the entire year."

One of Lefever's colleagues at Brookings who specializes in content analysis suspects the motives of a study that measures a 22½-minute television program against the *New York Times*, which is a comprehensive journal of record and unique among newspapers. Lefever quotes a former CBS correspondent as stating that CBS considers itself to be the network of record. But by its very nature and make-up, television cannot purport to be a journal of record; even within the industry itself, yesterday's television does not lend itself to clipping and filing in a morgue or scrapbook. As Lefever's Brookings colleagues suggest, the analysis should have compared CBS to its network rivals.

There is another unique quality that distinguishes television from other media. Newspapers try to enlarge their readership by including special-interest stories, and the reader scans each page selecting that which concerns him. But in radio and television, stories are not subject to such selectiveness; the audience is compelled to listen to or watch an item, and if it holds no interest, a hand hits the dial. As yet there is no device to turn a broadcast page, and as long as the three nightly news broadcasts are in a rating race in which a few percentage points can cost a producer or anchorman his job, there will be resistance to complicated technical stories. Unfortunately, a comparison between, say, the Soviet Foxbat interceptor and the U.S. B-1 bomber is just such a story.

As a dozen zealots in a dozen other life-and-death areas—energy, the environment, unemployment, hunger, cancer, the cities—will testify, television slights them too. Columnist James J. Kilpatrick questioned the institute's complaints that CBS gave far more time on a given night to the trial of Angela Davis than to the mission of the armed services. "The trouble is that 'the mission isn't news,' " said Kilpatrick, "and put to a choice between reporting Admiral Moorer on Soviet submarines and covering the trial of Angela Davis, 99 editors out of a 100 would take the Davis trial." The Institute for American Strategy is obsessed with defense, he continued. "But a thousand other outfits have a thousand other newsworthy obsessions: abortion, gun control, fluoridation, organic gardening, racial balance busing, women's rights, historic preservation. It is likely that every one of them could compile a statistical violation of the fairness doctrine."[34]

In varying degrees such gripes are all correct, but 22½ minutes is a very short time in which to cover all the news of the day; moreover, as every broadcast journalist understands, some news stories lend themselves to the special grammar of television better than others. Lefever says that he would like the Cronkite news program to be more like the twenty-five-paragraph news roundup in the *Wall Street Journal*, and he dismisses the contention that television's time limitations are "an excuse for its distortions."

To be sure, all news does not require film or video tape, and the amount of time devoted to such "tell" stories is known as the "magic number." This varies between 6 and 7½ minutes from night to night, and is the amount of time that the anchormen have to report, in brief, on those important events which do not lend themselves to pictorial treatment. There is a constant tug of war between anchorman and producer to increase this "magic number," and with all the stresses and balances of producing a nightly news show, with various correspondents and bureau chiefs pushing their own "must" stories, there is constant disagreement among the staff about which stories are used and which ones sacrificed to the tyranny of the stopwatch. After Sputnik and throughout the early sixties, rocket and other weapons stories were a cinch to sell to an executive producer or an anchorman; after Vietnam and repeated moon landings, they have become a hard sell.

Ironically, in 1960 television was severely criticized for its emphasis on the missile gap and space race. On several occasions

President Eisenhower privately admonished CBS News for over-playing those stories to the advantage of the Kennedy-Johnson ticket. "You news people created the fiction of the missile gap as much as Kennedy," he once remarked to this broadcaster. At the same time, some liberals and environmentalists were accusing the media of manipulating public opinion, so that by 1970 we would "have one foot on the moon, while standing with the other foot deep in garbage." Such television documentaries as "Year of Polaris" and "Biography of a Missile" won numerous awards, while today in retrospective showings they are derided by journalism students who view them as "sales pitches for the military." It was another time, and disillusionment over the war in Southeast Asia had not yet caused many Americans to ques-tion the integrity of the Pentagon's intelligence, motives and planning. Part of this backlash, which crossed political party lines, may have conditioned the news media to de-emphasize military reporting other than Vietnam.

In *TV and National Defense* the CBS Evening News coverage of the Vietnam war was studied as a separate category. A total of 1,092 minutes was devoted to reporting the war, second only to the presidential election, to which 1,455 minutes was given. By tabulating 760 separate news items on Vietnam, the study concluded that CBS relayed a "picture . . . that bore little re-semblance to realities . . ." The Cronkite broadcast was accused of "Glamorizing the enemy," of "Deprecating our ally," and of "Placing the U.S. Government on the defensive." The study concluded: ". . . all evidence suggests that CBS Evening News employed various techniques of selective reporting and presenta-tion to advocate a position opposed to U.S. military involvement in Vietnam. It failed to present a full or fair picture of opposing viewpoints on the issues of peace negotiations, the problem of American POWs, the nature of the U.S. military presence, or—on a larger canvas—the significance to the United States of the struggle between Communist and non-Communist forces in South-east Asia."[35]

While the analysis concludes that critical themes on the evening news exceeded those supporting the U.S. and South Vietnam posi-tion by more than 4 to 1, it does concede that 42 percent of CBS's reporting of North Vietnam was of a critical nature.

According to the IAS study, CBS erred in not broadcasting

enough blunt statements by Soviet leaders intensifying "the ideological struggle" and "supporting all revolutionary forces of our times,"[36] and the failure of the Cronkite broadcast to present such "blunt views on détente" and its "constant barrage against the U.S. military" is attributed to several factors. "It is difficult to know to what extent this undeniable, anti-authority, anti-establishment bias was attributable to the disenchantment of CBS newsmen with Vietnam or to a larger and more persistent anti-military complex."[37] The study blames this on the same liberal bias that was Agnew's target, and states that CBS's reporting on Vietnam "At best . . . confused many listeners and at worst . . . bred a distrust of government authority and military responsibility . . ."[38]

Although *TV and National Defense* was released at a full-dress news conference, it wasn't until January of 1975 that CBS and the Institute for American Strategy had a public, face-to-face confrontation, when Dr. Lefever and CBS News senior vice-president William Small debated before the Women's National Republican Club. Lefever defended his analytical techniques and explained the underlying premise of the study—that fairness can be quantified: "The nearest discipline to fairness is justice, and our symbol of justice in the Anglo-Saxon world . . . is a woman holding a scales with a cloth around her eyes. Fairness is something that can be objectively determined. It's not like aesthetics and art; fairness is more akin to justice."[39]

When his turn came, Small labeled the IAS study unfair to the integrity of CBS News, but it was not until near the end of the ninety-minute debate, in response to a question from a woman in the audience about the patriotic content of CBS's reporting, that he explained his concept of the mission of a news organization: ". . . unfortunately, people in high places would like to have the news molded to their concept of what is patriotic. Dean Rusk once said this to me, as he has said it to other newsmen. '. . . Whose side are you on?' . . . It isn't our job to be on the side of someone. Our job is to present the good news and the bad news, the news that patriots love to hear and the news they don't want to hear. I am sure no one in this room wanted to hear the story of Mylai; but if there is anyone in this room who feels it should not have been reported because . . . it was a reflection on America, then they're just fooling themselves."[40]

*   *   *

The Institute for American Strategy invested slightly under $5,000 in acquiring video tapes from the Vanderbilt Television News Archive, primarily for 1972, but estimates that the entire study cost $300,000. It was an expensive exercise, but it has had impact. Hundreds of newspapers and commentators accepted the IAS indictment of CBS at face value. Other organizations will probably conduct studies of news coverage in a variety of different areas, and this should disturb no one, though each such analysis should be subject to examination. And it is to be hoped that such studies will not be conducted by the same special-interest group that finances them.

Some disturbing questions about the IAS study concern the uses it will be put to, and particularly its application to a Fairness Doctrine complaint. Ernest Lefever says that he has no personal interest in pursuing a fairness complaint, and that he still rarely watches the nightly news. According to him, such litigation "would be seventy-five percent public relations to keep the issue alive, and twenty-five percent legal. . . . It is really up to IAS, if they wish to press it with the FCC."

John Fisher is certain that the institute will proceed. "We had the complaint and documents ready in early June [1975], and then decided to monitor CBS for a few months to see if we could detect any improvement in their coverage of view 'A' and the general defense picture. But there's been no real change, and we've asked our Washington lawyers to proceed."

When the Federal Communications Commission examines such a complex and subjective complaint, it will be faced with a unique and precedent-making challenge. The complaint will rest on far different grounds than the total good-faith performance of the network and its stations, and on much more than the fairness of a single documentary like "Pensions" or a brief personal attack like that of Hargis on Cook. Fisher expects IAS to win, and he will ask the FCC "to order CBS to grant compensatory programming to correct the omissions and distortions of the past."

How can the Commission make such a judgment without retracing all the steps of the study, and how can it begin to do this without becoming a super-referee of content? How can it measure one news program, major though the Cronkite broadcast is, without considering CBS's total output: the hour-long morning news, *CBS Reports, 60 Minutes, Face the Nation,* and all its specials including space shots, presidential appearances and congressional hearings, as well as its network radio coverage of all these events?

This particular study, the Commission may find, is flawed because of the "floating center" error, the omissions and the other problems described. But suppose it were not flawed. Think what the FCC would be faced with in handling a complaint of this nature:

1. It must review what the controversial issue of public importance is, and what the relevant viewpoints on that issue are. IAS will claim one formulation of the issue and the viewpoints, and CBS another. CBS may well claim that its 24½ hours of special space coverage in 1972 and 1973, in addition to the almost three hours on the Cronkite news, are pertinent. The military aspects of those space missions may be secondary, but America's commitment to be "number one" in space is dependent on rocket capability, satellites, guidance and control systems and related ground-support installations. The Space Shuttle, a multibillion-dollar project, is jointly sponsored by NASA and by the Department of Defense, and its military implications equal its space applications. U.S. military officers have played key roles in the civilian space effort. The FCC examiners would thus have to make a decision: whether or not to weigh CBS's emphasis on space activities against its alleged short-changing of military news. This peripheral area is messy, amorphous and impossible.

2. Assuming that the FCC could find its way out of this swamp and that it knows precisely the scope of the issue and the particular significant views relevant to that issue, it must now examine every snippet broadcast by CBS over this two-year period and make a judgment: is it pro, anti or just neutral? In some cases this will be easy to judge, but in many, categorizing the material will really be subjective. Obviously this process, while permissible by media critics (although it leads to intractable controversy), is not proper business for the government.

3. Finally, assuming that the government has cleared both the above hurdles, it must now state that this compendium of figures—for overall time spent on particular views; frequency of presentation; times when presented (prime, Sunday afternoon, late night)—is reasonable or unreasonable. There are no magic formulae here—not even one for overall time, much less taking into account the other factors. On what basis will the FCC label some amalgam of figures unreasonable? No one knows—least of all the

FCC, as former Chairman Dean Burch has confessed in grappling with such problems and admitting to complete confusion.

What the Institute for American Strategy and others who attempt to codify journalism often fail to account for in their computations is the relationship of the total environment, and the impact of a given minute, hour, sentence or image. A single two-minute sequence of U.S. Marines using cigarette lighters to burn the huts in the village of Cam Ne in 1965 was one of those scenes equal to a million words. That incident is a vivid lesson on the contrast between newspaper and television news, and illustrates the fallacy of Lefever's hypothesis that content can be measured by word count alone. Even on radio, Morley Safer's account, complete with the sound of crackling huts and terrorized peasants, caused slight reaction, but the filmed report by the same reporter on television set off a groundswell of public reaction which continued throughout the night as the broadcast moved through the time zones across the nation.

In his study Lefever is concerned that all three networks, with their "inherent TV demand for vivid and dramatic images, [have projected] . . . an unduly negative image of America." He added, "The painfully vivid TV portrayal of the Vietnam war prompted CBS Newsman Roger Mudd to wonder 'whether in the future a democracy which has uncensored TV in every home will ever be able to fight a war however moral or just.' "[41] Some, such as Lefever and Fisher, would condemn television for such negative influence; others might decide it was worth the Nobel Peace Prize.

The Ernest Lefever of 1975 is convinced that "Nobody can fight a war that's watched in the living room every night, no matter how just that cause is," and he deplores this fact. He resents Cronkite's "emphasis" on casualty figures: "I'm convinced that every night Cronkite was reporting the casualty figures, he was saying to the audience that the Vietnam war was cruel, inhuman and unjust." (If one takes a second look at twenty of those broadcasts in which the Pentagon's weekly list of casualties was reported, it appears to this observer that Cronkite, like Chancellor and Reasoner, read them straight.)

When the FCC considers the IAS list of grievances against one network, it might also consider Justice Potter Stewart's words: "Newspapers, television networks, and magazines have been outrageously abusive, untruthful, arrogant and hypercritical. But it hardly follows that elimination of a strong and independent press is the way to eliminate abusiveness, untruth, arrogance or hypocrisy from government itself."[42]

Justice Stewart also likes to point out that the Constitution is "neither a Freedom of Information Act, nor an Official Secrets Act." The Constitution poses the conflict of interest between government and the press, but it cannot resolve it. For one branch of government to regulate the amount and point of view of journalistic investigation of another branch—in this case the defense establishment—is as unthinkable as it is unworkable. Even if the Institute for American Strategy is right, the FCC and federal courts cannot referee the process by which information is collected and distributed to the American public, without bringing the federal government into the news process.

John Chancellor, who has worked in both journalism and government, where he was director of the Voice of America, is convinced that "Government cannot operate a news-gathering organization, and all attempts by government to control it or even administer it inevitably end by altering it." A mutation of the journalistic process may be an effective way to inform the public by offering them a safely edited version of official handouts, but as Chancellor points out, "it will not be journalism."

When it began, broadcasting did not consider journalism one of its basic ingredients, and serious broadcast journalism, as pioneered by Edward Klauber, Elmer Davis and Ed Murrow, and now practiced by hundreds of professionals at commercial and public stations, may not be able to survive in an atmosphere in which fairness is the government-mandated condition of a "free press." Television and radio are a vital element of that press, but it may turn out that the licensing of those franchises will force them to be so responsive to government agencies that what is left cannot truly be called journalism. This would be a tragic outcome to the government's aspirations, because most people depend on broadcasting for most of their news and information. This vast audience may not represent the citizens most concerned with serious national and international events, but those citizens have a role in the making of the mosaic that we call public opinion.

Before the courts have finished looking at broadcasting and the Bill of Rights, they may determine that television and radio are so powerful, that they offer such limited access, that their content must be minutely regulated. If the Institute for American Strat-

egy wins its demand for compensatory time, there will be a pro-
liferation of similar cases from every kind of pressure group—
including those who wish America to disarm completely. The
limitations and price of continuing to run responsible broadcast
news organizations could put their survival in jeopardy.

The IAS study and fairness complaint may soon cause the issue
of governmental control of broadcast content to be tested. Regardless of its merits, it is an idea in fairness regulation whose time
was bound to come. Ever since the FCC ordered the station in
Red Lion to grant Fred Cook free time, it was inevitable that
a complainant would ask for compensatory programing or for a
license denial based on content analysis.

The Institute for American Strategy proposes that this compen-
sation might consist of "one or two documentaries written from
'A' perspective." Of course, it is possible that the IAS lawyers will
persuade its clients to drop the complaint, or that the FCC will
dismiss it as having no merit. Nevertheless, the impact and implications of the Fisher-Lefever study cannot be dismissed. The research burden and legal costs of defending every such complaint
could come to hundreds of thousands of dollars and take years to
litigate. Some stations, or even a network, might decide that the
stamina needed for such investigation and litigation would strain
serious journalism beyond its means.

Moreover, if the FCC decides to investigate the IAS charges, a
new era of the Fairness Doctrine will have begun. A concluding
paragraph in *TV and National Defense* foreshadows the duties
that the FCC will have to shoulder because of the increasing flow
of fairness complaints. "If this occurs," Lefever anticipates with
enthusiasm, "the FCC may need a larger professional staff to process the heavier case load with all deliberate speed."[43]

On November 24, 1975, John Fisher told a class at the Columbia
Graduate School of Journalism that the IAS Fairness Doctrine
complaint would be filed with the FCC immediately after the first
of the year. As this chapter went to the binder, IAS had not yet
delivered its formal complaint. Some observers suspect that in the
end Fisher and his board will stop just short of entering costly
litigation. Whether or not an actual case develops from this study,
what emerges is an alarming demonstration of the dangers inherent in the proposition that the Fairness Doctrine can be
strictly applied to the vagaries of news content.

12

FAIR VS. FREE:
Squaring Tornillo
and Red Lion

~~~~~~

*The myth of the free press . . . has lumped
together the fighting colonial printer-editor
John Peter Zenger and the modern newspaper
chains and media conglomerates. The myth
says that if the press is kept "free," liberty of
discussion is assured. But in how few hands is
left the exercise of "freedom."*

JEROME A. BARRON, FREEDOM
OF THE PRESS FOR WHOM?

If there were no scarcity of broadcast frequencies, most arguments
for the Fairness Doctrine would disappear. If in the absence of
scarcity the government could still justify the constitutionality
of a Fairness Doctrine for television and radio, would it not follow that there was a compelling rationale for such a doctrine to
regulate newspapers and magazines? In fact, such serious scholars
of the Bill of Rights as Professor Jerome A. Barron of George
Washington University have advocated just such right-of-reply
laws. His book *Freedom of Speech for Whom?* is the definitive
document on this interpretation. "Attention is at last being given
to the idea that the First Amendment grants protection to others
in the opinion-making process besides those who own the media
of communication,"[1] he writes in his book. Professor Barron
played a prominent role in the case known as *Miami Herald* v.
Tornillo, and while it was being fought out in the courts, news-

papers all over the country suddenly became aware of the threat
of the Fairness Doctrine.

Patrick Tornillo, Jr., and Fred Cook have never met and know
little about each other's landmark cases, yet their complaints are
almost mirror images of each other. With the assistance of Professor Barron, Tornillo, the leader of the Dade County Teachers
Union, challenged the Miami *Herald* in what became the Fairness
Doctrine test case for newspapers. Understanding *Tornillo* and
its outcome provides a perspective for *Red Lion,* for each case
focused on virtually the same issue—the right of reply enforced by
government—and both were unanimous decisions. However, for
reasons that will emerge, neither the words "Red Lion" nor "Fairness Doctrine" appear any place in the *Tornillo* opinion.

In 1972 the Miami *Herald* published two editorials attacking
Tornillo, who was running for the Florida State Legislature. Both
editorials, published just prior to the primary, argued that the
nomination of the executive director of the teachers union would
be "inexcusable." The newspaper objected to Tornillo's leader-
ship of a recent teachers' strike in Dade County· "We cannot say
it would be illegal but certainly it would be inexcusable of the
voters if they sent Pat Tornillo to Tallahassee . . ."[2] In answer,
Tornillo wrote letters stating that he had done nothing illegal, and
demanded that the newspaper print his replies. He delivered his
demands for space in person, accompanied by his lawyer and a
copy of a fifty-year-old Florida statute which extended to each
candidate for public office the right to free space in which to reply
to a newspaper's attack on his character or record. Outraged by
the fact that he came accompanied by counsel threatening legal
action, the *Herald* turned down Tornillo. In its journalistic judgment, the candidate did not lack access, and in its legal opinion,
the right-of-reply statute was a violation of the First Amendment.

Tornillo lost the primary decisively and brought suit against
the *Herald* under the Florida reply statute, which had never before been tested in the state's courts. The case attracted national
attention both because the Florida Supreme Court upheld the
fifty-year-old law, and because Professor Barron had represented
Tornillo. Supported by the amicus curiae briefs of other major
newspapers and broadcasters, the *Herald* appealed the case to the
Supreme Court of the United States, where it was argued on April
24, 1974.

The *Miami Herald* v. *Tornillo* case centered on the First Amendment. The issue was simply whether the Florida statute furthered the goals of—and was consistent with—the constitutional protections of the press.

On argument day before the Supreme Court, Barron contended that some regulation of the press would be permissible as long as it served an overriding public purpose. He claimed that the Florida statute did not detract from free expression but added to it. Barron's language was almost interchangeable with the words of Solicitor General Erwin Griswold in *Red Lion.*

Representing the Miami *Herald,* Florida attorney Daniel Paul told the Supreme Court that Tornillo had not been censored by the newspaper, and that as boss of the classroom teachers union, Tornillo was a controversial public figure who did not have to rely on a paragraph in the Miami *Herald* to answer the attacks on him. Paul's main line of reasoning was that compulsion to print is equal to censorship under the First Amendment. The ultimate issue, he argued, is who decides what gets into a newspaper, the editors of the Miami *Herald* or the Florida Legislature.

There was some disagreement at the *Herald* as to whether Tornillo's letter should have been published. "I always thought we should have printed the damn letter voluntarily," said a high-ranking executive at the *Herald.* "But once the state tried to force us to print it, we had no choice but to fight it out in the courts."

To no one's surprise, Tornillo lost his case. The mood of the Court was evident long before the publication of the decision, in a comment made during oral arguments by Justice Harry Blackmun: "I want to ask a question—no, I guess I want to make a statement—for better or for worse we have opted in this country for a free press, not fair debate."

In the Court's unanimous decision, Chief Justice Burger restated this: "It has yet to be demonstrated how governmental regulation of this crucial process [the choice of material to go into a newspaper] can be exercised consistent with First Amendment guarantees of a free press."[3] Broadcasters who rejoiced in the sweeping tones of Burger's opinion hastened to compare it to the contrasting language of *Red Lion:* "But . . . we hold that Congress and the [Federal Communications] Commission do no violate the First Amendment when they require a radio or television station to give reply time to answer personal attacks and political editorials."[4]

There seemed to be a stunning contradiction between the two cases, and communications lawyers read the *Tornillo* opinion in a futile search for a *Red Lion* citation. The omission was no accident. Several of the Justices wished to explain why Red Lion Broadcasting and the rest of the broadcast industry were not entitled to the protections accorded to the Miami *Herald* under the First Amendment, but Chief Justice Burger and the majority thought it essential to make *Tornillo* a unanimous decision. However, the inclusion of language in *Tornillo* reaffirming *Red Lion* as being a different problem because of the scarcity issue would have cost the votes of Douglas and Stewart. Douglas, who supported the Miami *Herald* absolutely, made it clear that he would not vote for an opinion which would have the effect of strengthening the Fairness Doctrine. (He never stopped reminding his colleagues that he was absent when *Red Lion* was argued.)

The significance of the omission of any *Red Lion* citation was not lost on constitutional authorities such as Paul Freund of Harvard Law School. "What is remarkable about the *Tornillo* Opinion . . . is not that it failed to apply the precedent of *Red Lion*," wrote Freund, "but that it did not discuss the precedent at all. Perhaps the explanation lies in the fact that the right of reply even in the broadcast field is on shaky footing. Two members of the Court, Justices Douglas and Stewart, have elsewhere expressed serious doubts about the soundness of the Red Lion case. Perhaps in the circumstances Chief Justice Burger writing the *Tornillo* opinion chose to let sleeping lions lie."[5]

While most broadcasters and their lawyers feel strongly that *Tornillo* and *Red Lion* contradict each other, most of the Justices saw no reason to cite *Red Lion* in *Tornillo*. In *Red Lion* the Court had clearly stated: "There is nothing in the First Amendment which prevents the Government from requiring a licensee to share his frequency with others . . ."[6]

The focal point of the contradiction between the two cases is the scarcity argument. Aside from this theoretical distinction, squaring *Red Lion* and *Tornillo* is difficult. The Justices based their reasoning on the premise that because of frequency limitations, radio and television can only operate with government approval, whereas print is open to all.

Unfortunately, this philosophic rationale collides with reality. For example, there are far more television and radio stations available in the Red Lion–York market than there are newspapers in Miami. In fact, the Miami *Herald* dominates southern Florida like a colossus, while WGCB is a weak daytime signal which even in its primary Pennsylvania market is but one of a multitude of voices.

The real difference is that the Miami *Herald,* part of the Knight empire, won its virtual monopoly by economic survival in a time of fading competition, while WGCB has its exclusive place on the dial by order of the FCC. Unlike in the newspaper field, the government (FCC) put WGCB on the air, and enjoined all others from using its frequency in that area. And it did so on the grounds that WGCB would act as a public trustee or fiduciary. In point of fact, it is much easier to acquire a radio station—and perhaps even a television station—in Pennsylvania or Florida than it is to acquire or found a daily newspaper. All such ventures are virtual monopolies, but the varying reasons for the economic health of each medium are academic and not truly relevant to the consumer of news.

True, the Miami *Herald,* whose circulation is 396,797,[7] requires no government license, but except for a weak afternoon newspaper (the Cox chain's Miami *News,* which is printed in the same plant with the same advertising staff), the *Herald* is far less vulnerable to competition than the six VHF and three UHF television stations in the area.[8] The *Herald* is a giant, and its virtual monopoly is the result of its journalistic good management and of economic survival of the fittest.

Professor Barron points out that the 1970 Newspaper Preservation Act is government intrusion into the economic life of newspapers, and argues that "if Congress has constitutional power to enact legislation to encourage diversity of viewpoint in the press, the Congress can enact legislation to give readers rights of access to the press."[9] But the courts do not consider such antitrust exemptions analogous to government involvement in broadcast regulation. Both media are tightly controlled, one by economic strictures, the other by government license, and while both controls may affect the public equally, they are considered distinctly different by the Supreme Court.

Fred Cook won his case because the Supreme Court said that a government agency, the FCC, had the legal right to decide what a station is required to broadcast in order "to preserve an uninhibited marketplace of ideas."[10] Tornillo lost because the Court declared that it was unconstitutional for a state to order a newspaper to grant the right of reply to a person who had been attacked editorially.

What these two decisions suggest, and what the Supreme Court assumes, is that newspapers and other printed publications fully qualify for the protections of the First Amendment, while television and radio do not. The U.S. Court of Appeals once noted: "Written messages are not communicated unless they are read, and reading requires an affirmative act. Broadcast messages, in contrast, 'are in the air.' "[11] Stated another way, the government can be the ultimate referee for what Cronkite or Chancellor or their producers believe to be fair, because the stations which carry them are licensed, but it may not intrude on the news judgments of James Reston, *Time* or *Rolling Stone*, because the printed press is not subject to licensing.

The Supreme Court does not necessarily imply that broadcasting is second-class journalism—just that it is different: "This is not to say that the First Amendment is irrelevant to . . . broadcasting . . . but . . . It is the right of the viewers and listeners, not the right of the broadcasters, which is paramount."[12] The Court has consistently reserved for the printed press First Amendment protections which it is not prepared to extend to other, more recently developed channels of communication.

But the fact remains that Tornillo and Cook shared a common grievance: each felt he had been unfairly attacked and sought to defend himself. Two different media controlled their entry—the Miami *Herald* by its economic dominance; WGCB by its possession of a government franchise in Red Lion—but the Court determined that different rules apply.

If the people's right to know is the primary goal of a free press, and if government regulation of the crucial editorial process threatens the flow of information to the citizenry, does it matter how the instrument of communication acquired its power, even its monopoly?

Since most Americans today receive most of their news from broadcast sources, as survey after survey indicates, it follows that the protections of the First Amendment now only apply to the media which serve a minority of the population. Moreover, most citizens who get their news from daily newspapers live in communities where a single company owns the one or two newspapers in the town. Ninety-five percent of the major cities in America are now single-ownership towns, and some conglomerates, such as Knight-Ridder, have a circulation in excess of four million per day. Is this degree of monopoly not to be feared? If so, is the threat any less dangerous than that of a television or radio station, or network, even if the electronic monopoly is an accident of technology and the result of government license?

A prominent communications attorney who filed amicus curiae briefs for clients in both *Red Lion* and *Tornillo* contends that it is impossible to square the two cases. Although he has defended many broadcast clients against the Fairness Doctrine, he carefully stops short of denouncing it. "If you could hear some of those station owners at conventions," he says, "you'd worry about deregulation too. These owners, even if they are my clients, feel it is their air and that they own it, and no damn government is going to tell them who or what to put on their air. They claim it's theirs and they're going to use it for the purpose it was intended—to make money."

In spite of the ritual of renewal, most radio and television franchises are licenses virtually in perpetuity. And though there are enterprising stations and inadequate ones, responsible and irresponsible managements, their survival in the marketplace has only a marginal relationship to their performance in the arena of ideas.

That "license to print money,"[13] as Lord Thompson and some U.S. broadcasters have called it, includes the mandate to be a "public trustee," as the FCC puts it; the courts define the responsibility as a "fiduciary with obligations to present those views and voices which are representative of [the] community and which otherwise, by necessity, [would] be barred . . ."[14] This mandate is what so many serious broadcast journalists find discriminatory.

The Supreme Court's inability to cope with *Red Lion* and *Tornillo* in the same opinion suggests that it recognizes the inherent contradiction of the two cases.

13

ESCAPING THE
EITHER/OR TRAP

*For even when the editor is scrupulously
fair . . . fairness is not enough. There may
be several other sides, unmentioned by any of
the organized, financed and active partisans.*

WALTER LIPPMANN,
PUBLIC OPINION

*"I had hoped that you could unscrew the
unscrewable and enable me to understand
the difference between passing on the truth
and passing on whether the news is slanted."*

SENATOR SAM ERVIN
IN EXAMINING WITNESS,
FCC CHAIRMAN DEAN BURCH,
OCTOBER 20, 1971

*Impossible though they [the Bill of Rights]
be of literal interpretation, like a statute, as
counsels of moderation rather than as parts
of our constituent law, they represent a mood,
an attitude towards life, deep rooted in any
enduring society.*

JUDGE LEARNED HAND,
SPIRIT OF LIBERTY

When John Pastore was growing up in Providence in the early
twenties, he was exposed to the rantings of Jacob Conn, who
owned the Olympia Theater in Olneyville Square and used sta-

tion WCOT to push his particular brand of bigotry. "Jakey" Conn, who operated his 50-watt transmitter as his own "mouthpiece,"[1] was closed down by the Federal Radio Commission because he utilized it "for promotion of his own candidacy for Mayor of Providence, for expressing his views on all private matters [including the sex habits of a prominent industrialist], and as a medium for his attacks on his numerous personal enemies."[2] One of these was U.S. Senator Jesse Metcalf, who, Conn charged, was a member of the Ku Klux Klan, "a yellow dog"[3] and an exploiter of slaves. Pastore and others who lived in Rhode Island in the era of the crystal set have never quite forgotten that shrill voice from Olneyville Square.

At sixty-eight and in his last term, Senator Pastore, chairman of the powerful Subcommittee on Communications, is concerned with violence, obscenity, children's programing, public television and satellites, but he still talks about Jakey Conn: "If you didn't have a Fairness Doctrine, you might have the return of the likes of Conn. Do you want that?"

The senator believes that the First Amendment is an act of political genius. He also believes in the Fairness Doctrine as "a distillation of those lofty principles" laid down by Jefferson and Madison. He encourages broadcasters to do more in-depth documentaries and bold reporting, and believes the Fairness Doctrine is a "unique guideline" to assist journalists and protect the public. "When you consider the Fairness Doctrine in its essence and strip it of all the legal niceties, what it says to the broadcaster is simply, 'do your almighty best to assure that your listeners and viewers are fully and fairly informed on all issues of public importance you choose to present.' "[4]

There can be little criticism of the aspirations embodied in the present Fairness Doctrine. Taken as a signpost for the course of conduct for licensees to follow, its dictates are a noble goal. However, the controversy is not about the initial intent of the regulation, but about the manner in which the Federal Communications Commission has chosen to attain those goals. "This situation is ready-made for regulation by lifted eyebrow," said Robert Kintner when he was chief executive officer of NBC.

Supporters of the Fairness Doctrine believe that it is needed to prevent stations from acting like Jakey Conn, George A. Richards of WJR in Detroit or WLBT in Mississippi. The responsible station has nothing to fear, Doctrine supporters argue; a station should *want* to be fair. If there is a fairness complaint, its possible transgression is weighed by the Commission and the courts, and even if that transgression is occasionally found to be unreasonable, this doesn't put the station's license in jeopardy. It only means that the public hears more robust debate, which according to Doctrine proponents proves that the Fairness Doctrine reinforces the First Amendment.

Opponents of the Doctrine—who cross all political boundaries from Nat Hentoff to William Buckley—vigorously dispute this, and just as strongly they place their reliance on the First Amendment. It is the heavy hand of government, they argue, that is trying to ensure fairness by broadcast editors. Further, foes of the Doctrine remind us of what the Supreme Court said in 1974 in *Miami Herald* v. *Tornillo:*

> The choice of material to go into a newspaper, and the decisions made as to limitations on the size and content of the paper, and treatment of public issues and public officials—whether fair or unfair—constitutes the exercise of editorial control and judgment. It has yet to be demonstrated how governmental regulation of this crucial process can be exercised consistent with First Amendment guarantees of a free press as they have evolved to this time.[5]

Shouldn't this guarantee apply equally to broadcast journalism? Practitioners like Bill Small of CBS News ask, "Doesn't that inequity make broadcasters second-class journalists?" Critics of the Doctrine point to the activities of the Kennedy, Johnson and Nixon administrations to show the dangers of governmental supervision of the media. They remember when, after the flush of the 1972 landslide, Clay T. Whitehead as Director of Telecommunications Policy for President Nixon said that local broadcasters must be "responsible." But like "law and order," "responsible" was a code word to Whitehead; to him, it meant that the local station should take steps to end "ideological plugola" in the news, correcting a situation where "so-called professionals . . . dispense elitist gossip in the guise of news analysis."[6] Whitehead threatened station managers at license renewal time "who fail to act to correct imbalance or consistent bias from the networks."[7] He also used the Doctrine in a carrot-and-stick approach which in effect promised that the Administration would fight to get the broadcasters a five-year license (instead of the present three-year term) in return for their squelching anti-Administration viewpoints on network news programs.

Opponents of the Doctrine also point to the anomalies in its application. Sitting in his office on the third floor of the Post Office Annex in Providence, only four miles from where Jakey Conn used to broadcast, Senator Pastore is frank to concede these paradoxes and inconsistencies.

Q.: Senator, the Fairness Doctrine only applies to news and public affairs?

PASTORE: That's correct.

Q.: Isn't that inconsistent when the real impact of television is in the entertainment schedule, whose programs are also involved in controversial issues?

PASTORE: What about them?

Q.: Well, let's take *Maude*. They did a program about—

PASTORE: About abortion. I saw it. Pretty amusing.

Q.: And Archie Bunker did a program about birth control—

PASTORE: Yes, I saw that.

Q.: —as did Marcus Welby. And *The Mary Tyler Moore Show* did an episode about reporters' shield laws. Some people might think there were several sides to that controversy.

PASTORE: That's right.

Q.: And only recently ABC broadcast an entertainment motion picture about the Cuban missile crisis of 1962, using actors to portray the President and his advisers. It didn't happen to be very controversial, but if it had been about the Bay of Pigs or Tonkin Gulf or a film about law and order, there might have been opposing views.

PASTORE: Yes.

Q.: Well, doesn't it seem inconsistent to you that the FCC will tell the documentary and news people what fairness is and how to correct it, but don't do so to the producers of Archie Bunker, or on a re-enactment of the missile crisis?

PASTORE (*pounding his desk*): Absolutely not. That would be censorship!

Pastore's reasoning is based on the fact that since there are so many entertainment shows, the content of a particular program tends to be balanced by similar programs with a different point of view. Nevertheless, is there any justification for considering the Fairness Doctrine censorship when applied to entertainment programs, but perfectly proper when applied to news programs—the very material most entitled to First Amendment protection against government intrusion? If a station broadcast 80 percent news and only 20 percent entertainment, would it render the Fairness Doctrine redundant? Should the all-news radio stations be immune? Certainly they provide a wide spectrum of views.

The price of such rules for news has been a dangerously neutral and bland journalism. Opponents of the Doctrine assert—as do several former FCC commissioners—that one result of such regulation has been an inevitable slide into content analysis. In its current role of super-editor, the FCC may determine whether a documentary such as "Pensions" is balanced, or may act as a "fairness broker" to settle political complaints—as in the 1970 *Fair Committee*[8] decision that embraced complaints from opposite ends of the political spectrum.

Nor does it make sense to arm the FCC with stopwatches and calculators so that they can analyze by the time spent how fairly a network's nightly news has covered a continuing issue. In testimony before the Pastore committee, Henry Geller stressed the absurdity of this stopwatch technique as applied to NBC's coverage of the Alaska pipeline:

DATE OF BROADCAST	PRO-PIPELINE	ANTI-PIPELINE
June 7, 1970	4:40	5:35
September 10, 1970	:20	1:00
January 13, 1971	:06	:15
February 14, 1971	—	:10
February 16, 1971	:49	1:05
February 24, 1971	:15	1:30
February 28, 1971	1:32	—
June 4, 1971	1:58	—
July 11, 1971	:27	2:15
August 6, 1971	:45	1:10
August 26, 1971	—	:15
September 15, 1971	—	8:00
Total	10:52	21:15[9]

This analysis was stimulated by a complaint from the Wilderness Society over Esso commercials favoring the pipeline; the FCC's box score, providing a detailed, by-second count of NBC's coverage, purported to illustrate how the network had covered the pipeline news story. The FCC's minute-and-second count prove little, for they cannot measure the impact of the various treatments; for example, the analysis does not indicate that the ten-minute report on June 7, 1970, was on a weekend, when news audiences are comparatively small.

Fairness Doctrine detractors are particularly concerned about the burden on the small station. For instance, a Spokane television station was subjected to a thirty-month hassle over one fairness complaint about its editorials supporting Expo '74. Eventually the station was found to have been "fair" by the FCC, but at the cost of 480 man hours in station-management time, over $20,000 in legal fees, and with its license renewal held up during the complaint process.[10]

There has been the same interference with larger stations. WBBM-TV, the CBS-owned station in Chicago, had to submit to a long hearing, costing hundreds of thousands of dollars in legal fees, about alleged news staging because of a series on its evening newscasts about "pot parties" at Northwestern University. Admittedly, the ethics of the reporter (who had just graduated from Northwestern) appear to have been questionable. If he did not "stage" the marijuana party, the evidence before the FCC indicates that his zeal to demonstrate the widespread use of marijuana on college campuses caused him to go further than a journalist should in arranging for such an event to occur when cameras, lights and microphones were to be present. Paying participants even a few dollars to defray the costs of such a happening is unacceptable. CBS executives, from the Chicago general manager all the way up to Frank Stanton, were brought to Washington to testify before both the FCC and Congressman Harley O. Staggers' House Committee on Interstate and Foreign Commerce on why such journalistic practices were not better policed. In the end, the Commission lectured CBS for "a serious mistake and an inadequate report to the Commission . . . of deficient policies in . . . investigative journalism."[11]

While the FCC held up renewal for eighteen months, it stressed that WBBM-TV's valuable license was not "in jeopardy since such action would be to discourage robust wide-open debate on controversial issues."[12] However, the Commission did order CBS "to make appropriate revisions in its policies (including especially those with respect to its supervisory responsibilities) in order to make every reasonable effort to prevent recurrence of this type of mistake."[13] Commissioner Nicholas Johnson, himself an advocate of the Fairness Doctrine, dissented from the majority, believing that the order amounted to censorship. "This Commission should bend over backwards to encourage courageous investigative journalism—not reach out to stifle it."[14] Some FCC staff members agreed that in this case the government had gone too far in attempting to oversee a network's news-gathering policies.

Since 1969, the Commission had attempted to maintain a "hands-off policy" on allegations of slanted or staged news events. Even after the 1968 Democratic National Convention in Chicago, where a rash of complaints charged all three networks with covering and editing the riots in such a manner "as to present a distorted picture," the FCC refused to intrude in order to ascertain what truly had occurred the night of Hubert Humphrey's nomination for President. The Commission decided that to make a finding "of bias" by comparing truth to what the networks had actually broadcast [would] not be "appropriate for this Government licensing agency. It is important that the public understand that the fairness doctrine is not concerned with fairness in this sense. . . . We do not sit as a review body of the 'truth' concerning news events."[15]

Another case was the prize-winning documentary "Hunger in America," which opened as follows: "Hunger is easy to recognize when it looks like this. This baby is dying of starvation. He was an American. Now he is dead."[16] The charge by San Antonio Hospital officials that the scene had been falsified was considered by the FCC to be beyond its purview. The producer of the CBS broadcast, Martin Carr, testified that at the time, the hospital social worker told him "that the infant . . . died as the result of maternal malnutrition."[17] The hospital official for social work recalls saying that "there were high incidence of premature births due to malnutrition in mothers,"[18] but denied identifying any specific infant. The FCC refused to adjudicate the conflict and particularly to enter "the quagmire of investigating the credibility of the newsman and the interviewed party in such a type of case."[19]

Such government intervention, said the Commission, would be "a worse danger than the possible rigging itself,"[20] and it referred the alleged distortion in the program back "to the licensee for its own investigation and appropriate handling."[21]

Even in "The Selling of the Pentagon,"[22] the one-hour documentary that made broadcast history because it produced another major confrontation between Congressman Staggers' House Committee on Interstate and Foreign Commerce and CBS president Frank Stanton, the FCC declined to involve itself in adjudicating fairness. The program, produced by Peter Davis and narrated by Roger Mudd, charged that the Department of Defense spent $30 million a year in public-relations activities "to convince and persuade the public on vital issues of war and peace," and "that the military is a runaway bureaucracy selling the theory that America's role is to be 'the cop on every beat in the world.'" After the broadcast, military officers who had appeared in the documentary charged that their statements had been distorted by unfair editing and misrepresentation. Louisiana Congressman F. Edward Hébert, chairman of the Armed Services Committee, who had also appeared on the program, attacked it as "one of the most un-American things I've ever seen on the screen."[23] CBS provided considerable air time to its critics, and rescheduled the show one month later with film clips of its most vocal detractors stating their objections, followed by a rebuttal by CBS News president Richard Salant.

Though there were some minor errors of fact, none of those who attacked the documentary were able to counter its central thrust. Further, speaking for the FCC, Chairman Burch wrote to Chairman Staggers: "Lacking extrinsic evidence or documents that on their face reflect deliberate distortion, we believe that this government licensing agency cannot properly intervene. It would be unwise and probably impossible for the Commission to lay down some precise line of factual accuracy—dependent always on journalistic judgment—across which broadcasters must not stray. As we stated in the *Hunger in America* ruling, 'the Commission is not the national arbiter of the truth' . . . It would involve the Commission deeply and improperly in the journalistic functions of broadcasters."[24] Nor, the FCC said, could it determine in such circumstances whether editing involved deliberate distortion. Burch concluded: "Our objective is to encourage broadcast journalism, not to hurt or hinder it . . . For what ultimately is at stake in this entire matter is broadcasting's own reputation for probity and reliability, and thus its claim to public confidence."[25]

But Staggers refused to let "The Selling of the Pentagon" controversy drop, charging "Deception in broadcast news is like a cancer in today's society."[26] He asked his committee to subpoena Frank Stanton so that it could investigate the way CBS had edited the various interviews. When the CBS president agreed to appear, but without the footage and other materials demanded by the committee, and refused "to answer any questions that may be addressed to me relating to the preparation of 'The Selling of the Pentagon,' " the Committee voted to hold Stanton in contempt of Congress.[27]

There was every expectation that the full House of Representatives would sustain the citation. There were, however, some surprising speeches by such anti-media congressmen as Jack Edwards of Alabama, who told the full House, "I would not run CBS as Dr. Stanton does, not by a long shot. But Mr. Speaker, that is not the issue here today. You know, Dr. Stanton's problem is that he is right this time, but he has cried wolf so long that nobody believes him . . . When Vice President Agnew and others have taken the press to task, Stanton has cried like a stuck pig . . . He does not understand that we have as much right and duty to criticize the press as it has to criticize us . . . And frankly, I would like to stick it to him now. But my friends, we overstep our bounds and exceed our prerogatives, and offend the Constitution when we attempt by subpoena to go behind a news story or a television broadcast."[28]

Eventually Stanton and CBS won their case, not so much because of the First Amendment conscience of the Congress, as by some last-minute corporate strategy in which virtually every CBS affiliate put pressure on its local congressmen.* The House

---

* On November 26, 1975, *Variety* reported that the Nixon White House staff had made a deal with CBS to influence Republican congressmen to vote against the Staggers contempt citation in return for more favorable treatment of Nixon policies. Charles Colson, special counsel to the President, was the source of the information, but he admitted that his meeting with Frank Stanton, president of CBS, had taken place two or three days after the congressional vote. Dr. Stanton admitted that a meeting had taken place but denied to the *New York Times* (November 27) that "he had ever asked Colson or anyone in the White House for help in halting the contempt move."

208

voted 226 to 181 to send the Staggers contempt motion back to committee, where it died. Professor Jerome Barron, who supported the contempt resolution, wrote that the feeling among Staggers' allies was that they lost because "legislators . . . feared the CBS affiliates around the country whose good will they wished to retain if their faces and views were to be given exposure on the local news in their home communities."[29] Barron was also disappointed that "a case that might have resulted in a great judicial decision which would have identified the First Amendment responsibilities and obligations of government and broadcasting . . . was aborted."[30]

CBS may have won the battle of "The Selling of the Pentagon," but not the peace. Chairman Staggers and his many supporters have continued to apply congressional pressure that has pushed the FCC further into the journalistic process. For example, in 1972 the FCC informed CBS of six charges of staging and slanting the news that had been forwarded to them by Chairman Staggers. The FCC demanded an investigation and report within thirty days, and then sought to monitor CBS's investigation, including all the raw material. This is a deep intrusion by government into broadcast journalism. As in the "pot party" case, investigation of the charges meant a continuing burden on the station in time and expense—and to what purpose? The management of station WBBM in Chicago was never implicated, and the transgression was the fault of a novice reporter who had overstepped professional guidelines. But the pragmatic result was that broadcasters would avoid hard-hitting, investigative journalism because it is costly and can lead to trouble with the FCC and Congress.

To be concerned about the FCC's role as the arbiter of staged or distorted news is neither to condone such practices nor to deny that occasionally they occur. Certainly a reporter or producer who contrives to alter an event or makes something happen which otherwise would not have occurred is unacceptable and dishonest, but the remedy for such malpractice lies within the news organization. Guidelines of high professional standards must be established, and when they are breached it is the responsibility of the news chief to act swiftly, firmly and—if appropriate—publicly. Of course, if there is extrinsic evidence that the management of a station or network has knowingly permitted such staging, or has dictated the distortion or omission of certain news events, as in the WLBT and Richards cases, then the licensee has put his public trusteeship in jeopardy. However, when a regulatory agency of the federal government attempts to investigate and enforce professional codes of conduct, the result is what in medicine is called an iatrogenic, or doctor-induced, disease. Without using that term, Burch called the "remedy far worse than the disease."[31] The liberal commissioner, Nicholas Johnson, who shared few other views with his conservative chairman, agreed. ". . . the series of FCC decisions of which I am proudest is our steadfast refusal to discipline the networks in any way in response to charges of distortion in news and documentaries,"[32] Johnson told a Senate committee in 1971.

Newsmen cannot function properly when they are hip-deep in lawyers telling them to pull together every snippet or frame on an issue aired over many months. Walter Cronkite has testified that the profusion of fairness complaints discourages the central purpose of the Doctrine: "Newsmen are diverted from their jobs to provide documentation to support the station's answer. It is only natural that station management should become timid, and newsmen should sidestep controversial subjects rather than face the annoyance of such harassment."[33] In his testimony before the Senate Subcommittee on Constitutional Rights, Cronkite told Chairman Sam Ervin: "News and dissemination cannot be accomplished without fear of failure, that is the only way that counts, and if the reporter or editor constantly must be looking over his shoulder for those who would have this product reflect their standard of right and wrong, of fairness and bias, [it] can't be achieved."[34]

John J. O'Connor, the television critic of the *New York Times*, described how a 1975 documentary on gun control, "A Shooting Gallery Called America," was watered down to blandness. In a column which was as probing as it was critical, O'Connor revealed that the original broadcast had been postponed not because "it needed more reporting," as NBC had explained, but because the network considered it too "polemical." With the postponement, a "new, more 'balanced script' was devised," reported O'Connor, "one that NBC executives felt would fall within the requirements of the Fairness Doctrine." Calling his essay "Can a Documentary Be Too Fair?," O'Connor said that NBC had "pulled back too much from taking a stand." A staunch Fairness Doctrine supporter, the *Times* critic felt that the network had leaned over backwards to accommodate the Doctrine; he believed

that the documentary should have advocated a strong solution
to the hand-gun problem, and that NBC should then have set
aside future air time to permit its critics to shoot back. This point
is pivotal and will be explored presently, but the chilling force
of the Fairness Doctrine on a specific program was well documented by this reporter's observations. The public was never able
to see this tough documentary that passed "so silently in the
night,"[35] as O'Connor put it.

Nevertheless, O'Connor is suspicious of NBC's corporate concern about the Fairness Doctrine—a concern, he suggests, which
"may have less to do with the excellence of broadcast journalism
than with the existence of any regulation that might put a crimp
in network profits by taking time from entertainment [for]
news."

Bill Monroe, producer and moderator of the NBC program
Meet the Press, has contempt for print journalists who don't seem
to understand that the fairness regulations they wish to impose
on television and radio will one day be focused on their own
medium. A former president of the Radio-Television News Directors Association, Monroe says, "The newspapers have played a
shameful and short-sighted role . . . They have been complacent
witnesses to the weakening of first amendment rights for broadcasting. They have consistently consulted their own competitive
interests instead of the long-range needs of the Nation, which they
appeal to so loudly when print is attacked."[36]

Not all reporters and producers share the view that fairness
regulations are a restraining factor. Av Westin, executive in charge
of the ABC nightly news program as well as the documentary
series _Close-up_, would not repeal the Doctrine. "It wouldn't
change anything for the better, and it might make some stations
less responsible and less willing to run our kind of probing
documentaries." Westin feels that the presence of the Doctrine is
useful in the cutting room and may make local stations, caught
up in local passions, more conscious of their responsibilities.
But he is a minority among top network executives on this
subject.

While not an advocate of the Doctrine, Edwin Newman could
not, during the _Pensions_ litigation, bring himself to write an
affidavit denouncing the AIM complaint as did his colleague David
Brinkley and Reuven Frank. "I can understand both sides of the
argument," he says. "It's not our air, and we certainly have a duty

to be fair." But most of his colleagues are anti-Doctrine and share Reuven Frank's view that fairness regulations pose a constitutional threat to broadcast journalists. When he was president of NBC News, Frank suggested that the First Amendment might become "the first constitutional provision repealed by technological ad: vance."[37]

Professor Jerome Barron's caustic response to broadcast journalists is that "it is one of the great public-relations triumphs of the twentieth century over the eighteenth that broadcasters have managed to identify themselves so completely with the First Amendment."[38] After listening to Cronkite and others testify before Senator Ervin's Subcommittee on Constitutional Rights about the evils of the Fairness Doctrine, Barron commented sarcastically: ". . . if Dr. Stanton, Mr. Cronkite, Mr. Reasoner and Mr. Brinkley have their say, then freedom of speech in America is safe; but *they* are three or four people out of 200 million."[39]

Barron has unexpected allies in some conservative broadcast owners. Charles H. Crutchfield, a broadcast executive from Charlotte, North Carolina, who has been "feudin'" with CBS News for two decades, and who believes "the central government . . . bureaucrats should keep their cotton-pickin' hands off us," has serious doubts that broadcasters "would operate in the public interest absent the [Fairness Doctrine] compulsion . . ." Crutchfield, president of a group that owns television stations in Charlotte and Richmond, and radio outlets in Atlanta and Denver, hates big-government intrusion in business but accepts the Fairness Doctrine as a necessary force for broadcasters to achieve balance. "At no time has the government even remotely interfered with us or applied any pressure . . . as far as trying to limit what we say," says Crutchfield.

Aware that most of his broadcast colleagues would consider his views heresy, Crutchfield scoffs at self-deluded "untouchables in the media." He continues, "If we in the media spent half the time defending the rights of our people against the excesses of the federal government that we do in protesting the real and imagined assaults upon our own 'rights,' not only the public but we ourselves would be far better served." Crutchfield, probably the most vociferous CBS spokesman, represents more than a few broadcasters who feel that the FCC and the Fairness Doctrine protect their public from the liberal journalistic excesses of the networks.

Such is the essence of the conflict. Both sides profess to be the "good guys" wearing the white hats; both maintain that their position, and *only* theirs, serves the First Amendment. James Madison is the patron saint both of those who revere the Doctrine and of those who defy it.

The concept of fairness is strictly based on scarcity and the public-trustee responsibilities of licensees. One could look at the total number of broadcast outlets allocated throughout the electromagnetic spectrum and conclude that frequency scarcity no longer exists. Today there are thousands of radio stations on the air. Unfortunately, most articulate spokesmen continuously obfuscate the statistics for radio broadcasting by lumping them together with television to prove that there are more broadcast outlets than there are daily newspapers in the United States. The battle cry is, "There are more than 8,700 broadcast stations and fewer than 1,800 daily newspapers, so there is no longer any need for regulation." The reality is that there are only 535 commercial VHF television stations, and these figures are what properly should be compared to the 1,768 daily newspapers.

If one separates television from the broadcast total, the distribution of AM and FM radio stations is high—and far exceeds the number of daily newspapers. The reasoning that 7,807 radio outlets, with many communities having access to more stations than daily newspapers, is a valid point. Chicago alone has 65 commercial stations, Los Angeles has 59, and New Yorkers have access to 43, in addition to the public and other nonprofit stations such as those operated by the Pacifica Foundation. Only in a legalistic sense is there a scarcity situation requiring a Fairness Doctrine for radio broadcasting.

There are strong indications that even the FCC now feels that radio and television are two different creatures. FCC Chairman Richard W. Wiley, though still a firm believer in fairness regulations for television, is beginning to make speeches about an "experiment in which the Commission would discontinue enforcement of the Fairness Doctrine in the larger radio markets." In an address to the International Radio and Television Society in New York in September of 1975, Wiley cited statistics to demonstrate the lack of scarcity for radio in major markets and wondered "whether . . . there really is any practical need to maintain Fairness Doctrine enforcement." The FCC chairman speculated "that an extensive range of viewpoints would be presented even with no government oversight," and concluded that although a

few stations may abuse fairness by presenting "only one side of
a particular issue, a performance that I would consider to be
journalistically unprofessional," he did not believe that such
occasional abuses would "necessarily detract from a citizen's
access to contrasting opinion."[40]*

* In the same speech to the International Radio and Television Society in
New York, Wiley addressed himself to the equal-time requirement of Section
315(a) of the Communications Act. He criticized the "serious inhibiting
effect" of the requirement, which he claimed "frustrated broadcast coverage
of political candidates and campaigns." Wiley said he supported congressional proposals by Senator Pastore and Congressman Torbert H. Macdonald to eliminate the equal-time requirement for elections involving the
President and Vice-President.

Although the equal-time provision is not dealt with directly in this book,
it does have some fairness aspects. The requirement has four exemptions:
bona-fide newscasts, bona-fide news interviews, bona-fide documentaries and
bona-fide news coverage. Wiley was criticizing some of the Commission's past
interpretations of one of those exemptions, the bona-fide news event.

A 1962 Commission ruling limited the interpretation of a bona-fide news
event. A debate between two major-party gubernatorial candidates had been
arranged by the Economics Club of Detroit but was never broadcast because
the FCC ruled that a minor candidate of the Socialist Labor party was entitled to equal time.[41] In a similar case, said Wiley, a 1962 Nixon-Brown
debate in California, organized by the United Press International for its
annual convention, did not, according to his FCC predecessors, constitute
bona-fide news.[42] "If events such as these do not qualify as bona-fide news,
one might ask: What does qualify?" Wiley's answer was: "Not much." He
told his audience that such interpretation of 315(a) was "chilling political
discussion" and "was devastating to the welfare of our democracy. He recommended that the equal-time provision be reversed.

Nine days later Wiley's speech suddenly became an official order. Without
waiting for congressional action, the FCC chairman and all but two of the
Commissioners voted to revise the 1962 ban on political debates. Under the
new interpretation, radio and television stations would be permitted to
broadcast debates in their entirety as long as they are "on-the-spot coverage
of bona-fide news events,"[43] organized by civic or other groups. Put simply,
the League of Women Voters or a newspaper association could arrange the
debate, but a broadcaster could not.

Responding to a petition by the Aspen Institute Program for Communications and Society which asked the Commission to revise its ruling on Section 315(a) in order to facilitate broadcast coverage of presidential debates,
the FCC decided that the *Goodwill Station* and *National Broadcasting* rulings
constituted an "undue stifling of broadcast coverage of news events."[44] The
Commission said: ". . . this remedy will go a long way toward ameliorating the
paucity of coverage accorded these news events during the past fifteen years."[45]

The FCC ruling went even further. In response to a CBS request for a

Wiley is one of seven FCC commissioners, and Congress' and the Court of Appeals' territorial imperative on the Doctrine must be reckoned with, but it does seem that the time is ripe for a trial period in which the Fairness Doctrine would be suspended for radio.

It would be ironic if the Doctrine, which was given its initial constitutional test in the Red Lion case, no longer applied to this medium and was enforced only on television stations. The courts might rule that such a separation was unconstitutional, and industry advocates would certainly argue that such a rule would make the instrument by which most Americans get their news a second-class medium. But such an experiment on, radio is one on which the FCC and the Congress could conduct hearings.

When Chairman Wiley's trial balloon floated across John Pastore's hearing room less than twenty-four hours after it was launched, the senator exploded. "Mr. Wiley, you made a speech in New York . . . are you suggesting . . . that the Fairness Doctrine not be invoked with reference to radio in certain areas where there are a number of radio stations?" Wiley, slightly flustered, replied that he still supported the Fairness Doctrine but suggested that in cities such as Chicago and Los Angeles, "it may be that the marketplace would be able to handle the situation in the absence of governmental regulation."

---

declaratory ruling on presidential news conferences and their relation to the equal-time requirement, the FCC declared that the 1964 ruling, which refused to exempt such news conferences from the requirement, was a mistake. "Thus the press conferences of the President, and all other candidates for political office, broadcast live and in their entirety," said the Commission, "qualify for the exemption under section 315(a)(4)."[46]

The Democratic National Committee and others immediately voiced their objection; appeals have been initiated by Representative Shirley Chisholm and the National Organization of Women. The final word on the interpretation of 315 will come from the courts.

No matter how this matter is resolved, it is clear that there is a fairness obligation whenever any of the exemptions to 315 are invoked. Under the *Zapple Ruling* of 1970, a licensee has an obligation to "afford reasonable opportunity for the presentation of contrasting views"[47] or "quasi-equal opportunity." In other words, when the equal-time requirement is not applicable, the Fairness Doctrine is. If Candidate Ford appears on a news interview or during live coverage of a bona-fide news event, the broadcaster must provide his Democratic opponent reasonable opportunity to answer the President.

PASTORE: Will you inform the Congress before you institute this experiment?

WILEY: I think we have to make ultimately the decision as to whether or not the authority exists, and then Congress, as it always must, has to review these decisions as to whether or not this independent agency has made an appropriate decision.

PASTORE: At any rate before you do anything, you will inform the Congress.

WILEY: We always keep you informed, Senator, you can count on that.[48]

In this cool exchange Pastore was echoing what Speaker Sam Rayburn had said to FCC Chairman Newton Minow fifteen years before: "Remember, son, that the FCC is a child of the Congress and you'll be all right." What was also clear was that the Fairness Doctrine was not to be meddled with, except with the advice and consent of Senator Pastore and his committee.

Congressman Macdonald, Pastore's counterpart in the House, agreed that Congress would have to approve Wiley's experiment. "The Fairness Doctrine is our lifeblood," Macdonald said. "On the other hand, I'm not sure that [current] implementation . . . is 100% correct."[49]

Broadcasting magazine, always opposed to the Doctrine, was wary about the Wiley proposal for no regulation in large radio markets. In an editorial it warned that there is "a grave danger of the cure turning into something worse than the disease. Surely the FCC's suspension would be put to court appeal somewhere. An appellate ruling that confirmed the legislative underpinning of fairness could be as damaging to broadcast freedom as the Red Lion decision was."[50]

For the most part, the broadcast industry wants it both ways. A genuine First Amendment for radio and television would mean removal of *all* restraints, particularly those which inhibit or prevent new technologies such as pay-cable and satellite transmission directly to the home set. Yet the industry has consistently opposed these new developments as entrenchments on its turf. Since the primary reason for the existence of the present Fairness Doctrine is the scarcity argument, the opening up of other arteries of telecommunications and the insertion of new VHF television stations into the spectrum would remove most justifications for government-imposed fairness. All justifications other than technical ones would wither away. If all could enter, to paraphrase Justice White in *Red Lion*, there would be scant reason for the government to intrude.

The major networks and the National Association of Broadcasters admit this privately but are trying to stall the use of cable television—particularly pay cable—as long as possible. In an illustrated pamphlet against this new development CBS argues: "America doesn't need another mouth to feed." A cartoon shows a small boy before a blank television screen asking, "Dad, could I have a dollar to watch *Gunsmoke?*"[51] Arthur Taylor, the CBS president, warns broadcasters that pay cable is "less a revolution than a sneak attack on the family pocketbook."[52] One network president confides to friends, "We are going to continue our propaganda and lobbying battle against cable, and especially pay cable, as long as we can, but when the walls come tumbling down, we expect to enter the field and dominate it as we do over-the-air television."

In the end, such a free system open to all is the only one beneficial to society. Still, it must be admitted that the major networks will probably dominate such a system, and that conceivably CBS, NBC and ABC may have two or three additional channels in every home. But to insist on a limitation of channels —which is what the current status quo position of the broadcasters implies—is to proclaim that "Congress shall make no law abridging . . . freedom of speech and of the press" *except for* those organizations and individuals who by congressionally legislated rules operate the only printing plants in town.

Cable television, particularly in the major markets, may be long in coming, but to oppose it with all the power of the major networks simply because there are FCC limitations on the networks' ownership in cable is to stunt its freedom and curtail the choices of the viewing public. Today the broadcast industry may lobby against the Fairness Doctrine, but if it had an option between being saddled with it and of being forever rid of the threat of pay cable, or of extending the three-year license period, there would be no contest. One candid network executive has admitted as much: "If we have to choose between the [long-term] license-renewal bill or abolition of the Fairness Doctrine, we would choose the renewal bill and forgo our First Amendment rights."

If one examines all the evidence and the cynical arguments that broadcasters employ to camouflage their profit drive in the cloth of the First Amendment, it is difficult to resist asking whether

the industry doesn't deserve the Fairness Doctrine. But a better question is whether the Doctrine fairly serves the purpose of the American public, which depends more and more on the broadcast media for its picture of reality.

This dilemma cannot be resolved by assuming that new technology will eliminate scarcity, especially when the National Association of Broadcasters and the networks are fighting to prevent the growth of cable television. Certainly any interim solution must afford breathing space for these new developments so that eventually they can be part of a new national communications policy. But new methods of telecommunications will not spring up full-blown tomorrow or even by the end of the next decade, and we must face the question of the Fairness Doctrine now. During that interval, or as long as the scarcity exists, some kind of responsibility doctrine is required.

It is for this reason that Congress has chosen to license the scarce frequencies to those who volunteer to serve the public interest. While Congress might have chosen a number of other alternatives, the courts have held that this public-trustee approach is both rational and constitutional. Thus, even if the Fairness Doctrine were eliminated, it would not wipe out governmental regulation of the public-trustee franchise. In addition, the other requirements of the public-interest licensing and regulatory approach—e.g., initial licensing, renewal every three years, rules such as multiple ownership and prime-time access—would still apply and government could always use this power to keep the broadcaster under pressure. This authority could also be employed in a renewal hearing, by a new rule proposed for prime time, or by limiting the number of stations that one network or group can own.

Hence, broadcasters who believe that all their political troubles would disappear if there were no Fairness Doctrine are only kidding themselves. Who can forget President Nixon's remark that the Washington *Post*, which owned stations, was going to have a "damnable, damnable time" getting its licenses renewed, and that "the game has to be played awfully rough."[53] Fairness rules had little to do with the threat to take away the *Post*'s television stations in Miami and Jacksonville; the challenge was based on absentee ownership and multiple ownership.

There are many other weapons in a President's quiver by which he can intimidate and punish radio and television licensees.

Though initiated by the career staff of the Justice Department, the antitrust suit against the commercial networks is considered by many to have been politically motivated. In 1972 WHDH-TV in Boston was denied its valuable franchise for reasons having nothing to do with the Fairness Doctrine. Right now WPIX-TV in New York faces a serious challenge to its license for reasons beyond the Doctrine.*

* The WPIX–Forum Communications case, now in its seventh year of litigation, is a book in itself. Although distortion and falsification of certain news events are part of the saga, the case does not involve a Fairness Doctrine complaint. WPIX, Channel 11, one of the six commercial VHF stations in the Greater New York area, has been a revenue producer for its owner, the New York *Daily News*, but it has never exhibited its parent's enterprise or responsibility.

In 1969 Forum Communications, Inc., headed by Lawrence Grossman and funded by a group of concerned citizens, petitioned the FCC to transfer the WPIX license to Forum. The organization claimed that "during the license period under review . . . WPIX failed utterly in its obligation to provide adequate program service to the public."[54] Forum also told the Commission that its "local program service would be far superior to that proposed by WPIX."

In the WPIX renewal hearings, there emerged a pattern of questionable news policies and outright distortions on the part of the station. What WPIX had represented to be a direct report via satellite of the invasion of Czechoslovakia in 1968 was actually film made in Bucharest and other European cities. It was also proven that "combat film reports from Vietnam" were instead training films produced at Fort Belvoir, Virginia. Although the station management blamed fourteen admitted malpractices on zealous young subordinates, it became obvious that senior executives and officers knew that WPIX did not employ correspondents in the capitals of the world and had not contracted for satellite service.

In August of 1974 the staff of the FCC Broadcast Bureau recommended that WPIX's license not be renewed and that the license be granted to Forum Communications. But Administrative Law Judge James F. Tierney rejected the bureau's recommendation and decided that WPIX was better qualified to operate the station than Forum. Part of his reasoning was that Forum had not demonstrated the financial capability required to build and operate such a station. The $5 million which Forum had claimed to have available had been eroded by inflation, said Judge Tierney.

Unexpectedly, in April of 1975, Forum Communications reached an agreement with WPIX: Forum would be permitted to nominate a member to the WPIX board, the station would establish a special $100,000 fund for community service, and it would reimburse Forum for its $318,000 in legal fees. The Broadcast Bureau regarded the settlement as against the public interest because private negotiations were denying FCC options, and in August of 1975 the FCC rejected the settlement.

Even some strong advocates of a free broadcast press are troubled by the prospect of the Doctrine's complete repeal which Senator Proxmire now advocates in his bill "The First Amendment Clarification Act of 1975." Their concern is that repeal might be misconstrued by television and radio stations as a sign that Congress and the FCC had abandoned the intent and obligations of the Doctrine.

As long as Justice Douglas was on the Court, he continued to denounce the constitutionality of *Red Lion*, and Justice Potter Stewart too has some serious doubts about that decision. Even in his dissent in *Pensions,* Chief Judge Bazelon had held out little hope that the Doctrine would soon be declared unconstitutional. As he wrote, "For better or worse, the propriety of some government intervention into broadcast journalism under the Fairness Doctrine has been declared constitutional and there seems to be no serious effort under way to reconsider the assumption of that declaration."[58]

Despite this, as well as clear signals from other members of the Supreme Court itself, broadcasters continue to fantasize about waking up tomorrow and hearing that the Fairness Doctrine has been struck down by some majestic judicial revelation. Of course, there is always the chance of a special case working its way up through the regulatory process, but broadcasters would serve themselves and their public better by looking elsewhere for a remedy. To state that the judiciary has embraced the concept of fairness regulations does not necessarily mean that broadcasting must be governed by the Fairness Doctrine as shaped by the FCC at present. The place for the debate is in the Congress—

The dispute, now as much between the Broadcast Bureau and the Administrative Law Judge as between WPIX and Forum, reached new levels of acrimony when the bureau filed a brief against Judge Tierney, calling his findings for WPIX "erroneous,"[55] and adding that "WPIX was not qualified to be a Commission licensee" because of its news practices.[56] The bureau argued that the license to operate Channel 11 be taken from WPIX, Inc., and given to the opposing applicant, Forum Communications, Inc.[57]

The full Commission has yet to dispose of the case, and there is no indication that the litigation will be resolved in the near future. The Fairness Doctrine was never an issue, and there are sufficient other criteria by which the case can be decided. Whatever the final outcome, even WPIX's greatest detractors admit that the pressure of the litigation has forced the station to improve.

with perhaps a strong prod from the courts, which could review the FCC's implementation of present provisions.

Unfortunately, current debate in the Senate on the subject has become a contest between extremes. Listening to Senate testimony on the Doctrine, one has the uneasy feeling of being caught in the polemics of polarity, and that there is no negotiable middle ground. A commentator who is not prepared to denounce the Doctrine is likely to be labeled a coward, while an activist in public-interest law who concedes that it may have some negative aspects risks being dubbed a propagandist for Paley or Sarnoff. If you are for the Doctrine, you have turned your back on the Bill of Rights; if you are concerned with its misuse and want to analyze its inhibiting factors, you are automatically opposed to access and are likely to be branded an ally of Hargis and McIntire. Such frozen positions begin to sound like a simplistic debate where an overzealous producer pits two bitter advocates against each other and asks his audience to assume that there is no solution between the two extremes.

Congress should take a hard look at the language of the Doctrine and examine closely the way the FCC interprets its two basic tenets: (1) that a reasonable amount of broadcast time must be devoted to the discussion of controversial issues; and (2) that a reasonable amount of time must be given to opposing viewpoints.

Given these standards, what has twenty-seven years of experience taught Congress? In truth, the Fairness Doctrine has not really stimulated radio and television stations to devote a reasonable amount of time to controversial issues of public importance. Many radio and television stations translate "reasonable" into "as little as possible," and those which broadcast documentaries steadily, particularly the networks, do so for a variety of reasons other than the Doctrine: prestige, economics and license-renewal considerations. Indeed, in the twenty-seven years since the FCC was founded it has never denied renewal or even scheduled a station for a hearing because of nonfulfillment of that first tenet. If a station were to regularly produce a hard-hitting series of documentaries and thereby accrued a file of fairness complaints, it would not be judged affirmatively for responsible, aggressive public-affairs programing. But a bland, penny-pinching or lazy station that never ventured into controversy or the discussion of vital public issues and received no complaints would have a clean slate, with no bad marks to show for its caution.

Penalizing initiative and rewarding inaction makes no sense, but the FCC has focused all its energy on the second part of the Doctrine, which was never intended to create rigid standards of fairness, to interfere with day-to-day broadcasting decisions or to make the Commission a "super-referee." But this is exactly what the Commission has done; the Wilderness Society and Pensions cases are only two examples of many.

Congress should compare the differences between the Commission's enforcement of the two parts of the Doctrine. At this moment stations are assayed in a way that so weights negative complaints against positive performance that it puts a premium on timidity. There is an old saying that "A man who never made a mistake never did anything," and one of the deadliest journalistic failings is the sin of omission.

If encouraging licensees to broadcast more public-affairs programs was the primary intent of the Doctrine, how did the FCC lapse into its present ad hoc policy of acting only on complaints? (Senator Ervin claims that "the First Amendment was drafted not only for the brave but also for the timid. One of the dangers that arises out of government regulation is that the timid will cease from printing anything which Government doesn't like."[59])History records that the change developed in the early sixties, first with the *Mapoles* and *Billings* cases, then with *Cullman* and the controversy over the nuclear test-ban treaty, and finally with *Red Lion* and the personal-attack rule.*

* It is important to remember that the personal-attack rule is supposed to be applicable only when it is part of a controversial issue of public importance; yet in recent complaints, such as Congressman Benjamin Rosenthal's suit against station WMCA in New York, the attack was separated from any substantive discussion of national or local policy. Bob Grant, the host of a program on that station, gratuitously called the congressman from New York a coward for not accepting an invitation to participate on a call-in show discussing meat controls, on which Rosenthal is an authority. Grant was guilty of bad manners, but it is difficult to relate his derogatory comment, made in response to an unrelated question asked two hours later, to a controversial issue of public importance. The Commission sustained the congressman's complaint but rescinded the $1,000 fine imposed by its staff.

WMCA and its licensee R. Peter Strauss appealed the ruling, which was reversed on January 16, 1976, by the U. S. Court of Appeals for the District of Columbia Circuit. This significant ruling virtually reinstates the aborted ruling in the *Pensions* case: that the FCC must respect the reasonable judgment of broadcasters on fairness doctrine questions, and must not substitute its administrative views on a broadcaster's performance unless the broadcaster has committed an abuse of discretion. The ruling thus gives broadcasters acting in good faith a considerable amount of editorial discretion in determining what the fairness doctrine requires in any particular situation.

After the personal-attack rulings of the early sixties, the Commission extended the case-by-case principle to all Fairness Doctrine complaints, without any major debate ever taking place before the agency or in Congress. Congressman Oren Harris, now a federal judge but then chairman of the House Committee on Interstate and Foreign Commerce, was critical of this procedure, considering it antithetical to the original goals of the Doctrine. After rejecting Harris' warning, in 1964 the FCC issued its Fairness Primer, and its Complaints and Compliance Bureau had a new mandate. What had once been a benign Doctrine became a law with sharp teeth which were to grow ever sharper. The Commission was off on its quest for measurable fairness, issue by issue, program by program.

The dilemma we now face is agonizingly clear: to enforce the Fairness Doctrine on a case-by-case basis is clumsy and unworkable; yet to deny the goals of the Doctrine by completely repealing it would be unrealistic, if not irresponsible. To examine government and fairness as if the issue were a "yes" or "no" referendum is only to entrap ourselves further. There is a sensible middle ground—no panacea, but a constructive measure to alleviate the present tug of war. "It's like everything else in the world," Justice Learned Hand once told his law clerk: "It's the mid-course, and there's no rule for that."[60]

For Congress to chart a course between the extremes of complete repeal and rigid enforcement will be neither popular nor easy, but perhaps it is the only sane alternative. It is unrealistic to look to the courts for a rejection of the Doctrine, though they may ameliorate its present intrusive application. Moreover, the FCC, a prisoner of its own bureaucratic rigidity, has shown itself to be wed to the ghost of *Red Lion*. The full Congress did consider the issue of fairness in 1959, but only in its hastily written amendment to the Section 315(a) equal-time provision, and it is significant that while it incorporated the language of the Fairness Doctrine into the statute, its debates make it explicitly clear that Congress regarded the Doctrine as applicable only on an overall basis at renewal time. Leaving an important, sensitive matter to unlikely correction by its agent, the FCC, or to an unsure fate by the courts is an abdication of Congress' responsibilities. It is high time for that body to focus directly on the FCC's implementation of the Doctrine, and to make explicit the intent of its original legislation.

14

WALKING THE
TIGER BACK

~~~~~~~~~~~~~~~~~~~~~~~~~~~~~~~~~~~~~

*This role of the government as an "overseer"
and ultimate arbiter and guardian of the public interest and the role of the licensee as a
journalistic "free agent" call for . . . both the
regulators and the licensees to walk a "tightrope" to preserve the First Amendment values
written into . . . the Communications Act.*

CHIEF JUSTICE WARREN E. BURGER
CBS ET AL. V. DNC, 1973

*It is time—indeed, long past time—for the FCC
to go forward by going back to prior, sounder
process. In its post-1962 reach for perfect fairness, the Commission has lost sight of the real
goal—robust, wide open debate. However well
intentioned, its actions now thwart or tend to
discourage such debate. If the Commission
does not walk the tiger back, a crucial aspect
of free speech may end up in its belly.*

HENRY GELLER
GENERAL COUNSEL, FCC
1964–1970

Recently NBC's Bill Monroe was asked if his 1971 congressional
testimony still reflected his opposition to the Fairness Doctrine.
His immediate response was "Hell, yes!" but then there was a
pause and he added, "but we are never going to get rid of it until
we do something about voluntary access . . . We're almost arro-

gant about not letting viewers who disagree with us or think we made a big error have access to some kind of air time to rebut us."

Other broadcast journalists, including Ed Newman and Eric Sevareid, share this view. "Nobody like me should be able to sit there night after night nattering away, without some provision for answering back," says Sevareid, who feels that much of Vice-President Agnew's success can be explained by latent public frustration on this point. "It's like gas building up in the boiler, and there's no way for the pressure to escape. Twenty years ago a psychologist prophesied, and I agree, that the Achilles heel of television would come to be the viewers' inability to talk back to the black box."

In the fairness deadlock that now exists, one side has to make the first move. Nothing the broadcast industry could do would impress the Congress, the courts and the FCC as much as a commitment to voluntary access for those who want to talk back. Newspapers and magazines, especially those with a commitment to bold reporting and vigorous commentary, have long recognized the need for a forum for those who feel that their views have been misrepresented or their reputations maligned, or who may feel there is another side to the issue. When the *New York Times* inaugurated its Op-Ed page in 1970 for just this purpose, its editorial stated:

> The purpose of the Op.Ed page is neither to reinforce nor to counterbalance The Times's own editorial position, which will continue to be presented as usual in these columns. The objective is . . . to afford greater opportunity for exploration of issues and presentations of new insights and new ideas by writers and thinkers who have no institutional connection with The Times and whose views will very frequently be completely divergent from our own. . . .
>
> In furtherance of our belief that the diverse voices of our society must be given the greatest possible opportunity to be heard, we are at the same time approximately doubling the weekday space devoted to letters from our readers.[1]

The Op-Ed page concept did not originate with the *Times.* Many newspapers—the Louisville *Courier-Journal*, the Washington *Post,* the Los Angeles *Times,* etc.—had already pioneered such reader access. The Chicago *Daily News* operates a Bureau of Fairness and Accuracy. In a prominent box on its editorial page it urges readers to communicate their "complaints and comments" as a means of "maintaining standards of fairness and accuracy, which will be published as promptly as possible." In Dallas the public-television station, KERA, utilizes the last five minutes of its nightly *Newsroom* program for "Feedback" in which a broad cross section of viewer complaints are ventilated. It is a yeasty highlight of the broadcast, and its anchorwoman-producer Lee Clark is certain that without it, *Newsroom*'s aggressive style of reporting would not be possible. In the same city the ABC affiliate, WFAA, has a regularly scheduled program, "Let Me Speak to the Manager," in which Mike Shapiro permits himself to be questioned by critical members of the audience. It has the highest rating of any program, network or local, broadcast by the Dallas stations.

At the network level, innovation in the area of corrections and complaints has been scant. In 1964 CBS News experimented with a monthly "Letters to CBS," broadcast with Harry Reasoner and Garry Moore, and produced and edited by Andrew Rooney; it was scheduled in prime time. All CBS shows were fair game, not just those produced by the news division, but we were unwilling to permit our detractors the last word, and I suspect that the truly devastating indictments of our sins and omissions never quite made it to air. After two months, we lost patience with it. NBC and John Chancellor now reserve a few minutes nearly every week for correction and amplification, and would schedule more if the limitations of time were not such a constriction. Called "Editors Notebook," this "line of communications" is regarded by Chancellor as an essential link between his viewers and the program's staff.

Most recently, in September of 1975, CBS demonstrated its interest in broadcasting reaction to the news division's coverage of a specific "matter of public importance." The network aired a one-hour explosive documentary on hunting, "The Guns of Autumn." Three weeks later it returned to that topic when it broadcast "Echoes of the Guns of Autumn," which was a one-hour examination of the issues raised in and by the initial documentary. Not a detailed rebuttal program, "Echoes" demonstrates the technique by which reply time can be provided in the network structure. But the problem with "Echoes," as with "Letters to CBS," was that the network had the last word.

The kind of access given to newspaper readers, which is in the highest tradition of journalism, should be a significant part of the station's or network's continuing commitment to provide a wide spectrum of voices. Such a broadcast should be voluntary and should be scheduled regularly in prime time. It need not be a consecutive half-hour; it can be divided into a number of smaller segments. As part of its discretion and responsibility, the individual station's management would make the determination of who, where, and for how long.

Such a talk-back forum would require flair and imagination, for it is easier to write a persuasive and provocative letter than to present such views on television and radio. But it can be done, as *60 Minutes* and some BBC experiments have begun to demonstrate. Given this kind of ombudsman assignment, people like Ed Newman, Mike Wallace, Bill Moyers and Andy Rooney could create a program as engrossing as it is necessary. Local stations have similar talented personalities capable of designing and presenting such a forum. It will cost money, but broadcasters should decide which is more chilling—the Fairness Doctrine as now enforced, or this minimal sacrifice of revenue?

This formula for rebuttal should not be confused with the techniques employed by most call-in shows, where the broadcaster always has the last word. Often the belligerent host bangs down the receiver with a rude rejoinder when it suits his purposes. It will require a voluntary, long-term commitment to taking it as well as dishing it out, but this is the kind of free-speech formula that can keep the FCC out of the newsroom and the broadcasters out of the courtroom.

If such programing was initiated, the most compelling reasons for renewal would be a station's record in complying with the goal of devoting prime time to the discussion of controversial issues of public importance, and its active policy of affording reasonable opportunity for opposing viewpoints. This means not playing it safe but playing it fair in the truest sense of the word. By establishing an Op-Ed page, the most aggressive or sloppy journalism can be held up to account by those who disagree. As one long-time critic of Henry Luce's style once observed, "I'd rip up my subscription to *Time* if it weren't for these marvelous letters that tear Harry apart." Luce understood that such a safety valve was not only sound journalism, but good business.

Five years ago a proposal like this would have been ridiculed by broadcasters as bad for business ("Who's going to watch or listen to an Op-Ed page?") and scoffed at by Fairness Doctrine advocates as too visionary ("The selfish broadcasters just won't provide time for such an innovation"). But this is 1975, and radio and television executives are finally aware that thoughtful citizens and powerful forces in government are disturbed by the one-way nature of broadcast speech. First Amendment disciples who for a generation fought for Murrow's and Elmer Davis' right to use the electronic press without pressure from sponsors, nervous networks and heavy-handed government are now willing to listen to those who argue that Fairness Doctrine and even more constricting forms of regulation are inevitable. Even those most insensitive to criticism are mindful of sober voices, conservative and liberal, who are raising questions about access, if not industry-provided, then mandated by government; an Op-Ed page of the air or its equivalent is not unrealistically visionary but almost a condition of survival. The Achilles heel that Sevareid referred to and that Newman, Chancellor and others worry about, cannot be treated by cosmetics. Broadcasting may be a business, but at its best it is a creative business. The industry will require innovations and imagination to satisfy the public's emerging and very real need for two-way communication.

An Op-Ed page concept that truly provides space for dissent need not be dull nor a money loser. It cannot be sloughed off as a mere bone to the FCC or constructed as a fool's soapbox where inarticulate or bumptious loudmouths are tricked into using the air to harm the cause they are there to defend. There was an *All in the Family* episode in which Archie Bunker managed to get some air time to answer a television editorial in favor of gun control, only to fall on his face.[2] Those who produce and edit the Op-Ed pages of the air will need to be committed to its success by constantly searching for eloquent, effective, diverse voices of dissent, capable of holding the attention of broadcast audiences. Indeed, an entire new breed of commentators might emerge similar to those who now inform, inspire and entertain millions in hundreds of newspapers which have come to understand that voluntary access is the foundation of a free press.

This Op-Ed concept relates to both parts of the Fairness Doctrine. The *intent* to be fair is generally honored, but for most stations the commitment "to devote a reasonable amount of time to the discussion of controversial issues" is a broken promise. Just as NBC argued that the problems of pension plans were hardly a controversial issue, it is hardly controversial that most licensees do not broadcast enough public-affairs programs. The most notorious abdication is the premise that nightly national and international news can be shoe-horned into 22 minutes and sandwiched between six or more commercials. Broadcast journalists are all too aware that they are short-changing their 50 million consumers. Several anchormen and their producers have made public statements about the need for an hourly nightly news program in prime time. "What we provide now is little more than indexing the day's news," says one anchorman. A major effort, combining bulletin and headline type of news, together with the kind of miniature documentaries now seen on the Chancellor, Cronkite and Reasoner programs, and the in-depth features of *60 Minutes, Close-up* or *Bill Moyers' Journal,* is long overdue. Such formats would also provide room for a regularly designated space during which the public could talk back. Until such commitments are made by the networks and independent stations, broadcasting will remain the second-class medium that its practitioners claim the Fairness Doctrine now makes it.

Advocates of a government-enforced Fairness Doctrine may argue that more news and public-affairs programing in prime time will not ensure fairness. The answer to this criticism is that of course rebuttal time is not the only or the perfect solution, but when combined with increased news, it should certainly help in stimulating the most critical areas of daily journalism: investigative reporting, analysis and comment.

One criticism of the Op-Ed page concept is that the public might not be informed about each side of every issue. Some would argue that the only way to ensure objectivity and fairness is to have the government controlling the daily broadcast scene, but such a drastic remedy ignores history. The FCC has never been able to ensure fairness. It waits for complaints—a haphazard process at best—and takes forever to adjudicate them. Is the public really served when another audience hears five or ten minutes more about an issue a year or two later? Would the people of Red Lion, Pennsylvania, have been better informed if they had heard Fred Cook's reply years later? But if WGCB had a regularly scheduled rebuttal column, Cook's complaint would have been broadcast in December 1964, and the FCC and the courts would never have intervened. And if the management of WLBT had had such a forum, it might never have lost its license. And if the nightly news programs had such a device, Spiro Agnew might not have gained such a following.

Broadcasters, who like to remind us of the intentions of the founding fathers, would be wise to recall that the first Congress was willing to forgo all laws "abridging freedom of speech and the press" because they understood that the secret of democratic government was based on the right of every citizen to criticize that government. In 1976 the 94th Congress is not likely to grant full press freedom to radio and television franchises, when those broadcasters are unwilling to create a mechanism by which their performance can be subject to the same kind of healthy criticism.

The history of fairness regulations in the last decade illustrates the pitfalls of a program-by-program examination of fairness questions. The Pensions case is like a documentary of the absurd, illustrating the quagmire that the FCC stumbles into when it attempts to assess a specific program. The FCC had to beat a hasty retreat on the grounds of mootness lest the entire Fairness Doctrine be destroyed in the litigation. The endless adjudicatory process, the channeling of the licensee's resources away from programing to deal with legal questions, and when a station is found to have violated the Doctrine, the delay in having the contrasting viewpoint broadcast, all combine to make present Fairness Doctrine regulation irrelevant to the one group it was designed to protect: the public. What is needed is a policy that, while continuing to hold the licensee responsible to overall FCC review, encourages the stations to invent formats for handling opposing viewpoints as part of their regular programing.

The crux of the solution would be that the FCC would view a station's entire output, not just one aspect of it. Viewed in the context of its total broadcast schedule, a licensee's fairness would become an integral part of the renewal process. Such a *modus operandi* would stress a broadcaster's voluntary responsiveness to his obligations through innovations such as an Op-Ed page of the air. Simply stated, the objective is to relieve the FCC of the responsibility of making decisions it cannot possibly make competently. As Chief Justice Burger wrote in *CBS et al. v. DNC,* "Editing is what editors are for," and the record of cases such as *Red Lion* and *Pensions* demonstrate that FCC involvement in the daily editing process leads to an inevitable blurring of the boundaries between government and broadcasters—a blurring that in turn exposes the communications process to intrusion by political appointees and special-interest pressure groups.

(In all fairness, it must be noted that Judge Tamm insists that Burger's "Editing is what editors are for" is "a much misapplied passage." Perhaps the staunchest defender of the Fairness Doctrine on the bench, Tamm feels that the Commission's role is limited and that broadcasters and others mislead the public in contending that the FCC substitutes its judgment for the licensees.)*

What the FCC and the courts have concluded in the paid-access areas of the Fairness Doctrine is that the complexities of adjudication make specific regulation unworkable. By necessity they are now compelled to rely on licensee discretion. Is the FCC any better equipped to referee the ephemeral images of news and public affairs? For this reason, the proposal outlined earlier is purposefully broad. Complaints would be filed with the FCC, as they are now. As with the present procedure, the Commission would notify the licensee of the fairness complaint lodged against it, then place it in the station's renewal file. Responsible complaints would be referred to the licensee, so that just as now, when the Commission refers less than 5 percent of the complaints it receives to licensees, the "crackpot" or frivolous protest would stop at the FCC.

The FCC would be prohibited from taking action on any specific fairness complaint except those involving political broadcasts. The 315(a) equal-time rulings must be made promptly; it serves no useful purpose to tell a candidate *after* the election that he had a valid complaint. Congress has specified that fairness is the standard in certain programs exempt from equal time, so the congressional scheme of prompt rulings within the election period should be observed.

* Referring to excerpts from this book which appeared in the *New York Times,* March 30, 1975, Judge Tamm rejected the author's opinion that an FCC victory in the Pensions case "would legitimize the idea that government could, in effect, substitute its judgment for that of the network as to what issue was involved in a broadcast documentary and order that more time be given to elements that the journalist never thought central to the story." Judge Tamm's rejoinder: "That is exactly what this case is not about. The Commission did *not* substitute its judgment for the licensee's; it found the broadcaster's judgment to be unreasonable. It did *not* order equal time; it only required reasonable opportunity."[3]

Unlike the present fairness procedures, in which complaints are decided individually, the proposal would limit the Commission's role to judging specific complaints in the context of a station's total performance at renewal hearings. In the interim, a licensee would have a variety of options for handling a complaint. It could simply be ignored, as newspapers ignore the most inflammatory and irresponsible of their readers' letters. If the station decided that the criticism was spurious or had already been acknowledged in other programing, it would be under no obligation to offer air time to the complainant. However, if the station viewed the grievance as a sound one, it could make what it deemed to be the proper response, up to offering the complainant free time to rebut.

The key is that the licensee would decide what course to follow, but its decision would not necessarily end the matter, for the FCC would review the station's actions at renewal time. With this approach, a licensee that broadcast a substantial number of programs on controversial issues and therefore had received a large number of complaints would not be punished for its compliance with the first part of the Doctrine; indeed, the station would be encouraged to continue to broadcast controversial programs, and at the renewal hearing it would be considered an affirmative indication that the licensee was living up to its obligations as a public trustee.

To be sure, the station vigorously discharging this obligation may attract a large number of fairness grievances, but all substantial ones would be referred to him so that he would have an opportunity to respond. Also, at renewal the FCC might have a number of complaints against such a broadcaster, and in some cases there might be an honest error of judgment. But this should not jeopardize the station's renewal, even if there were many close judgments; the FCC should be concerned solely with determining whether a flagrant pattern of violation was indicated, either of bad faith or a reckless disregard of fairness obligations. In effect, this would be akin to the famous *New York Times* v. *Sullivan*[4]*

---

* In *The New York Times* v. *Sullivan* case the Supreme Court found that a newspaper could not be held liable for the publication of defamatory material about a public official unless it was published with actual malice, a term which the Court defined as knowing publication of a falsehood or the publication with serious doubts as to its truth.

standard promulgated by the Supreme Court in the libel field—to promote and protect "uninhibited, robust, wide-open debate."

In its examination of how well the licensee honored the second part of the Doctrine—presenting controversial programs fairly—the FCC would also consider the station's overall attempts to obtain contrasting viewpoints. Barring unusual cases like WLBT, the focus would not be on the content of specific complaints, and even in such cases it would take a *pattern* of violations, not an isolated failure, to warrant a renewal hearing. And such hearings, though rare, would serve to remind all licensees that fairness remained a *sine qua non* for renewal.

Thus, the FCC's judgment of the overall performance of the licensee would give wide latitude to the handling of fairness complaints. Following the logic of the *Cullman*[5] ruling, stations would be asked to demonstrate that they had shown an affirmative willingness to comply with the Fairness Doctrine, and would carry the burden of demonstrating that they had complied with it. But it is the *character* of the licensee, not the broadcasts, that would be crucial. Character was and still is the bedrock of the Communications Act.

In the hearing, the Commission would be required to establish that there had been a flagrant pattern of abuse. If no such pattern clearly emerged, the renewal would be granted. In the rare case where the evidence showed a sloppy effort to achieve fairness, an alternative would be a short-term renewal of one year—in effect, probation.

Criticism of a station's fairness could be produced at renewal hearings by those seeking to challenge a licensee's renewal application, and the failure of a station to satisfy the affirmative spirit of the Doctrine would be a damaging indication that it was unable to serve as a public trustee.

The recommendations outlined here would not eliminate fairness or complaints by individuals, public-interest groups or competing organizations that wished to challenge license renewal; it would simply preclude the FCC from acting on individual grievances and becoming a fairness bargainer.

The personal-attack rule—the basis of the Red Lion case—should be rescinded, but this facet of fairness should be considered at renewal, along with other aspects of the Doctrine. The FCC now exempts newscasts, news interviews, and coverage of spot-news events from the personal-attack rule. If the broadcaster can be trusted to operate under the Doctrine in these categories, which are by far the most frequent, why can't he be trusted across the board? If the licensee's record at renewal shows a *pattern* of personal attacks without giving the other side rebuttal time, the FCC can and should take remedial action. But if the overall record shows good faith here and in other areas, the Commission should renew. The road that it started down in 1962 and in *Red Lion*— that of giving the licensee detailed instructions on how to meet fairness obligations in certain situations—has been a twisted one, and should be abandoned.

To continue the present application of the Fairness Doctrine is to accept the continued surveillance of journalistic and editorial decisions by the government in the form of the FCC, and necessarily these will continue to become more and more exact, more finicky and, inevitably, more inhibiting to the free flow of ideas. To follow the present course is to reject Lord Devlin's warning: "If freedom of the press . . . perishes, it will not be by sudden death. . . . It will be a long time dying from a debilitating disease caused by a series of erosive measures, each of which, if examined singly, would have a good deal said for it."[6]

It will be argued that this proposed restructuring amounts to the weakening of the Fairness Doctrine. On the contrary, it corrects an unenforceable and misapplied formula and restores its initial purpose and guidelines. The FCC would adhere to its established policy of considering only overall broadcast performance. "But it is clear that the standard of public interest is not so rigid that an honest mistake or error in judgement on the part of a licensee will be or should be condemned where his overall record demonstrates a reasonable effort to provide a balanced presentation of comment and opinion . . ."[7] This interpretation of the Doctrine is hardly revolutionary or even original; it happens to be the verbatim language of the report on the Doctrine made by the staff of John Pastore's Senate Subcommittee on Communications in a three-year study released in September of 1967, just a year and a half before the final *Red Lion* decision.

This report based its conclusion on the 1949 FCC Report on Editorializing which is where "the foundations of the modern Fairness Doctrine were laid." It noted:

. . . The question is necessarily one of the reasonableness of the station's actions, not whether any absolute standard of fairness has been achieved. It does not require any appraisal of the merits of the particular issue to determine whether reasonable efforts have been made to present both sides of the question.[8]

This approach continued through the fifties and into the early sixties in a series of rulings which maintained that "it is no business of the Commission to say that any particular program should or should not be presented. The licensee itself, however, possesses an extensive discretion to select or reject programs."[9]

To return to the 1949 or even the 1963 intent of the Fairness Doctrine is not a retreat to the past, and is far from a submission to the broadcasters' propaganda war. Rather, it is a considerable step forward in that it recognizes that the present use of the Doctrine sets part one and part two against each other. The proposals recommended here do not permit television and radio stations to abdicate any of their voluntarily undertaken public-trustee duties; instead, they demand far more of them in terms of creativity and programing. The question is, how much of a commitment are broadcasters willing to make in order to liberate themselves and their public from the regulations that they claim prevent them from achieving their full potential?

The debate over the Fairness Doctrine has been healthy. The excesses of the regulators, no less than those of some broadcasters, have provided useful lessons. The United Church of Christ used the tool effectively against WLBT, and because of that case it seems likely that no such drastic action against a station may ever be required again. It is also doubtful that another President or political party will again attempt covertly to use the Doctrine to silence what they consider to be noxious views. In its misapplication by regulators and its breach by the regulated, the Fairness Doctrine may have made all parties wiser to the dangers of too much government regulation brought on by an absence of self-regulation.

In the end, the open marketplace will determine what's on the air and what's fair. A station or network which ignores its public-affairs responsibility and a sense of fairness will ultimately lose its following. Broadcast news at its professional best needs no government to enforce fairness, and at its worst, no government can really ensure it.

Dr. Lefever notwithstanding, fairness is not "a woman holding a scales with a cloth around her eyes,"[10] and a regulatory process which attempts to impose its standards of fairness by way of millions of decisions made in thousands of newsrooms 365 days a year, is violating an obligation of restraint proclaimed 144 years before the FCC came into existence.

In spite of self-made promises never to become a super-referee, in the Pensions case five members of the Commission played precisely that role. Dean Burch says that earlier on that day, November 26, 1973, he told his colleagues, "This is the worst piece of crap we've ever put our hands on." But at the meeting, Burch, who as chairman was the last to vote, hesitated and then affirmed the ruling "because we had turned down so many foolish AIM complaints in the past." Commissioner Nicholas Johnson says that he doesn't remember how he voted in the case; the record shows that he and Commissioner H. Rex Lee were absent on that fateful morning.

Freedom can ill afford such capricious runs of luck when it affects how a nation of 210 million citizens informs itself. Fairness should not be a deterrent but an aspiration. It is better left to a marketplace of 8,500 licensees, even if some of them are named Norris and McIntire, than to seven politically appointed bureaucrats on M Street, even if their names are Burch, Johnson and Minow.

The telecommunications revolution and the anticipated multiplicity of outlets may never materialize, and broadcasters may yet prove, as their most cynical critics prophesy, that the goals of responsibility and fairness must be enforced by saber-toothed laws. If so, the industry will get the restraints it invites, but in the meantime the nation cannot afford the price of what could amount to a government-controlled press. We need to extricate ourselves from the trap set by the two extremes, if only to give us time to send a final signal to both sides.

To the licensees: it may be your frequency, but it's everybody's Bill of Rights. To demand the First Amendment's protections without providing free speech for those who seek to talk back and to attempt to stunt the growth of all new channels of telecommunications is to impugn broadcasting's credibility.

To the FCC: Fair debate is the product of free speech, and the genius of the First Amendment is that it prescribes what the government is restrained from doing. Fairness goals are benevolent yearnings, like the Bill of Rights, which Judge Learned Hand once interpreted as "merely a counsel of perfection and an ideal of temperance, always to be kept in mind . . ."[11]

For the government to seek the goals of free speech and fair debate is fitting and proper. To enforce them by rigid rules of content is to place these two noble dreams in perpetual conflict with each other.

The American system works because it is able to weigh competing social values whenever two rights collide, and to determine which part of the Constitution shall prevail. The Fairness Doctrine has taxed the system's balancing mechanism to its limits without achieving its goals. Both the regulators and the courts have entered areas from which the Constitution has traditionally excluded them.

Government enforcement of the Fairness Doctrine will vanish when scarcity of channels is no longer a prior restraint. Until then, access voluntarily granted by broadcasters to those who seek to talk back is the only sure remedy. More than all the briefs and test cases, demonstrations of good faith will cause the Fairness Doctrine to wither away.

SOURCE NOTES

Foreword

1. Speech of Lyndon Johnson before the National Association of Broadcasters, Chicago, Illinois, April 1, 1968.
2. Leonard W. Levy, *Freedom of Speech and Press in Early American History: The Legacy of Suppression* (New York: Harper Torchbooks, 1970), p. 3.
3. *Ibid.*, p. 267.
4. Gaillard Hunt, ed., *The Writings of James Madison*, Vol. V (New York: Putnam, 1904) , p. 377.
5. Paul Leicester, ed., *The Writings of Thomas Jefferson*, Vol. V (New York: Putnam, 1895), p. 112. (Letter from Thomas Jefferson to James Madison, August 28, 1789.)

1 Red Lion: The Attack Lasted Two Minutes

1. *Editor and Publisher* (January 11, 1969), p. 70.
2. Fred J. Cook, "Hate Clubs of America," *The Nation* (May 25, 1964), p. 525.
3. *Ibid.*, pp. 525–526.
4. Letter from John M. Norris to Fred J. Cook, January 7, 1965.
5. Cook, "Hate Clubs of America," p. 526.
6. "Christian Crusade," WGCB broadcast, November 25, 1964. Narrator: Reverend Billy James Hargis.
7. Letter from Fred J. Cook to station WGCB, December 19, 1964.
8. 47 C.F.R. Sec. 73.123(a); see also *In the Matter of Editorializing by Broadcast Licensees*, 13 FCC 1246 (1949). Hereafter referred to as "Report on Editorializing by Broadcast Licensees."

2 The Birth of the Fairness Doctrine: From Aimee Semple McPherson to Red Lion

1. "Report on Editorializing by Broadcast Licensees," 13 FCC 1246, 1249 (1949).
2. Gilbert Seldes, "Murrow, McCarthy and the Empty Formula," *Saturday Review* (April 24, 1954), p. 26.
3. Lawrence Lessing, *Man of High Fidelity* (Philadelphia: Lippincott, 1956), pp. 132–134.

4. Erik Barnouw, *A Tower in Babel* (New York: Oxford University Press, 1966), p. 95.

5. *National Broadcasting Co., Inc., et al.* v. *United States et al.*, 319 U.S. 190, 212, 63 S. Ct. 997, 1008, 87 L.Ed. 1344 (1943).

6. Barnouw, *A Tower in Babel*, p. 95.

7. *Ibid.*

8. *Ibid.*, p. 96.

9. *Ibid.*, p. 180.

10. Testimony of Secretary of Commerce Herbert Hoover, Hearings of the House Committee on the Merchant Marine and Fisheries, Hearings on H.R. 7357, 68th Cong., 1st Sess. (March 11, 1924), p. 8.

11. Remarks of Representatives Fiorello LaGuardia and Wallace H. White, Cong. Rec. Vol. 67, p. 5480 (1926).

12. Barnouw, *A Tower in Babel*, p. 216.

13. Communications Act of 1934, Title 47 USC 151 et seq. (1934).

14. *Great Lakes Broadcasting Co.*, 3 FRC An. Rep. 32–34 (1929).

15. Senate Commerce Committee, Subcommittee on Communications, Staff Report on FCC's Action and the Broadcaster's Operations in connection with the Fairness Doctrine, 90th Cong. 2d Sess., p. 10 (1968).

16. Erik Barnouw, *The Golden Web* (New York: Oxford University Press, 1968), p. 29, footnote 4.

17. *In the Matter of The Mayflower Broadcasting Corporation, and The Yankee Network, Inc. (WAAB)*, 8 FCC 333, 340 (1940).

18. Staff Report of Senate Commerce Subcommittee on Communications, p. 20.

19. *Ibid.*, pp. 21–22 (excerpt from "Public Service Responsibility of Broadcast Licensees," March 7, 1946).

20. *Ibid.*, p. 23.

21. *KMPC (Richards)*, 14 Fed. Reg. 4831 (1949).

22. Barnouw, *The Golden Web*, p. 223.

23. *Ibid.*, p. 222.

24. *Ibid.*

25. *Ibid.*, p. 223.

26. "Report on Editorializing by Broadcast Licensees," 13 FCC 1246, 1248 (1949). (Paraphrase.)

27. Staff Report of Senate Commerce Subcommittee on Communications, p. 27.

28. "Report on Editorializing," p. 1255.

29. Testimony of Senators Proxmire and Pastore, Cong. Rec. Vol. 105, pp. 14446–14457 (July 28, 1959).

30. *Ibid.*, p. 14457.

31. 47 USC 315(a) (1959).

32. *Cullman Broadcasting Co., Inc.*, 25 Pike and Fischer RR 895, 896 (1963).

34. *NBC*, 14 FCC2d 713 (1968).

35. *NBC*, 25 FCC2d 735 (1970).

36. *In Re Application of Clayton W. Mapoles, tra Milton Broadcasting Co.* 23 Pike and Fischer, RR 586, 589 (1961).

37. *Ibid.*, p. 591.

38. *Ibid.*, p. 586.

39. *Billings Broadcasting Co. (KBMY)*, 23 Pike and Fischer, RR 951, 952 (1961).

40. *Ibid.*, p. 953.

41. The official title of the Fairness Primer is "Applicability of the Fairness Doctrine in the Handling of Controversial Issues of Public Importance."

3 Red Lion: Conversation in the Fish Room

1. Letter from John Pastore to the FCC, August 27, 1963.

2. Marquis Childs, "Kennedy Thinks Rightists Use Tax Exemption for Propaganda," St. Louis *Post Dispatch* (October 10, 1963), p. 1 B.

3. Letter from Wayne Phillips to Richard Seaver, Grove Press, Inc., August 6, 1964; letter from Richard Seaver to Wayne Phillips, August 10, 1964. (Letters on file at George Arents Library, Syracuse University.)

4. Advertisement, *New York Times* (October 8, 1964), p. 12.

5. "Anti-Birch Group Presses an 'Exposé,'" *New York Times* (October 18, 1964), p. 18.

6. Confidential memo from Martin E. Firestone to Wayne Phillips, October 28, 1964, p. 4.

7. *Ibid.*, p. 6.

4 Red Lion: The Race to the Circuits

1. Letter from Fred J. Cook to Ben F. Walpole, Secretary, FCC, February 7, 1965.

2. *Ibid.*

3. Taken from tape of Cook reply to Hargis broadcast.

4. Letter from John M. Norris to Fred J. Cook, December 28, 1964.

5. Letter from Fred J. Cook to John M. Norris, December 31, 1964.

6. Letter from John M. Norris to Fred J. Cook, January 7, 1965.

7. Letter from Red Lion Broadcasting to the FCC, May 19, 1965.

8. Letter from the Democratic National Committee to the FCC, February 1, 1965.

9. Letter from John M. Norris to ten stations cited by the Democratic National Committee, February 12, 1965. (Norris quoting James 4:7.)

10. Letter from John M. Norris to the FCC, February 12, 1965. (Norris quoting Matthew 5:11.)

11. Order of Chief Judge David Bazelon, U.S. District Court of Appeals (D.C.) in *Red Lion Broadcasting Co. v. FCC*, Case No. 2331-65, December 3, 1965.

12. Letter from the FCC to John M. Norris, 1 FCC2d 934 (October 6, 1965).

13. Letter from the FCC to John H. Norris, 1 FCC2d 1587, 1588 (December 9, 1965).

14. Psalms 5:10.

15. Order of U.S. District Court of Appeals (D.C.), *Red Lion Broadcasting Co.* v. *FCC*, 381 F.2d 908 (1967), Case No. 19938.

16. *Red Lion Broadcasting Co., Inc. et al.* v. *Federal Communications Commission and United States of America*, 381 F.2d 908, 924 (1967).

17. *Ibid.*, p. 930.

18. *Ibid.*, p. 929.

19. *Ibid.*, p. 930.

20. *Notice of Proposed Rule Making, 3 FCC2d 991 (1966).* (Adopted July 5, 1967. *In the Matter of Amendment of Part 73 of the Rules to Provide Procedures in the event of a Personal Attack or Where a Station Editorializes as to a Political Candidate,* 8 FCC2d 721 [1967]).

21. Brief of the RTNDA for Court of Appeals (Seventh Circuit), *RTNDA et al.* v. *FCC*, 400 F.2d 1002 (1968), Case No. 16369, p. 31.

22. *In the Matter of Amendment of Part 73 of the Rules to Provide Procedures in the event of a Personal Attack or Where a Station Editorializes as to a Political Candidate,* 9 FCC2d 539 (1967).

23. Brief of CBS in *RTNDA et al.* v. *FCC*, 400 F.2d 1002 (1968), U.S. Court of Appeals for the Seventh Circuit, Case No. 16498, p. 49.

24. *Ibid.*, p. 48.

25. *Ibid.*, p. 45.

26. *Ibid.*, p. 27.

27. Letter from Assistant Attorney General Donald F. Turner to Chairman Rosel Hyde, February 29, 1968.

28. *In the Matter of Amendment of Part 73 of the Rules Relating to the Procedures in the event of a Personal Attack,* 12 FCC2d 250, 252 (1968).

29. *Ibid.*, 260 (Loevinger dissent).

30. *Ibid.*, 257 (Loevinger dissent).

31. Brief of NBC in *RTNDA et al.* v. *FCC*, 400 F.2d 1002 (1968), U.S. Court of Appeals for the Seventh Circuit, Case Nos. 16369, 16498, 16499, p. 12.

32. *Ibid.*, p. 22.

33. *Radio Television News Directors Association et al.* v. *United States of America and Federal Communications Commission; Columbia Broadcasting System, Inc.* v. *United States of America and Federal Communications Commission; National Broadcasting Company, Inc.* v. *United States of America and Federal Communications Commission,* 400 F.2d 10002, 1021 (1968).

34. *Ibid.*, pp. 1017–1018.

35. *Ibid.*

36. *Ibid.*, pp. 1018–1019.

5 Red Lion: Judgment Day in the Supreme Court

1. Transcript of oral argument of *Red Lion Broadcasting, Inc.* v. *Federal Communications Commission,* Supreme Court of the United States, 395 U.S. 367, April 2, 1969, p. 4.

2. *Ibid.*, p. 5.

3. *Ibid.*, p. 6.

4. *Ibid.*, p. 8.
5. *Ibid.*, p. 7.
6. *Ibid.*, p. 9.
7. *Ibid.*, p. 15.
8. *Ibid.*, pt. II, p. 39 (April 3).
9. *Ibid.*, p. 40.
10. *Ibid.*, pt. I, p. 19 (April 2).
11. *Ibid.*, pt. II, p. 33 (April 3).
12. *Ibid.*, pt. I, p. 29 (April 2).
13. *Ibid.*
14. *Ibid.*, p. 30.
15. *Ibid.*, pt. II, p. 47 (April 3).
16. *Ibid.*, p. 41.
17. *Ibid.*, p. 42.
18. *Ibid.*
19. *Ibid.*, p. 43.
20. *Ibid.*, p. 44.
21. *Ibid.*, p. 46.
22. Transcript of oral argument before Supreme Court of *RTNDA*, 395 U.S. 367, April 3, 1969, p. 10.
23. *Ibid.*, p. 3.
24. *Ibid.*, p. 15.
25. *Ibid.*, p. 42.
26. *Ibid.*
27. *Ibid.*, p. 44.
28. *Ibid.*
29. *Ibid.*, p. 45.
30. *Ibid.*, pp. 45–46.
31. *Ibid.*, p. 46.
32. *Ibid.*, p. 51.
33. *Ibid.*, p. 56.
34. *Ibid.*, p. 57.
35. *Ibid.*, p. 58.
36. *Red Lion* transcript, pp. 9, 17.
37. *RTNDA* transcript, p. 37.
38. *Ibid.*, p. 23.
39. *Red Lion Broadcasting Co., Inc., et al.* v. *Federal Communications Commission et al.*, 395 U.S. 367, 395, 23 L. Ed. 2d 371, 89 S. Ct. 1794 (1969).
40. *Ibid.*, p. 396.
41. *Ibid.*, p. 385.
42. *Ibid.*, 384.
43. *Ibid.*, p. 396–397.
44. *Ibid.*, p. 388.
45. *Ibid.*, p. 389.
46. *Ibid.*, pp. 389–390.
47. *Ibid.*, p. 393.
48. *Ibid.*, p. 401.

6 WXUR: Killing Gnats with a Sledgehammer

Epigraph: Chief Judge David L. Bazelon dissenting in *Brandywine-Main Line Radio, Inc.* v. *Federal Communications Commission*, 473 F.2d 16, 64 (1972).

1. *In Re Application of George E. Borst et al.*, 4 Pike and Fischer, RR 2d 697, 699 (1965).
2. *Ibid.*, p. 700.
3. *In Re Application of Brandywine-Main Line Radio, Inc.*, 24 FCC2d 18, 35–37 (1970).
4. Bernard McCormick, "McCormick," Delaware County *Daily Times* (October 6, 1967), p. 15.
5. General Assembly of Pennsylvania, House Resolution No. 160, December 17, 1965.
6. *Initial Decision of Hearing Examiner*, 24 FCC 2d 42, 122 (Conclusions, par. 4) (December 13, 1968).
7. *Ibid.*, p. 125, Conclusions, par. 11.
8. *In Re Application of Brandywine-Main Line Radio, Inc.*, 24 FCC2d 18, 34–35 (1970).
9. Lawrence Laurent, "FCC, Acting on Fairness Doctrine, Lifts Licenses of Two Pa. Stations," Washington *Post* (July 3, 1970), p. A 6.
10. *In Re Application of Brandywine-Main Line Radio, Inc.*, 27 FCC2d 565 (1971).
11. *Brandywine-Main Line Radio, Inc.* v. *Federal Communications Commission*, 473 F.2d 16, 46–47 (1972).
12. *Ibid.*, p. 52.
13. *Ibid.*, p. 63.
14. *Ibid.*, p. 80 (quoting Justice Jackson quoting Baron Bramwell in *McGrath* v. *Kristensen*, 340 U.S. 162, 178, 71 S. Ct. 224, 233, 95 L. Ed. 173 [1950]).
15. *Ibid.*, pp. 63–64.
16. *Ibid.*, p. 80.
17. *Ibid.*, pp. 78–79.
18. *Ibid.*, p. 70.
19. *Ibid.*, p. 80.
20. *Ibid.*, p. 81.
21. Editorial, *News of Delaware County* (October 26, 1967), p. 26.
22. *Brandywine*, p. 71.
23. *Ibid.*, p. 70.
24. Cong. Rec., 93rd Cong., 1st Sess., Vol. 119, p. 37048, Wednesday, November 14, 1973.

7 WLBT: Line Trouble in Mississippi

1. Letter from WLBT to the FCC, July 17, 1958, quoted in *In Re Application of Lamar Life Broadcasting Co.*, 38 FCC 1143, 5 Pike and Fischer, RR 2d

205, 209 (1965).

2. *Ibid.*, 1164.

3. Mrs. Medgar Evers, with William Peters, *For Us, the Living* (New York: Doubleday, 1967), p. 309.

4. *Lamar Life,* 38 FCC 1143, 1153 (1965).

5. *Ibid.*, pp. 1153–54.

6. *Ibid.*, p. 1154.

7. *Ibid.*

8. *Ibid.*, p. 1164 (dissent of Henry and Cox).

9. *Ibid.*, p. 1160 (dissent of Henry and Cox).

10. *Ibid.*, p. 1158 (dissent of Henry and Cox).

11. *Office of Communication of United Church of Christ, Aaron Henry, Robert L.T. Smith and United Church of Christ at Tougaloo* v. *Federal Communications Commission,* 359 F.2d 994, 1000 (1966).

12. *Ibid.*

13. *Ibid.*

14. *Ibid.*, p. 1002.

15. *Ibid.*, p. 1005.

16. *Ibid.*, p. 1007.

17. *Ibid.*, p. 1008.

18. *Ibid.*, p. 1009.

19. *Ibid.*

20. Transcript of oral argument of Paul Porter, counsel of Lamar Life, before FCC, p. 1737, June 4, 1968.

21. *Ibid.*, p. 1753.

22. *Ibid.*, p. 1724.

23. *Ibid.*, pp. 1751–1752.

24. *Lamar Life,* 11 FCC2d 431, 437–438 (1968).

25. *Ibid.*, pp. 430–437.

26. *Ibid.*, p. 463 (dissent of Cox and Johnson).

27. *Ibid.*, pp. 466–467 (dissent of Cox and Johnson).

28. *United Church of Christ* v. *FCC,* 425 F.2d 543, 549–550 (1969).

29. *Ibid.*, p. 550.

30. *Office of Communication of United Church of Christ* v. *FCC,* 359 F.2d 994, 1003 (1966).

8 Unprotected Speech: Some Commercials May Be Hazardous to Your Health

Epigraphs: John F. Banzhaf III v. *FCC,* 405 F.2d 1082, 1096–1097 (1968). Advertisement in the *Wall Street Journal* (June 18, 1962), p. 13.

1. *Capital Broadcasting Company et al.* v. *John Mitchell, Attorney General of the United States, and Thomas Flannery, United States Attorney for the District of Columbia,* 333 F. Supp. 582, 587 (1971).

2. Advertisement, *Wall Street Journal* (June 18, 1962), p. 13.

3. Federal Cigarette Labeling and Advertising Act, 79 Stat. 282 (1965), 15 U.S.C. at 1331–40 (Supp. 1966).

4. *In Re Complaint Directed to Station WCBS-TV, New York, N.Y., Concerning Fairness Doctrine*, 8 FCC2d 381, 382 (1967).

5. Letter from John F. Banzhaf III to television station WCBS-TV, New York, December 1, 1966.

6. Letter from Clark S. George, vice-president and general manager, WCBS-TV, to John F. Banzhaf III, December 30, 1966.

7. *WCBS-TV*, 8 FCC2d 381, 382 (1967).

8. *Ibid.*

9. *In the Matter of Television Station WCBS-TV, New York, N.Y. (Applicability of the Fairness Doctrine to Cigarette Advertising)*, 9 FCC2d 921 (1967). (This is usually called *Cigarette Advertising*.)

10. *In Re Applicability of Fairness Doctrine to Cigarette Advertising*, 10 FCC2d 16 (1967).

11. *John F. Banzhaf III* v. *Federal Communications Commission*, 405 F.2d 1082, 1086 (1968).

12. Cigarette Labeling and Advertising Act of 1965, 15 U.S.C., 1333 (amended in 1970).

13. *Banzhaf* v. *FCC*, 405 F.2d 1082, 1099 (1968).

14. *Ibid.*

15. *Ibid.*, p. 1101.

16. *Ibid.*, p. 1103.

17. *Ibid.*, p. 1096.

18. *Ibid.*, pp. 1096–1097.

19. *Ibid., cert denied,* 396 U.S. 842 (1969).

20. *Capital Broadcasting* v. *Mitchell,* 333 F. Supp. 582, 586 (1971) (referring to *U.S.* v. *Carolene Products,* 304 U.S. 144, 151, 58 S. Ct. 778, 783).

21. *Ibid.*, pp. 593–594 (Wright's dissent).

22. *Ibid.*, p. 594 (Wright's dissent).

23. *Ibid.*, p. 587 (Wright's dissent).

24. *Ibid.*, pp. 588–589 (Wright's dissent).

25. Testimony of Leonard Goldenson, Hearings before Consumer Subcommittee of Senate Committee on Commerce on H.R. 6543, 91st Cong., 1st Sess. (1969), p. 137.

26. *Banzhaf* v. *FCC*, 405 F.2d 1082, 1093 (1968), quoting 9 FCC2d 921, 949 (1967).

27. Letter from Friends of the Earth to television station WNBC-TV, New York, February 6, 1970.

28. *Ibid.*

29. *Banzhaf*, 9 FCC2d 921, 943 (1967).

30. Letter from WNBC-TV to Friends of the Earth, February 18, 1970.

31. Letter from Friends of the Earth to FCC, March 14, 1970.

32. Letter from WNBC-TV to the FCC, June 13, 1970.

33. Letter from the FCC to Friends of the Earth, August 5, 1970 (quoting 24 FCC2d 743, 746 [1970] from S. Rep. No. 91–745, 91st Cong., 2d Sess., p. 3 [1970]).

34. *Ibid.*, p. 748.

35. *Banzhaf* v. *FCC*, 405 F.2d 1082, 1099 (1968).

36. *Friends of the Earth and Garie A. Soucie* v. *Federal Communications Commission and United States of America*, 449 F.2d 1164, 1169 (1971).

37. *Ibid.*

38. *Ibid.*

39. *Ibid.*, p. 1170.

40. *In Re Complaint by Wilderness Society and Friends of the Earth Concerning Fairness Doctrine Re National Broadcasting*, 30 FCC2d 643, 643–644 (1971).

41. *Friends of the Earth and Garie A. Soucie* v. *FCC*, 449 F.2d 1164, 1170 (1971).

42. *Ibid.*, pp. 1164–1165.

43. *In Re Complaint by David C. Green Concerning Fairness Doctrine Re Stations WRC and WMAL*, 24 FCC2d 171 (1970).

In Re Complaint by Alan F. Neckritz, Berkeley, Calif. Concerning Fairness Doctrine by Station KFRC, 24 FCC2d 175 (1970).

44. *David Green, Individually and as Chairman of the Peace Committee of the Baltimore Meetings of the Religious Society of Friends*, 447 F.2d 323 (1971).

Alan F. Neckritz v. *Federal Communications Commission*, 446 F.2d 501 (1971).

45. *Alan F. Neckritz* v. *FCC*, 502 F.2d 411 (1974).

46. *In the Matter of the Handling of Public Issues Under the Fairness Doctrine and the Public Interest Standards of the Communications Act*, 48 FCC2d 1, 26 (1974). (Usually cited as *Fairness Report.*)

47. *Ibid.*

48. *Ibid.*

49. *Ibid.*, p. 28.

50. *Banzhaf* v. *FCC*, 405 F.2d 1082, 1093 (1968).

51. Les Brown, "Networks Reject Mobil Equal-Ad Plan," *New York Times* (March 16, 1974), p. 1.

52. Speech of Herbert Schmertz to the Advertising Club of New Jersey, Newark, New Jersey, November 21, 1974, p. 1.

53. Brown, "Networks Reject . . . ," p. 63.

54. *Ibid.*

55. Advertisement, *New York Times* (June 17, 1974).

56. S.1 is a Senate bill which many journalists find objectionable. It was introduced in January 1975 to amend the Federal Rules of Criminal Procedure. Among the sweeping changes proposed is a section that would make it a felony to publish classified material which might endanger national security. Another section of the bill would impose a maximum three-year sentence on a person who refused to answer a presiding officer during a congressional investigation, or who refused to produce records or documents requested by the Congress. The new code would make a felony of disobeying or resisting a court's temporary restraining order or preliminary injunction (i.e., gag orders). See S.1, 94th Cong., 1st Sess., Chapter 11, Section 1122(a) Section 1123(a)(2)(A), Section (1)(2)(B) and Chapter 13, Subchapter D, Section 1333 (a)(1)(A), Section 1333 (a)(1)(B) and Section 1335(a).

57. Letter from Arthur Taylor to Editors, July 10, 1974.

9 The Paid-Time Case: The President's Use of Television

Epigraph: Columbia Broadcasting System et al. v. *Democratic National Committee*, 412 U.S. 94, 93 S. Ct. 2080, 2098 (1973).

1. Letter from Daniel Gold to Business Executives' Move for Peace, January 7, 1970.
2. Request for Declaratory Ruling Concerning Access to Time on Broadcast Stations from the Democratic National Committee to the FCC, May 19, 1970, p. 19.
3. Lawrence F. O'Brien, *No Final Victories* (Garden City, New York: Doubleday, 1974), p. 275.
4. *Ibid.*
5. *Ibid.*, p. 276.
6. *Ibid.*
7. *Ibid.*
8. *Ibid.*
9. Request for Declaratory Ruling, p. 1.
10. *Ibid.*, pp. 10–11.
11. *Ibid.*, p. 17.
12. *Ibid.*
13. *In Re Complaint by Business Executives' Move for Vietnam Peace Concerning Fairness Doctrine Re Station WTOP, Washington, D.C.*, 25 FCC2d 242, 246 (1970).
14. O'Brien, *No Final Victories*, p. 277.
15. *Ibid.*
16. *In Re Complaints of Committee for the Fair Broadcasting of Controversial Issues, Against Columbia Broadcasting System, Inc. (WCBS-TV, Channel 2), et al.*, 25 FCC2d 283, 289 (1970). (This is usually referred to as either *Fairness Doctrine Ruling* or *Fair Committee Ruling*.)
17. CBS reply to RNC complaint, July 23, 1970.
18. *Fair Committee Ruling*, 25 FCC2d 283 (1970).
19. *Ibid.*, p. 305 (separate statement of Chairman Burch).
20. *Ibid.*, p. 309 (Johnson's concurring opinion).
21. *Ibid.*, p. 314 (Johnson's concurring opinion).
22. Testimony of Senator Robert Griffin and of CBS president Frank Stanton, before the Subcommittee on Communications, Senate Commerce Committee, August 4, 1970, transcript p. 140 *et seq.*
23. *In Re Democratic National Committee, Washington, D.C. Request for Declaratory Ruling Concerning Access Time on Broadcast Stations*, 25 FCC2d 216, 221 (1970).
24. *Ibid.*, p. 233 (dissent of Commissioner Johnson).
25. *Ibid.*, p. 234 (dissent of Commissioner Johnson).
26. *In Re Petition of Republican National Committee for Relief Against Columbia Broadcasting System, Inc.* 25 FCC2d 739, 746 (1970).
27. Memo from Charles Colson to H. R. Haldeman, September 25, 1970.

28. *Columbia Broadcasting System, Inc.* v. *Federal Communications Commission and United States of America, Democratic National Committee* v. *Federal Communications Commission and United States of America,* 454 F.2d 1018 (1971).

29. *Democratic National Committee* v. *Federal Communications Commission and United States of America, Republican National Committee* v. *Federal Communications Commission and United States of America,* 460 F.2d 891, 913 (1972).

30. *Fair Committee Ruling,* 25 FCC2d 283 (1970).

31. *In Re Complaint of Democratic National Committee Against National Broadcasting Co., Inc., Columbia Broadcasting System, Inc., American Broadcasting Co.,* 33 FCC2d 631, 637 (1972).

32. *Democratic National Committee* v. *Federal Communications Commission and United States of America, American Broadcasting Companies,* 481 F.2d 543 (1973).

33. *Business Executives' Move for Vietnam Peace* v. *Federal Communications Commission; Democratic National Committee* v. *Federal Communications Commission,* 450 F.2d 642, 646 (1971).

34. *Ibid.*

35. *Ibid.,* p. 667 (dissent of Judge McGowan).

36. *Columbia Broadcasting System, Inc.* v. *Democratic National Committee, Federal Communications Commission et al.* v. *Business Executives' Move for Vietnam Peace, Post Newsweek Stations, Capital Area, Inc.* v. *Business Executives' Move for Peace,* 412 U.S. 94, 36 L. Ed. 772, 93 S. Ct. 2080, 2095 (1973).

37. *Ibid.,* p. 2098.

38. *Ibid.,* p. 2095.

39. *Ibid.,* p. 2091.

40. *Ibid.,* p. 2097.

41. *Ibid.,* p. 2090

42. *Ibid.*

43. *Ibid.,* p. 2100.

44. *Ibid.,* p. 2096

45. *Ibid.*

46. *Ibid.*

47. *Ibid.*

48. *Ibid.,* p. 2094.

49. *Ibid.*

50. *Ibid.,* p. 2109 (Douglas' concurring opinion).

51. *Ibid.,* p. 2112 (Douglas' concurring opinion).

52. *Ibid.,* p. 2096.

53. *Ibid.,* p. 2101 (Stewart's concurring opinion).

54. *Ibid.,* p. 2108 (Stewart's concurring opinion).

55. *Ibid.,* p. 2109 (White's concurring opinion).

56. *Ibid.,* p. 2120 (Brennan and Marshall's dissent).

57. *Ibid.,* p. 2133 (Brennan and Marshall's dissent).

58. *Ibid.,* p. 2136.

59. *Ibid.*

60. *Ibid.*, p. 2137.
61. *Ibid.*, p. 2130.
62. *Ibid.*
63. *Ibid.*, p. 2138 (quoting from 450 F.2d, at 665–666).

10 Pensions: The Broken Promise and the Splintered Bench

Epigraphs: Judge Harold Leventhal: *National Broadcasting Co. Inc.* v. *FCC*, 516 F.2d 1101, 1153 (1975).
Judge Edward A. Tamm: *Ibid.*, p. 1196.
Chief Judge David L. Bazelon: *Ibid.*, p. 1179.

1. All quotes from the "Pensions" broadcast are taken from an NBC transcript of the program.
2. *Accuracy in Media, Inc.* v. *FCC*, 521 F.2d 288, 297 (1975).
3. Letter from Richard H. Solomon to the author, December 9, 1974, p. 1, summarizing the complaints he had made at the time of the broadcast.
4. *Ibid.*, p. 2.
5. *Ibid.*
6. *Ibid.*, p. 3.
7. *In the Matter of Complaint of Wilderness Society and Friends of the Earth Against National Broadcasting Co. Regarding Applicability of Fairness Doctrine to Commercial Announcements Sponsored by Standard Oil of New Jersey (ESSO)*, 31 FCC2d 729, 737 (1971).
8. Letter from AIM to the FCC, November 27, 1972.
9. Letter from AIM to the FCC, February 20, 1973.
10. Letter from AIM to the FCC, April 11, 1973.
11. AIM letter of November 27, 1972.
12. AIM letter of April 11, 1973.
13. Letter from NBC to the FCC, February 14, 1973.
14. *In Re Complaint of Accuracy in Media, Inc., Concerning Fairness Doctrine Re NBC*, 40 FCC2d 958, 966 (1973).
15. Letter from AIM to NBC affiliates, May 23, 1973.
16. *Accuracy in Media, Inc.*, 44 FCC2d 1027, 1044 (1973).
17. Affidavit of David S. Brinkley, *In Re Complaint by Accuracy in Media, Inc.*, concerning Fairness Doctrine re NBC, p. 3 (1973).
18. Reply Brief to NBC in Support of a Motion for Stay, etc., in *NBC* v. *FCC*, 516 F.2d 1101, U.S. Court of Appeals for the District of Columbia, Case No. 73-2256 (February 6, 1974), pp. 7–8.
19. *Ibid.*, p. 8.
20. Quotes from the oral argument of *NBC* v. *FCC* before U.S. Court of Appeals for the District of Columbia, Case No. 73-2256, 516 F.2d 1101 (1974), were taken from a tape made by the Clerk of the Court, February 21, 1974.
21. *National Broadcasting Company, Inc.* v. *Federal Communications Commission and the United States of America*, 516 F.2d 1101, 1109 (1974).
22. *Ibid.*, p. 1130.
23. *Ibid.*, p. 1132.

24. *Ibid.*
25. *Ibid.*, pp. 1132–1133.
26. *Ibid.*, p. 1133.
27. *Ibid.*
28. *Ibid.*
29. *Ibid.*
30. *Ibid.*
31. *Ibid.*
32. *Ibid.*, p. 1115.
33. *Ibid.*
34. Amicus brief of Henry Geller, Esq., for *NBC* v. *FCC*, U.S. Court of Appeals for the District of Columbia, 516 F 2d 1101, p. 6.
35. *NBC* v. *FCC*, 516 F.2d 1101, 1116 (1974).
36. *Ibid.*
37. *Ibid.*, p. 1152 (Fahy's concurring opinion).
38. *Ibid.* (footnote 1).
39. *Ibid.*
40. *Ibid.*, p. 1154 (Tamm's dissent).
41. *Ibid.*, p. 1153.
42. *Ibid.*, p. 1154.
43. *Ibid.*
44. *Ibid.*, p. 1155.
45. *Ibid.*, p. 1152 (Leventhal's supplemental concurring statement).
46. *Ibid.*, p. 1153.
47. Petition for a Rehearing and Suggestion for a Rehearing En Banc by AIM, p. 1.
48. *Ibid.*, p. 15.
49. Federal Rules of Appellate Procedure, Section 35.
50. *NBC* v. *FCC*, 516 F.2d 1101, 1178 (1974). (Bazelon's dissent to order vacating the en banc hearing.)
51. *Ibid.* (Bazelon's dissent).
52. *Ibid.*, p. 1179.
53. *Ibid.*, p. 1177.
54. *Ibid.*, p. 1180.
55. *Ibid.*, p. 1179.
56. *Ibid.*
57. *Ibid.*, p. 1182 (Fahy's opinion).
58. *Ibid.* (Fahy's opinion).
59. *Ibid.*, p. 1201 (Leventhal's concurring and dissenting opinions).
60. *Ibid.*, p. 1203 (Leventhal's concurring and dissenting opinions).
61. *Ibid.*, p. 1186 (Tamm's concurring opinion).
62. *Ibid.*, p. 1196 (Tamm's concurring opinion).
63. *Ibid.*, p. 1182 (Fahy's opinion).
64. *Ibid.*, p. 1184 (Fahy's opinion).
65. *Ibid.*, p. 1122 (Leventhal's original opinion).
66. *Ibid.*, p. 1182 (Fahy's opinion).
67. *Ibid.*, p. 1201 (Tamm's concurring opinion).

11 Distortion in the News . . . or about the News? The Case against the Cronkite Show

1. Richard J. Levine, "Anti-Communist Group Lobbies to Keep U.S. a Military Superpower," *Wall Street Journal,* August 1, 1972, p. 1.
2. Ernest W. Lefever, *TV and National Defense* (Boston, Virginia: Institute for American Strategy Press, 1974), p. 78.
3. *Ibid.,* p. 146.
4. James J. Kilpatrick, "How 'Fair' Can TV Be?," Washington *Star-News* (November 27, 1974), p. A 10.
5. Wallace Turner, "Anti-Communist Council Prepares a Voting 'Index' on Congress," *New York Times* (August 17, 1970), p. 21.
6. Letter from John M. Fisher to station managers, September 28, 1972, p. 2.
7. *Ibid.*
8. TV film produced by the Institute for American Strategy, "Only the Strong" (Boston, Virginia: Institute for American Strategy, 1972), transcript, p. 4.
9. Letter from W. C. Foster and Rear Admiral Gene LaRocque to station managers, August 28, 1972.
10. Lefever, *TV and National Defense,* p. 158.
11. *Ibid.*
12. *Ibid.,* p. 151.
13. *Ibid.,* p. 46.
14. *Ibid.,* p. 85.
15. *Ibid.,* p. 86.
16. *Ibid.,* p. 75.
17. CBS Evening News with Walter Cronkite (Vanderbilt University, Virginia: Television News Archive, June 27, 1972).
18. *Ibid.*
19. Lefever, *TV and National Defense,* p. 82.
20. *Ibid.,* p. 107.
21. "How CBS Responds to Criticism," Institute for American Strategy's printed answer to CBS's response to IAS study, April 15, 1975, p. 10.
22. Lefever, *TV and National Defense,* p. 127.
23. *Ibid.,* p. 81.
24. *Ibid.*
25. *Ibid.,* p. 63.
26. CBS Evening News with Walter Cronkite, December 12, 1972.
27. Lefever, *TV and National Defense,* p. 25.
28. *Ibid.*
29. *Ibid.,* p. 74.
30. *Ibid.,* p. 51.
31. *Ibid.*
32. CBS Evening News with Walter Cronkite, August 24, 1972.
33. Lefever, *TV and National Defense,* p. 26.
34. Kilpatrick, "How 'Fair' Can TV Be?," Washington *Star-News* (November 27, 1974), p. A 10.

35. Lefever, *TV and National Defense*, pp. 129–131.
36. *Ibid.*, p. 51.
37. *Ibid.*, p. 157.
38. *Ibid.*, p. 158.
39. Debate between William Small and Dr. Ernest Lefever at Women's National Republican Club, New York, January 15, 1975. Program Transcripts Special Projects Department, CBS News, p. 11.
40. *Ibid.*, p. 19.
41. Lefever, *TV and National Defense*, p. 14.
42. "Or of the Press"—Speech by Justice Potter Stewart at Yale Law School, New Haven, Connecticut, November 2, 1974.
43. Lefever, *TV and National Defense*, p. 161.

12 Fair vs. Free: Squaring *Tornillo* and *Red Lion*

Epigraph: Jerome A. Barron, *Freedom of the Press for Whom?* (Bloomington, Illinois: Indiana University Press, 1973), p. 5.

1. *Ibid.*, p. 343.
2. Editorial, Miami *Herald* (September 20 and 29, 1972).
3. *Miami Herald Publishing Co. v. Pat L. Tornillo, Jr.*, 418 U.S. 241, 258 (1974).
4. *Red Lion* v. *FCC,* 395 U.S. 367, 390 (1969).
5. Paul A. Freund, "The Legal Framework of the Tornillo Case," in *The Miami Herald v. Tornillo: The Trial of the First Amendment* (Columbia, Mo.: Freedom of Information Center, 1975) p. 27.
6. *Red Lion* v. *FCC,* 395 U.S. 367, 389 (1969).
7. This figure is the daily circulation of the Miami *Herald* based on an in-house audit of the period July 1, 1974, to June 30, 1975. Based on that same audit, the Sunday circulation is 497,415.
8. There are currently six Miami-based VHF stations and three UHF stations. However, Channel 2 has both a VHF and a UHF permit and has been included in both groupings. Not included in the UHF group is Channel 51 from Fort Lauderdale, which is also viewable in Miami.
9. Barron, *Freedom of Press,* p. 19.
10. *Red Lion,* 395 U.S. 367, 390.
11. *Banzhaf* v. *FCC,* 405 F.2d 1082, 1100 (1968).
12. *Red Lion,* 395 U.S. 367, 389-390.
13. *Editor and Publisher* (July 11, 1969), p. 70.
14. *Red Lion,* 395 U.S. 367, 389.

13 Escaping the Either/Or Trap

Epigraphs: Walter Lippmann, *Public Opinion* (New York: The Free Press, 1922, 1949), p. 252.
Spirit of Liberty; Papers and Addresses of Learned Hand, ed. by Irving Dilliard. 3rd rev. ed. (New York: Knopf, 1960). p. 73.

1. "Conn's Station Ruled Off Air Permanently by Radio Board," Providence *Journal* (August 22, 1928), p. 9.

2. "Full-Time Radio Stations in State to be Cut in Two," Providence *Journal* (September 1, 1928), p. 1.

3. "Providence Woman Pleads With U.S. Board to Ban Conn From Air," Providence *Journal* (July 21, 1928), p. 5.

4. Speech of Senator John O. Pastore to the Associated Press Broadcasters Association, Alameda Plaza Hotel, Kansas City, Missouri, May 31, 1974.

5. *Miami Herald* v. *Tornillo,* 418 U.S. 241, 258 (1974).

6. Speech of Clay T. Whitehead to the Indianapolis Sigma Delta Chi Chapter on December 18, 1972.

7. *Ibid.*

8. *Committee for the Fair Broadcasting of Controversial Issues (Fair Committee Ruling),* 25 FCC2d 283 (1970).

9. *Complaint of Wilderness Society against NBC (Esso),* 31 FCC2d 729, 738-739 (1971).

10. *In Re Complaint of Sherwyn H. Heckt, Spokane, Washington, Concerning Fairness Doctrine Re Station KREM-TV,* 40 FCC2d 1150 (1973), *(Fairness Doctrine Ruling).* See Hearings on S.2 (First Amendment Clarification Act of 1975) before Senate Subcommittee on Communications, 94th Cong., 1st Sess.

11. *In the Matter of Inquiry Into WBBM-TV's Broadcast on November 1 and 2, 1967, of a Report on a Marijuana Party,* 18 FCC2d, 124, 139–140 (1969).

12. *Ibid.,* p. 139.

13. *Ibid.,* p. 140.

14. *Ibid.,* p. 161 (Commissioner Johnson's dissent).

15. *In Re Complaints Concerning Network Coverage of the Democratic National Convention,* 16 FCC2d 650, 655 (1969). (Letter to ABC, CBS and NBC dated February 28, 1969, p. 7.)

16. *CBS Reports,* CBS telecast, May 21, 1968: "Hunger in America." Narrator: Charles Kuralt.

17. *In Re Complaints Covering CBS Program "Hunger in America,"* 20 FCC2d 143, 146 (1969).

18. *Ibid.*

19. *Ibid.,* p. 151.

20. *Ibid.*

21. *Ibid.*

22. *CBS Reports,* CBS telecast, Feburary 23 (and follow-up, March 23), 1971: "The Selling of the Pentagon." Narrator: Roger Mudd.

23. Fred W. Friendly, "The Unselling of the Selling of the Pentagon," *Harper's* magazine (June 1971), p. 31.

24. *In Re Complaint Concerning the CBS Program "The Selling of the Pentagon,"* 30 FCC2d 150, 152 (1971).

25. *Ibid.,* p. 154.

26. Statement of Harley O. Staggers, Chairman, Committee on Interstate and Foreign Commerce, House Report 92-349, Proceedings Against Frank Stanton and CBS. See S. Edward Foote, ed., *CBS and Congress: "The Selling of the Pentagon Papers"* (A Special Issue of the Educational Broadcasting

Review) (Washington: National Association of Educational Broadcasters, 1971), p. 43.

27. *Ibid.*, p. 48.

28. *Ibid.*, pp. 139–140.

29. *Ibid.*, p. xiii.

30. *Ibid.*, p. ix.

31. *Selling of the Pentagon,* 30 FCC2d 150, 153 (1971).

32. Testimony of Nicholas Johnson, Senate Subcommittee on Constitutional Rights, Judiciary Committee, 92d Cong., 1st & 2d Sess. (1971–72), p. 401.

33. Testimony of Walter Cronkite, *ibid.*, p. 81.

34. *Ibid.*, p. 80.

35. John J. O'Connor, "Can a Documentary Be Too Fair?" *New York Times* (May 18, 1975), p. 35.

36. Testimony of Bill Monroe, Senate Subcommittee on Constitutional Rights, p. 562.

37. Speech of Reuven Frank to Sigma Delta Chi National Convention, Washington, D. C., November 11, 1971.

38. Testimony of Jerome Barron, Senate Subcommittee on Constitutional Rights, p. 106.

39. *Ibid.*

40. Address of Richard E. Wiley before the International Radio and Television Society, Inc., New York, N.Y., September 16, 1975.

41. *The Goodwill Station, Inc.,* 40 FCC 362 (1962).

42. *National Broadcasting Co.,* 40 FCC 370 (1962).

43. *In the Matter of Petitions of the Aspen Institute Program on Communications et al.,* 55 FCC2d 697, 703 (1975).

44. *Ibid.*, p. 712.

45. *Ibid.*

46. *Ibid.*, p. 703.

47. *Letter to Nicolas Zapple,* 23 FCC2d 707 (1970).

48. Transcript of Remarks of Senators John O. Pastore and FCC Chairman Richard W. Wiley, before Subcommittee on Communications, Senate Commerce Committee, September 17, 1975.

49. *TV Digest,* Vol. 15, No. 38 (September 22, 1975), p. 1.

50. Editorial, *Broadcasting* magazine (September 22, 1975), p. 82.

51. Arthur R. Taylor, "Does the American Family Need Another Mouth to Feed?" (a pamphlet published by CBS), p. 18.

52. Speech by Arthur R. Taylor to Arizona Broadcasters Association, Phoenix, December 7, 1973.

53. Transcripts of presidential conversations of September 15, 1972, Washington *Post* (May 17, 1974).

54. Brief of Forum Communications, Inc., in support of Exceptions to Initial Decision, before the Federal Communications Commission, Docket No. 18711, File No. BRCT-98 *(WPIX),* and Docket No. 18712, File No. BPCT-4249 *(Forum Communications),* p. 3.

55. Brief of the Broadcast Bureau in Support of Exceptions to Initial Decision, before the Federal Communications Commission, Docket No. 18711,

File No. BRCT-98 *(WPIX)*, and Docket No. 18712, File No. BPCT-4249 *(Forum Communications)*, p. 2.

56. *Ibid.*, p. 4.

57. *Ibid.*, pp. 34–42.

58. *NBC* v. *FCC*, 516 F.2d 1101, 1156 (1974).

59. Testimony of Senator Sam Ervin, Hearings before the Subcommittee on Constitutional Rights, Senate Committee on the Judiciary, 92d Cong., 1st and 2d Sess., 1971–72.

60. Hershel Shanks, ed., *The Art and Craft of Judging: The Decisions of Judge Learned Hand* (New York: Macmillan, 1968), p. 99.

14 Walking the Tiger Back

Epigraph: Chief Justice Warren E. Burger in *CBS et al.* v. *DNC*, 412 U.S. 94, 117, 93 S. Ct. 2080, 2094 (1973).

1. Editorial, *New York Times* (September 21, 1970).

2. *All in the Family*, CBS telecast, September 16, 1972: "Archie and the Editorial."

3. *NBC* v. *FCC*, 516 F.2d 1101, 1200-1201 (1974).

4. *New York Times* v. *Sullivan*, 376 U.S. 254 (1964).

5. *Cullman Broadcasting Company*, 40 FCC 576 (1963).

6. *Yale Broadcasting Co.* v. *FCC*, 478 F.2d 594, 606 (1973). (Judge Bazelon quoting from remarks by Richard S. Salant to the Boston University School of Public Broadcasting, Boston, Mass., April 28, 1971; Salant quoting Lord Devlin.)

7. *Report on Editorializing*, 13 FCC 1246, 1255 (1949).

8. *Ibid.*, pp. 1255-1256.

9. *In Re Complaint under Fairness Doctrine Requirements and License Renewal*, 40 FCC 499, 499-500 (1960). (The Commission was quoting from *In the Matter of WBNX Broadcasting Co., Inc., et al.*, 4 Pike and Fischer RR 242, 248 [1948].)

10. Debate of Ernest Lefever and William Small before Women's National Republican Club, New York City, January 15, 1975.

11. Hershel Shanks, ed., *The Art and Craft of Judging: The Decisions of Judge Learned Hand* (New York, Macmillan, 1968), p. 23.

SELECT BIBLIOGRAPHY

Arlen, Michael J. *Living Room War*. New York: Viking, 1969.

Bagdikian, Ben H. *The Information Machines*. New York: Harper & Row, 1971.

Barnouw, Erik. *A History of Broadcasting in the United States*. Vol. 1: *A Tower in Babel: To 1933*. Vol. II: *The Golden Web: 1933 to 1953*. Vol. III: *The Image Empire: From 1950*. New York: Oxford University Press, 1966, 1968, 1970, respectively.

—————. *Tube of Plenty: The Evolution of American Television*. New York: Oxford University Press, 1975.

Barrett, Marvin G., ed. *Survey of Broadcast Journalism 1968-69*. New York: Grosset & Dunlap, 1970.

—————, ed. *Survey of Broadcast Journalism—Year of Challenge, Year of Crisis 1969-70*. New York: Grosset & Dunlap, 1971.

—————, ed. *Survey of Broadcast Journalism 1970-71—A State of Siege*. New York: Grosset & Dunlap, 1972.

—————, ed. *Survey of Broadcast Journalism 1971-72, Politics of Broadcasting*. New York: Crowell, 1973.

—————, ed. *Survey of Broadcast Journalism, Moments of Truth*. New York: Crowell, 1975.

Barron, Jerome A. *Freedom of the Press for Whom?* Bloomington, Ill.: Indiana University Press, 1973.

Bliss, Edward Jr., ed. *In Search of Light: The Broadcasts of Edward R. Murrow 1938-1960*. New York: Knopf, 1967.

Brown, Lester L. *Television: The Business Behind the Box*. New York: Harcourt Brace Jovanovich, 1971.

Dilliard, Irving, ed. *The Spirit of Liberty*. New York: Knopf, 1952.

Epstein, Edward Jay. *News From Nowhere*. New York: Random House, 1973.

Etzioni, Amitai. *The Moon-Doggle*. New York: Doubleday, 1964.

Evers, Mrs. Medgar. *For Us, the Living*. New York: Doubleday, 1967.

Foote, S. Edward, ed. *CBS & Congress: "The Selling of the Pentagon" Papers*. Washington, D.C.: National Association of Educational Broadcasters, 1971.

Geller, Henry. *The Fairness Doctrine in Broadcasting*. Santa Monica, Calif.: Rand, 1973.

Goodell, James, ed. *Communications Law Explosion*. New York: Practicing Law Institute, 1973.

Johnson, Nicholas. *How to Talk Back to Your Television Set*. Boston, Mass.: Little, Brown, 1970.

Kahn, Frank J., ed. *Documents of American Broadcasting*. New York: Appleton-Century-Crofts, 1968.

Kendrick, Alexander. *Prime Time*. Boston, Mass.: Little, Brown, 1969.

Lefever, Ernest. *TV and National Defense*. Boston, Va.: Institute of American Strategy, 1974.

Levy, Leonard W. *Freedom of Speech and Press in Early American History: Legacy of Suppression*. New York: Harper Torchbooks, 1963.

Lippmann, Walter. *Public Opinion*. New York: The Free Press, 1922, 1949.

MacNeil, Robert. *The People Machine*. New York: Harper & Row, 1968.

Mayer, Martin. *About Television*. New York: Harper & Row, 1972.

Minow, Newton. *Equal Time*. New York: Atheneum, 1969.

Minow, Newton; Martin, John Bartlow; and Mitchell, Lee M. *Presidential Television*. New York: Basic Books, 1973.

O'Brien, Lawrence. *No Final Victories*. New York: Doubleday, 1974.

Robinson, Glen O., "The FCC and the First Amendment," 52 Minn.L.Rev. at 88.

———— and Ernest Gellhorn. *The Administrative Process*. St. Paul: West Publishing Co., 1974.

Schmidt, Benno. *Freedom of the Press v. Public Access*. New York: Praeger, 1975.

Shanks, Hershel, ed. *The Art and Craft of Judging: The Decisions of Judge Learned Hand*. New York: Macmillan, 1968.

Smith, Anthony. *The Shadow in the Cave*. London: George Allen & Unwin, 1973.

United States. Congress. Senate. *Hearing before the Subcommittee on Constitutional Rights of the Committee on the Judiciary*. 92d Cong., 1st and 2d Sess., 1971–72.

United States. Congress. Senate. *Staff Report of the Subcommittee on Communications of the Committee on Commerce*. 90th Cong., 2d Sess., 1968.

United States. Federal Communications Commission. *Federal Communications Commission Reports*. 15 Series Vols. 1–45, 2nd Series Vols. 1–40.

Variety and *Broadcasting* magazine. These two weekly publications provide a unique and comprehensive history of broadcasting's first half-century.

ACKNOWLEDGMENTS

This book grew out of a course, Journalism and the First Amendment, which Professor Benno Schmidt of the Law School and I teach at the Columbia Graduate School of Journalism. For the five years of its existence, the course has benefited from support from the John and Mary Markle Foundation and from the New York State Bar Association. This assistance has enabled Professor Schmidt to prepare a comprehensive study, *Freedom of the Press vs. Public Access*, published for the National News Council by the Aspen Institute Program on Communications and Society, and has made it possible for many experts to visit our seminars.

Sitting in the classroom with Schmidt on one side and a former teaching assistant, Dan Werner, on the other, I once commented that I was being guided and often taught by two colleagues whose combined age was less than mine. For anyone who has not been exposed to such an experience, it is a crash course in perspective, endurance and humility.

The work of another young scholar of journalism has had impact on this book. Walter Lippmann's *Public Opinion*, written when he was thirty-two and long before even radio had emerged as a prime source of news, has been scripture to me in both newsroom and classroom. In his eighty-fifth and last year, Mr. Lippmann encouraged me to write this book.

Of the three teaching assistants who contributed to this work, Dan Werner, Columbia Law School '72, Columbia Journalism '73, labored longest. Martha Elliott, Columbia Journalism '75, who succeeded him, and who ably handled the intricate process of organizing the source notes, left her mark on many chapters. Jennifer Siebens, '73, wrote critiques of the book's initial chapters.

Year after year, the most rewarding visiting lecturer at our course has been Henry Geller, who served as general counsel to the Federal Communications Commission from 1964 to 1970. His admirers include a variety of FCC chairmen, from Newton Minow to Dean Burch, and if the nation is lucky, Mr. Geller will someday head the agency. His scholarly treatise of the Fairness

Doctrine for the Rand Corporation is required reading for the course and for all who wish to understand how broadcast regulation is written. He is a pleasure to debate with, and though he must be counted as one of the fathers of the Fairness Doctrine, he is a useful resource for anyone seeking a sane way out of the dilemmas it poses.

Three books, all by the same author, have been constant companions during this expedition: Erik Barnouw's trilogy on the History of Broadcasting in the United States, *A Tower in Babel, The Golden Web* and *The Image Empire.* As John Leonard wrote in a *New York Times* book review of the single-volume edition of this monumental work, *Tube of Plenty,* ". . . everybody who writes about television steals from . . . Mr. Barnouw."

I want to acknowledge the patience and wisdom of my colleague Stuart Sucherman, a former lawyer at the FCC and now a program officer for the Ford Foundation. Mr. Sucherman is responsible for teaching me what judges and lawyers mean when they say, "It won't write." I also express my special gratitude to two other communications authorities who are on opposite sides of the Fairness Doctrine: New York attorney Floyd Abrams and Nicholas Zapple, who for twenty-five years, until 1975, was counsel to the Senate Subcommittee on Communications. I also wish to thank Marcus Cohn, a Washington communications attorney whose experience goes back to the Federal Radio Commission and who started me on the road to Red Lion; Ben Cottone, a former FCC general counsel and now a Washington communications attorney; and Wayne Phillips, formerly of the Democratic National Committee, who opened several closed doors for me.

Earl K. Moore, who successfully represented John F. Banzhaf III in the cigarette case and the United Church of Christ in the WLBT litigation, was patiently generous in sharing with me his unique knowledge of both cases. Reverends Carl McIntire and Everett Parker, who differ with each other and me on a broad front of issues, provided my classes and me with rare glimpses into their spirit and character.

My two bosses, McGeorge Bundy, president of the Ford Foundation, and Elie Abel, dean of the Graduate School of Journalism at Columbia University, deserve to have it known that they were not exposed to a single word of this book until it appeared in print. They encouraged and tolerated me—not necessarily in that order.

About the Author

FRED FRIENDLY was born in New York City in 1915, but spent much of his boyhood in Providence, R.I., and began his broadcasting career there in 1938. After serving in the CBI theater during World War II, he returned to New York, where in 1948 he met Edward R. Murrow. Their partnership lasted for twelve years, and together they were responsible for many of television's most distinguished moments. Mr. Friendly was also the originator of *CBS Reports*, and for five years, beginning in 1959, its executive producer; thereafter, from 1964 to 1966, he was president of CBS News.

For the last ten years Mr. Friendly has been the Edward R. Murrow Professor of Journalism at the Columbia School of Journalism, as well as serving the Ford Foundation as Advisor on Communications. In the latter capacity he was one of the designers of the "News and the Law" seminars, a series of programs designed to make journalists and those in the legal profession more aware of the issues and problems they face, both mutually and separately, in civil rights and the defense of freedom in this country.

Married, and with six children, Mr. Friendly lives in Riverdale, N.Y.